THE TROPOHOLIC'S GUIDE TO EXTERNAL ROMANCE TROPES

CINDY DEES

CYNTHIA DEES PUBLISHING INC

Thanks to my family for enduring endless conversations about tropes they couldn't care less about.

Thanks to Damon for insisting that I take on this project and for both cheering me on and delivering swift kicks when I needed each.

Thanks most of all to my hundreds of writing students over the years, who taught me most of what I know about writing, and for your endless curiosity that pushed me to always keep learning.

CONTENTS

Introduction   vii

1. HOW TROPE WRITE-UPS ARE ORGANIZED   1

2. WHAT ARE TROPES AND WHY DO THEY MATTER?   17
   What is a trope?   32
   What trope isn't   34
   Why bother with tropes?   39
   Obligatory Scenes   43

3. HOW TO USE THIS BOOK   47
   How to Use Trope to Build Story   51
   Developing Plot from Trope   53
   Romantic Tragedies   53
   Developing Characters from Trope   59
   Layering Tropes   65

4. ACROSS THE TRACKS/WRONG SIDE OF THE
   TRACKS   71

5. BEST FRIEND'S SIBLING/SIBLING'S BEST FRIEND   81

6. BEST FRIEND'S/SIBLING'S EX   89

7. BEST FRIEND'S WIDOW/WIDOWER   99

8. CHILDHOOD SWEETHEARTS   105

9. COUPLES' THERAPY   113

10. CROSS CULTURAL/INTERRACIAL   121

11. DIVIDED LOYALTIES   129

12. EVERYONE ELSE CAN SEE IT   139

13. EVIL/DYSFUNCTIONAL FAMILY   151

14. FEUDING FAMILIES   163

15. FISH OUT OF WATER/COWBOY IN THE CITY   171

16. FOLLOWING YOUR HEART   181

17. FORBIDDEN LOVE   193

18. FRIENDS TO LOVERS   203

19. GIRL/BOY NEXT DOOR   213

20. HERO/HEROINE IN HIDING   223

21. HIDDEN/SECRET WEALTH   233

22. HOME FOR THE HOLIDAY/VACATION FLING   243

23. LONG DISTANCE ROMANCE   251

24. LOVE TRIANGLE   261

25. MARRIAGE PACT/MARRIAGE BARGAIN
COMES DUE   271

26. MARRIAGE OF CONVENIENCE/FAKE MARRIAGE   281

27. NO ONE THINKS IT WILL WORK   289

28. NURSING BACK TO HEALTH   299

29. ON THE RUN/CHASE   311

30. QUEST/SEARCH FOR THE MACGUFFIN   319

31. RAGS TO RICHES/CINDERELLA   327

32. RESCUE ROMANCE/DAMSEL OR DUDE IN
DISTRESS   337

33. RICHES TO RAGS   345

34. RIVALS/WORK ENEMIES   357

35. SECRET BABY   369

36. SECRET IDENTITY   379

37. SECRET ORGANIZATION/SECRET WORLD   389

38. TWINS SWITCH PLACES/LOOKALIKES   399

39. APPENDIX A - UNIVERSAL ROMANCE TROPES
LISTED BY VOLUME   411

Also by Cindy Dees   417

About the Author   419

INTRODUCTION

Go ahead. Groan. Everyone does when they hear the word trope.

In recent decades, the word trope has come to stand for clichéd, trite, boring, predictable plots and plot devices.

Writers have been encouraged to layer trope upon trope, overusing and abusing them until they've become a bad joke in the publishing industry and a thing to be assiduously avoided in the screenwriting industry.

Authors, editors, producers, readers, and viewers alike have turned their noses up at tropes, unfairly maligning them without understanding them at all. But in reality, tropes are absolutely fundamental to the writing process and form the foundation of all stories.

That's right. *All* stories.

They're big. They're powerful. They're archetypal. They're the stuff of myth and legend. They shape all the great epic love stories and give structure to all your favorite plots on the page and on the screen.

In fact, they form the core of every great story ever told.

It's time to bring tropes out of the ridiculed corner and restore them to their proper and prominent place as essential tools for all writers. I plan to do this by:

- properly defining what tropes are
- showing how they're the vital building blocks of all storytelling
- demonstrating why they're the key to creating unforgettable stories that resonate powerfully with readers and viewers

You might want to read that last bullet point again. I'll wait for you.

First, a note about how this and the subsequent books in this series are organized.

When I first set out to make a list of all, or almost all, of the classic tropes used in romance novels of *any* romance sub-genre, my initial list came out at well over a hundred of what I started calling universal romance tropes—meaning each trope is applicable to every genre of romance and any type of love story.

> **To be clear, you don't have to be writing a romance novel or a romantic screenplay for these tropes to be useful to you. If you're writing a story of any genre that also happens to contain a love story, or even just a romantic relationship, read on.**

When I started writing detailed analyses of each trope, it quickly became obvious that a single volume containing every universal romance trope would come out to well over a thousand pages. Hence, I launched into the daunting exercise of trying to figure out how to divide them into some sort of logical groupings.

After many failed experiments, I finally hit upon a way to divide tropes into four categories that made sense in the context of how they get used by writers.

I will be the first to admit that these divisions are somewhat arbitrary. It could easily be argued that any of the tropes might fit one or more of the other categories. However, I will show you in a later exercise how to choose one trope from each of the four categories I've established to create a complex, layered, multi-dimensional story.

That said, here are the four categories of universal romance tropes I came up with:

> **INTERNAL TROPES – These are the tropes of personal affliction: the wounds, fears, and personality traits that form obstacles to love inside the hearts and minds of your story's hero and heroine.**

> **EXTERNAL TROPES – These are comprised of people, situations, and problems around your hero and heroine that prevent them from blissfully and naturally falling in love and finding their happily ever after.**

> **BACKSTORY TROPES –As the name implies, these tropes are made up of the lingering problems, scars, and needs from your hero's and heroine's pasts that must be overcome before they can achieve happiness and true love.**

HOOK TROPES – **These tropes might more accurately be called Inciting Incident Tropes. They're the trope-based way your hero and heroine meet and come together as a couple and how that initial meeting establishes a set of problems that must be overcome before the hero and heroine can achieve their happily ever after.**

All of the universal romance tropes resonate through the history of storytelling and continue to adapt to any time, place, or format.

- They work in novels, comics, TV, film, video games—you name it.
- They can be found in any genre or sub-genre of fiction, regardless of whether the tale is comic or tragic, a suspenseful thriller, taut murder mystery, science fiction adventure, or madcap farce.
- They adapt readily to any situation in which two people fall in love over the course of a story.

Story is story is story. Any story with a romantic element is a candidate for using one or more romance tropes to give it structure and movement.

These are truly the universal tropes of love.

In this series of universal romance tropes, I am confining myself to the tropes that apply to any type of fiction in any format.

If you're writing an epic fantasy novel, a hardboiled crime thriller, a giant MMO video game, or the next Oscar-nominated family saga screenplay, and you have a romantic relationship in your project, these tropes apply to you.

These universal romance tropes also apply to **any** genre of romance. Meaning, it doesn't matter whether you're writing historical romance or alien-abduction romance, inspirational romance, romantic suspense, or romantic comedy. All of the tropes I've identified as universal are applicable to pretty much all romance genres and sub-genres.

Each of these trope types is no more or no less important, valuable, or powerful as a foundation for your story than another. They all are the stuff of classic romance story structure.

> **HELPFUL HINT: In this book, the two main love interests in each trope are referred to by the terms "hero" and "heroine" purely as a device for telling apart the main protagonists. Gender identity is interchangeable and exchangeable in every example, and not limited to just two people.**

1

HOW TROPE WRITE-UPS ARE ORGANIZED

The table of contents lists in alphabetical order every trope included in this volume of the universal romance trope series. An appendix at the back of this book includes a list of all 146 universal romance tropes I've analyzed and which volume they appear in.

As for the write-up on each trope, it's probably easier to show you how it's broken down than it is to describe it to you. Below, I've randomly chosen the FORBIDDEN LOVE trope as a sample of this book's organization. My annotations for each section of the trope's entry are added in bold text for ease of identification.

Feel free to skim over the write-up itself. It's merely included here to give you an idea of how the rest of this book is organized and how granular the detail is on each trope.

And yes, EACH write-up on EACH trope in this series of books on universal romance tropes runs from six to eight pages in length. This is meant to be an encyclopedic reference providing complete information on each trope—gathered in one place for you.

I've developed this book as a handy guide for working writers. It's meant to streamline your plotting and planning, speed up your drafting, keep you from getting stuck or unstick you when you do stall mid-story, ensure your revisions catch all the big plot holes and pitfalls, and help you aim your story squarely at your audience in a way that will be deeply satisfying to your readers or viewers.

TITLE

We'll talk more about what tropes are titled in a bit, but I've tried to choose the most common names in use today and which are also the most self-explanatory and easily recognizable to you. In this case, Forbidden Love is self-explanatory. This trope will tell the story of two people who are forbidden from falling in love doing exactly that.

FORBIDDEN LOVE

DEFINITION

This is where I break down the trope in detail, analyze it in depth, and discuss any variations on the trope that are common.

DEFINITION of Forbidden Love

This is a trope of two people who are, for some reason, forbidden to love each other. There may be an excellent or deeply entrenched reason why they're not supposed to be together, or it can be an altogether specious reason. Regardless, the act of ignoring this prohibition is fraught with danger and will exact a very high price upon the lovers if they are caught...which they inevitably will be in your story.

This story typically features distraught lovers, a great deal of drama, sneaking around, fear of getting caught, and angst galore. These people know they shouldn't love each other or be together, and yet they simply can't stop themselves. Their passion is too great to resist or even restrain.

It's also possible the lovers see some compelling reason why they should be together. They may think the reason they're forbidden from being together is stupid, ridiculous, outdated, or in need of reversal, and in this case, they may defiantly pursue their love and unconsciously—or consciously—hope to get caught. They may want to flaunt the rules and openly challenge them.

Either type of couple—the worried, secretive one or the openly defiantly one—is in for a rough road when they do finally get caught. They have their work cut out for them not coming to a tragic end.

At its core, this is a trope of rebellion and the price of that rebellion. The culture, system, or rules against which the hero and heroine are rebelling will set the tone for your story and its level of darkness, danger, fear, or its level of farce, silliness, and humor.

Unlike the Across the Tracks/Wrong Side of the Tracks or a Cross Cultural/Interracial/Interethnic tropes, in which the lovers *may* face strong disapproval, anger, and pushback, in the Forbidden Love trope, the lovers *will* face serious and inevitable legal consequences, punishment, or even death for disobeying a hard and fast rule, law, or taboo (along with the disapproval, disappointment, anger, and pushback of family and friends).

ADJACENT TROPES

If this particular trope is close to what you want to write, but not quite right, you might want to check out the trope write-ups for one or more of these similar, but not exactly the same, tropes I've collected for you here.

Also, if you're looking for further inspiration or more things to think about while working with this trope (in this case, Forbidden Love), you can check out these similar tropes and find additional elements to add to your characters and plot.

ADJACENT TROPES of Forbidden Love

- Following Your Heart
- Feuding Families
- Rebellious Hero/Heroine
- Dangerous Secret
- Across the Tracks/Wrong Side of the Tracks
- Cross Cultural/Interracial/Interethnic Romance

WHY READERS/VIEWERS LOVE THIS TROPE

This is a deceptively useful little list. It's worth thinking seriously about the kind of experience you want to give your reader or viewer.

This list will give you some starting insights as to why your audience is drawn to this particular story arc. This list will also give you some idea of what kind of experience you need to deliver to your readers or viewers if they're going to fall in love with your project.

This list is not meant to be exhaustive by any means. It's merely a jumping off point for you to consider what your audience wants from this trope and if you're delivering that experience.

WHY READERS/VIEWERS LOVE FORBIDDEN LOVE

- it's typically a highly charged trope that takes the audience on a roller coaster emotional journey
- we love to root for the underdog who's up against impossible odds
- your partner loves you enough to risk his/her *life* to be with you
- your partner will *die* for you
- we all like to think we would be heroic enough to defend our deepest values and/or true love with our lives

OBLIGATORY SCENES

As the title suggests, each trope has a traditional starting point, it develops in a predictable way, it reaches a crisis in a certain way, and it resolves predictably. This is where we explore in detail the archetypal requirements of telling this story in a satisfying way to your audience.

Keep in mind, your audience already KNOWS how every classic story trope should go. Deviate from some version of these obligatory scenes at your own risk...

OBLIGATORY SCENES of Forbidden Love

THE BEGINNING:

The hero and heroine are introduced to the audience, possibly separately or just before their paths cross. They may need to start the story apart while the writer establishes the forbidden-ness of any potential relationship between these two people.

In this scenario, when the hero and heroine do meet, they know up front that any relationship between them is a very, very bad idea. Hence, their decision to pursue a relationship is probably driven by overwhelming attraction and informed by a shared sense of understood risk.

OR

The hero and heroine may meet without understanding who the other person is or that a relationship between them would be a terrible idea. They may enter into the early stages of a relationship before they find out who the other person is and how forbidden continuing with the relationship would be.

In this scenario, they have a terrible choice to make right away—a choice they will have to make again and again as the story progresses —of whether to continue on with the relationship or call it quits before they get caught.

The consequences of getting caught may be spelled out right up front such that the audience is fully aware of the risk, or these consequences may only be hinted at, creating a sense of questioning and suspense in your audience. Of course, it's possible the hero and heroine don't yet know the full consequences of their actions, in which case the audience may not find out right away, either.

The early stages of the relationship may happen completely in secret, or the couple may enlist the aid of a few trusted confidantes. These confidantes will undoubtedly advise strongly against continuing the relationship and serve to heighten the tension and sense of risk. If you choose to add confidantes as accomplices to your story, the stakes are raised as the hero and heroine put other peoples' lives in danger, too.

Remember that, at its core, this is a trope of rebellion and the consequences of that rebellion...on steroids. The beginning typically introduces the system, rules, situation, or person(s) the lovers will spending most of the story rebelling against. The sky-high stakes these lovers are flirting with are almost always established early in the story for your audience, as well.

THE MIDDLE:

The hero and heroine begin to fall in love. Much of the action of the story revolves around arranging and pulling off their trysts, and on scenes with the hero and heroine in their separate worlds, living a lie where they pretend not to be in love with the forbidden person.

If the consequences of the hero and heroine getting caught haven't been made clear before now, they definitely will be spelled out in the middle of the story.

The middle typically includes desperately romantic stolen moments, near misses with getting caught, and a rising sense of desperation in the hero and heroine the more they fall in love with each other.

It's not uncommon for lovers of this type to fall in love fast and for the relationship to move quickly. They probably have very limited time together for the relationship to develop, so each scene in which they're together is likely a significant scene with substance and that moves the relationship forward.

There won't be many or any scenes where they just hang out together casually. Every moment is stolen, and every moment counts for these two.

The middle is characterized by increasing emotion, increasing stakes, and increasing risk. As the lovers continue to get away with spending time together, they may be emboldened to go for something bigger—consummating the relationship, eloping, getting married in secret, or the like. This bigger goal they try to pull off is often the one that will ultimately lead to a crisis and disaster.

BLACK MOMENT:

The lovers are caught. All is lost. They are pulled apart and the consequences of their ill-advised romance lands upon them (and possibly on anyone around them who helped them). Their gamble hasn't paid off. Not only have they lost their relationship, but they may now lose the person they love and face terrible repercussions themselves.

A black moment in this trope is bad. Really bad. As a writer, do not hold back on letting fly with all the terrible consequences you've promised earlier in the story. The devastation should be complete as you rake your characters and your audience over the coals.

THE END:

The hero and heroine are rescued, redeemed, or forgiven in the happy version of this trope. The lovers find a way to convince the authorities around them, those responsible for enforcing the rules, norms, customs, or taboos they've broken, to forgive them. The lovers snatch victory from the jaws of terrible defeat and are allowed to be together, after all. They may be forced to leave their home and go into exile, or they may flee to a place where they're safe or where nobody knows them.

Even though they end up together, in this trope they usually pay a great price before the story is over. It can be a price paid as punishment for their transgression, or a price levied upon them in return for their freedom. Often it is both.

Remember: this couple did break the rules. Depending on what that rule is, your audience may be angry if the lovers don't pay a price of some kind for their rebellion or infraction. If it was an unjust rule, your audience may cheer if the lovers find a way not only to escape but also to avoid retribution or punishment for their transgression.

KEY SCENES

Of course, it takes more than four major scenes to fill a novel, take up an entire movie, etc. Most tropes suggest other important events or moments between your main characters as their relationship and the story unfold in a way unique to this particular story arc.

The additional scenes in this list are not mandatory in the same way the obligatory scenes are. These are just a few typical scenes you might choose to include in your story as you flesh out the plot. They're meant to help you brainstorm and suggest things to consider doing next if you get stuck.

KEY SCENES of Forbidden Love

- the moment when the hero and heroine realize that their love is forbidden
- the moment when the real penalties for getting caught are made clear to the lovers and to the audience
- the moment when the hero and heroine (maybe together or maybe individually) have a crisis of doubt about their decision to pursue this forbidden relationship
- the moment when a friend, family member, or other supporter finds out about the forbidden and secret relationship and we see that person's reaction
- the hero and heroine's last moment together before they're torn apart forever
- the hero and heroine's moment of reunion at the end

THINGS TO THINK ABOUT WHEN WRITING THIS TROPE

This section is a detailed list of questions to guide your plot/character development and prompt thought about many of the major decisions you will need to make before you tackle writing your story or you'll want to ponder as you're discovering your way forward through your story.

Many writers tell me they come back to this list when they get stuck in the middle of drafting their project. Often, browsing through a bunch of questions like this can provoke a new idea or story direction. If you're REALLY stuck, you may also want to browse through the Things To Think About When Writing This Trope for one or more of the adjacent tropes listed earlier in this trope write-up.

You can also use this list as an editing/revision checklist. Have you included the major decisions and developments these questions cover, or are there areas in your story that need fleshing out, beefing up, or further explanation?

THINGS TO THINK ABOUT WHEN WRITING FORBIDDEN LOVE

How do the hero and heroine meet? It is an accident or chance? Do they recognize each other immediately, or do they have no idea who the other one is?

Do the hero and heroine know a relationship between them is forbidden when they meet, or do they not learn that until later? If later, when and how?

Why is this relationship forbidden? Do the hero and heroine think this is a good, reasonable, or just reason *before* they meet each other? If so, how do they feel about the restriction on being in a relationship *after* they've met? Is it still a good rule?

Who enforces this prohibition on a relationship between the hero and heroine? Is this person the villain in your story? Is this person reasonable and right to enforce the prohibition? Does more or less everyone around this authority figure agree with the rule that makes the relationship forbidden? Are they right to agree or not?

What are the consequences to the lovers of being caught together in a relationship?

Who around them finds out about their relationship but keeps it secret or aids and abets the relationship? Why does this person help?

What will the consequences be to anyone who helps the lovers be together? Are the consequences less or the same as those faced by the lovers?

Who sends a warning shot across the bow to the hero and heroine that there will be bad consequences for anyone who breaks the rule(s) that the lovers are secretly flouting? How is this warning sent?

How will the hero and heroine sneak away for stolen moments and trysts together? They may use different tactics every time they meet, or they may repeat the same tactic.

How does each tryst get slightly more dangerous than the last one? What causes the stakes to go up each time?

Do the hero and heroine meet in a situation where they have to pretend not to know each other or to be in love with each other? How does that go? Does anyone around them pick up on something...off... between the lovers or get suspicious?

How far will they take their relationship in secret? Will they sleep together? Get married? Get pregnant?

What are they trying to do when they finally get caught? Is it just another tryst, or is this tryst special in some way?

How do the lovers get caught? Are they betrayed? Is it accidental? Do they make a mistake?

Who separates them, and how are they kept apart?

Are the full consequences promised earlier in the book leveled at the hero and heroine or not? If not, why not?

Are the consequences for the hero and heroine the same or different? Are they punished by the same person or by completely different people? For example, do their own individual families, clans, kingdoms, or governments punish them separately under different sets of rules? Or does the same official or person in authority punish them both under the same set of rules?

Does the hero or heroine own up to having done a bad thing by breaking the rules? Are they defiant about having broken the rules? Do they try to bargain with whoever's going to enforce their punishment?

Will the hero and heroine finish suffering the consequences before they get back together, or will they be pardoned, escape, or in some other way evade the full measure of the consequences? If they avoid some or all of their punishment, how do they do this? Do they do it together, or individually in separate pardons or escapes?

If the hero and heroine escape punishment, this may be the most difficult part of the story to pull off plausibly. Systems of control and punishment are typically designed to prevent escapes and are very hard to break free of. Also, your hero and heroine are probably separated, so two different escapes must be coordinated and timed simultaneously.

Where will they go after they're reunited? Can they stay home or will they have to leave? If they must leave, where do they go?

Are they known where they go or not?

What happens to their friends who helped them be together in secret? Are these people okay at the end of the story? How will the hero and heroine ensure these people are okay, assuming they're still alive?

TROPE TRAPS

While I make no claim to have thought of every trap

you can fall into with any given trope, I've done my best to capture as many landmines lurking within each trope as I can. This is where they're listed.

This list is also useful to read through and use as a thought exercise as you plan your story. I'm told by many writers that they find it, too, to be a source of ideas and inspirations as they plot, draft, or get unstuck.

TROPE TRAPS of Forbidden Love

Creating a hero and/or heroine who is more in love with the idea of love than their actual partner. Meaning, one or both of the characters gets so caught up in the tragic romance of it all that they lose sight of the very real risk and of the person they're actually in a relationship with.

Creating a couple that doesn't seem plausible for the long run. It may be all drama and danger now, but when all of that is gone, these two people are going to drive each other to distraction in a bad way and never survive as a couple for a happily ever after.

Creating a TSTL (too stupid to live) villain who enforces the rules even if they're silly or stupid rules.

Bonus trope trap: Failing to have the rule(s) the lovers are breaking make sense to the person(s) enforcing them. (although it's okay for the rules not necessarily to make sense to the lovers or your audience).

Not creating serious enough consequences for getting caught to sustain all the drama and secrecy the hero and heroine engage in. It's not enough for the hero and heroine to think the consequences would be horrible—the reader or viewer has to believe it, too.

Creating implausible situations where the hero and heroine get away with stealing a moment together but in which the audience knows they would normally be caught and should have been caught.

The lovers using the same tactics to be together over and over—

when someone with an ounce of common sense around them would have caught on long ago to the tactic and caught them.

Not creating near enough misses with the lovers getting caught, which is to say, failing to keep your audience on the edge of its seats.

Creating a lame scenario in which the lovers are caught.

The lovers themselves create a lame or overcomplicated plan to be together that goes awry.

Failing to follow through on the consequences that were promised to the lovers and the audience at the beginning of the story.

Relying on a lame save to pull the hero and heroine out of the proverbial fire so they can be together at the end of the story.

Relying on an abrupt about face or change of heart in the person meting out punishment to relent and let the lovers be together out of the (brand new and heretofore unseen) goodness of his or her heart.

I can't tell you how many of my Asian friends loved the movie, Crazy Rich Asians right up to the moment where the dragon mother sees her son unhappy, has a change of heart, and gives him her engagement ring so he can go get the girl. That's when my friends universally groaned and said something to the effect of, "No Asian dragon mother would ever back down after having successfully chased off the woman she doesn't like or approve of for her son!" While I'm sure that's not universally the case, don't create a villain who suddenly acts completely out of character for no good reason to let the lovers be together in the end.

FORBIDDEN LOVERS TROPE IN ACTION

Last but not least, these are lists of movies, in some cases television shows, and books that use this particular trope. If you're looking for further inspiration for your story or want to see what this particular trope looks like in action, I've gone ahead and collected examples for you here.

. . .

Movies:

- Romeo and Juliet (the personification of the tragic version of this trope)
- The Thornbirds
- Dirty Dancing
- Titanic
- Guess Who's Coming to Dinner?
- Pride and Prejudice
- Clueless

Books:

- Birthday Girl by Penelope Douglas
- Twisted Games by Ana Huang
- Slammed by Colleen Hoover
- Matched by Allie Condy
- Daughter of Smoke & Bone by Laini Taylor
- Vampire Academy by Richelle Mead
- Delirium by Lauren Oliver
- The Sweetest Oblivion by Danielle Lori
- Red, White & Royal Blue by Casey McQuiston

2
WHAT ARE TROPES AND WHY DO THEY MATTER?

The term *trope* gets bandied about frequently in the publishing world and screenwriting world. Editors and producers watch carefully which tropes are selling well and chase those trends. Marketers and publicity departments aggressively signal tropes in back cover copy, trailers, and advertising posters. Artists faithfully convey tropes on book covers—cue the cowboy, cute baby, or Greek typhoon. Even online fiction retailers sort fiction by trope, although they typically call it category or keyword. Moviemakers follow their structure faithfully while filming and go out of their way to signal which tropes they've used even in movie titles.

Why do these tropes matter, you ask?

Because **the vast majority of readers choose their reading material largely based on the tropes inside stories, and the vast majority of TV and film viewers choose their content based on the tropes inside the shows and movies**.

Sure, readers fall in love with the work of individual authors and become devoted fans. Likewise, TV/film viewers fall in love with the work of a specific screenwriter or director.

But this is probably because most authors, screenwriters, and directors tend to return to the same tropes (or related and similar tropes) over and over in their creative projects. I propose that one reason why readers and viewers become super fans of individual story creators is, in part, because they all share an affinity for a similar set of tropes.

Authors and screenwriters explore and write about what they know, what they're comfortable with, or what's fascinating to them. Like readers and viewers, most story creators have favorite tropes they go back to again and again in telling their stories.

This tendency to repeat tropes is an important source of consistency in reading/viewing experience and, in fact, largely defines that writer's brand.

Let me repeat that.

Your brand is defined by the tropes you write over and over again.

You can try like the dickens to brand yourself as a Sally Sunshine rom-com writer and put all the cute, cartoon covers you'd like on your books or movie posters. But if the stories you deliver to the reader/viewer are the tortured journeys of lonely vampires, cowboys, and gothic recluses, no amount of marketing is going to change the type of story readers and viewers associate with your name.

So, let me state what I said above in a slightly different way.

The stories you write over and over ARE your brand.

I hear some of you out there saying, "But I write all over the map. I might do a cute secretary-boss rom com, then a dark, tortured historical set piece with a wounded hero, then a western-themed opposites attract story, and as a palate cleanser I might play around with a bit of alien menage-à-trois."

Congratulations! You're a really versatile writer! However...you have a branding problem. How will any reader or viewer see your name attached to a project and immediately know what to expect from the story you want them to buy or watch? Keep in mind the purpose of branding is to help readers and viewers find, as easily as humanly possible, a book, TV show, or film (or play, comic, graphic novel, video game, or song lyric) that they'll love and tell all their friends about.

We could spend a chapter or two of this book debating whether or not a great cover and title are enough to fully brand a book or if a great title and great trailer are enough to fully brand a TV show or film, but I stand by my statement that your NAME will be closely identified with the repeating tropes in the stories you create.

It's also likely that, as you develop a decent-sized backlist over time, you will start to see tropes repeating themselves in your projects no matter how many genres or sub-genres of fiction you write in, no matter how varied the screenplays you write.

All human beings have tropes that personally resonate with them and hold particular importance in our psyches and lives. We all tend to read and write those tropes, not to the exclusion of all others, of course, but with the most frequently.

We are drawn to reflecting on the things that have caused us pleasure or pain, trauma or healing, and we all tend to spend years chewing on and examining those life events, themes, and lessons that have had the most significance in our own lives.

There are a bunch terrific books on the market about self-branding (I highly recommend Your A Game: Winning Promo for Genre Fiction by Damon Suede and Heidi Cullinan) if you'd like to explore the subject more.

The important takeaway: the majority of readers and viewers return to the same tropes over and over in their reading and viewing preferences.

A second key takeaway: it might behoove you to consider how this tendency in readers or viewers will affect your branding, sales, and audience loyalty.

This idea is so important that we should probably dive into it a little deeper.

In Lisa Cron's seminal work, <u>Wired for Story</u>, she compellingly argues that mankind survives and thrives because of stories, so much so that our brains are literally hard-wired to crave them. We live vicariously and learn through reading, watching, or hearing about the fictional or real experiences of others, and we're literally drawn to stories as a survival instinct.

In his book <u>Hit Makers</u>, a study of what makes some stories, songs, movies, fashions, or fads mega-popular, Derek Thompson presents overwhelming evidence that the stories people are most drawn to—in whatever form they happen to be told—have a strong element of familiarity with just enough newness to it to keep it interesting.

Thompson cites study after study proving that people gravitate to stories they're familiar with.

Readers don't want to work too hard to have a good idea of where a story is going, and they actually prefer to have a good idea of how a story is going to end.

Indeed, in one study, some people were given spoilers of books, including descriptions of their endings before they read the books while others in the study read the same books without any advance knowledge of them. Consistently, the people who knew in advance how the story would end, and even what the big twists in the stories would be, rated the books *higher* in enjoyability.

Why does this matter to us as writers?

Because tropes are predictable.

Tropes have a predictable beginning, middle, and end. And consumers of stories like this. In fact, they crave this predictability.

I hear some of you howling that readers and viewers get bored of consuming the same story over and over. You're not wrong—readers and viewers want enough surprises and twists to keep a story from being completely predictable. But they are comforted by and happier reading or watching a story that doesn't make them work *too* hard to follow it.

Thompson calls this *fluency*. Readers and viewers want to feel smart and grasp the general bones of a story without having to hurt their brains to figure out where it's going.

I propose that one of the most powerfully familiar elements in any story is its trope(s). It is the trope that defines the shape of the story and reliably predicts for the reader where this story is going to go.

We all grow up absorbing and memorizing tropes whether we're aware of it or not. Everywhere we look we see tropes in action—from cartoons we watched as little kids, to literature taught in schools, to our entertainment—be it television, movies, video games, comic books, music lyrics, or some other format of story.

If I were to ask anyone, anywhere, at pretty much any time in human history, to tell me a story about two people who've grown up together as friends and then suddenly realize they're more than friends, I would get told a story that follows the classic friends-to-lovers trope **every single time**. If I specified that it should be a love story, the friends would overcome their reservations about the changing nature of their relationship and end up happily ever after, every single time.

Some stories are so universal they follow the same pattern every time they're told. The lessons we learn from these classically patterned stories are relatively the same every time, as well. And yet, we go back to them over and over and over.

They're familiar. They resonate with us at a deep, visceral level. We want to see them come out the same way every time. In fact, we *need* them to come out the same way every time as a means of reassuring us that the world we live in is predictable and safe.

These universal story patterns *that we all know already* are tropes. I'm merely naming, writing down, clarifying, and expanding on classic patterns of storytelling that have existed pretty much since the first stories were ever told by mankind. Obviously, new variations on ancient tropes get added over time and as societies evolve, but the cores of all classic tropes remain pretty much unchanged.

It's worth pointing out that, in the same way readers and viewers tend to be drawn to certain tropes that have special significance in or applicability to their lives, most readers, viewers, and writers also avoid certain tropes like the plague.

Perhaps a trope reminds a reader or viewer of something painful in their own past, or perhaps they personally disagree with the premise of a certain trope. Or maybe, they just don't like a particular kind of story.

Whatever the reason for their dislike of a particular trope, a viewer will change the TV channel or walk out of a movie in the middle, and a reader will put a book down—or throw it against a wall —and never finish it if they discover they've accidentally started consuming a story with a trope they despise.

And heaven help the writer who doesn't deliver on the promise of the trope(s) they've set up in a story or promised in its marketing materials. Readers and viewers are *outraged—*

Wait, let me shout that.

Readers and viewers are OUTRAGED— when tropes aren't followed through on...but we'll come back to that in a minute.

PRO TIP: You have to pick your battles in the publishing and TV/film businesses. But fight, and fight for all you're worth, with your editor, producer, and marketing department to make sure your title, cover, blurb, back cover copy, trailer, posters, marketing materials, and advertising do not mislead readers or viewers into expecting a different trope than you deliver in your story. If you're self-publishing or independently producing your work, make this an absolute priority as you choose the packaging, marketing materials, and sales strategies for your work.

I wrote a novel that a publisher tried to title, <u>Diving Deep</u>, and wanted to put a male Navy SEAL on the cover of the book in diving gear about to plunge off a boat into water. Deep sea treasure or ocean rescue adventure by a hunky soldier, right?

Nope. The book focuses on a woman trying to prove she's good enough to become a SEAL, and she spends the entire book in a land-locked, arid, mountainous region struggling to keep up with her SEAL instructor and rescue a kidnapped friend. She never even comes near water and neither she nor her boss ever puts on scuba gear.

How furious would readers have been if they bought this book expecting an underwater adventure focusing on a hot guy along with oceans, danger at sea, maybe sunken treasure, and they got my story instead?

Not to mention, how many sales would I have lost from readers who like a good kidnapping-and-rescue tale or a story of a spunky woman proving her worth to her boss, but who had no idea my story was about those?

Bottom line: Get the packaging, marketing, and advertising right when it comes to letting readers and viewers know what tropes will be in your story.

As an aside, this is why no story you ever create will ever be all things to all people. There is no such thing as a story that appeals to everyone. There are always bound to be readers or viewers who despise the tropes you've used in your story. But luckily, there are also bound to be readers and viewers who love them.

All you can do is faithfully tell the story dictated by the trope or tropes you chose to write about and hope that like-minded readers or viewers who particularly enjoy that trope or trope combination will find your story and love it.

This is also why there is no such thing as a marketing campaign or ad that will make everyone who sees it go buy your book or go watch your movie. All you can do is accurately signal to potential audience members what tropes are in your story and hope people who love that trope will give your work a try.

It's fine for potential consumers not to click through to your story or choose not to watch it. In fact, you want some readers or viewers— those who despise the tropes you wrote about—to stay far, far away from your story and never, ever write a scathing review of your work!

Your tribe of readers, viewers, or other story consumers is out there. For every trope or combination of tropes you can imagine to write about, there are plenty of like-minded people who have a special affinity for exactly those tropes and who crave stories built around that story structure.

EXERCISE: FINDING THE TROPES YOU LOVE

In order to find out which tropes you are most drawn to and tend to return to over and over, let's do a brainstorming exercise.

1. Take a few minutes to write down as many of your favorite things as you can think of.
2. Because this is a writing exercise, be sure also to think about things that make your favorite stories your favorites. What do you absolutely adore about them? You can draw from books, movies, video games, chitchat among friends, or any other way you consume stories.
3. If you've written stories before, you can include the tropes from those stories that you particularly enjoyed writing in your list.
4. Also, if you've noticed repeating trends in the stories you prefer to read, or the television/films you prefer to watch, you may have already started identifying the tropes that are totally your jam (and the ones you won't go near with a ten-foot pole). Add the tropes you know you love to your list.
5. Because tropes do not always have happy endings, now add to your list negative events or themes that tend to recur over and over in your life or in the stories you consume. I was shocked years ago when a reader pointed out to me, some thirty books into my career, that I tended to write absent or disengaged fathers over and over again in my work. And yes, my own father was both of those things. Go figure.

6. Don't forget to include settings you like, types of characters that really excite, delight, or fascinate you, favorite endings, or favorite plot twists. While these aren't tropes in and of themselves, they may suggest tropes you might particularly enjoy.

7. What are the movies or TV shows you rewatch over and over and the books you've read so many times they're falling apart? Write down what you love most about those stories. Pay particular attention to the moments you tend to re-watch or re-read or include versions of in every story you imagine, plot, or write.

8. Jot down favorite foods, colors, weather, seasons, places— sky's the limit. The key is to capture many, many things you really, really like or that you repeat over and over in your life.

I keep a running list of these things in a spreadsheet on my computer, and I add to it as I discover new things that fascinate me. As of this writing, my list is over a thousand entries long. It includes things like horses, dogs, military men, spaghetti, rain, secret societies, and smart women in jeopardy.

I hear you pointing out, but these aren't tropes. Correct! (And yay for you understanding what a trope is already!) But, by looking through our lists of favorite things, we can find plenty of elements that are common to various tropes.

Let's take my love of secret societies, for example While that's not a trope in and of itself, a secret society might make an appearance in a hero-in-disguise trope, a reclusive hero trope, a secret identity trope, a secret world story, or perhaps a rescue story.

Spaghetti might lead me to thinking about a restaurant or maybe a big family dinner...and those might lead me to an employee-boss story of a chef on the hunt for the perfect spaghetti recipe and an

Italian restaurant employee, or an other-side-of-the-tracks story about a person from a tiny family falling for a person from a huge family and spaghetti acting as a metaphor for love in this story.

1. Pick out something you're particularly drawn to from your list. Now, browse through this book (or the other volumes in my series) and search for tropes that might work well with that thing you love and that appeal to you to write.

2. If you're the ultra-organized type, you might start a second list of tropes that relate to things you love. They're likely to be tropes you'll find comfortable and enjoyable to write.

3. If you're a more spontaneous type, pick out something you're drawn to from your list and browse through this book with that thing in mind. I'll bet an idea (or several) for a story are triggered by some one of the tropes you explore. That's likely a trope you'll find to be a good fit if you sit down to play with it.

I can tell you with assurance, there are certain tropes that, no matter how much I might like something that relates closely to them, I will never, ever, be drawn to or want to write. You will find the same. The tropes you absolutely hate will not resonate with you, no matter what.

SIDE NOTE: It's worth noting that the names of tropes can and do evolve over time, sometimes quite rapidly. In fact, historically, tropes were often referred to by the name of a classic character, fable, or even a nursery rhyme that perfectly illustrated that story arc. What was once called the Heathcliff

trope has become the reclusive hero or brooding hero trope. The Frankenstein trope has become loving-a-monster or simply, monstrous lover trope.

In this book, I have chosen the most descriptive names I can come up with unless there is already a name so commonly used that just about everyone will automatically understand what it refers to.

Regardless of how a classic, universal trope is currently being labeled, the basic story will remain the same, unchanged, recognizable, and archetypal.

It's also important to note that some tropes lose their acceptability in cultural, societal, and political environments as those environments evolve and grow.

While nobody thought twice about writing an enslaved hero or heroine several hundred years ago (or sadly, much more recently than that), this trope is not widely accepted as a positive trope to write about in contemporary fiction today.

Likewise, writing a romance between an interracial couple several hundred years ago would have been highly controversial but is widely accepted today.

Side note: I chose the two examples in the previous paragraph as a blunt reminder of just how fraught certain tropes have the potential to be.

Secretary-boss romances can be a minefield in today's #MeToo environment. Makeover stories where the hero doesn't notice the heroine until she gets thin aren't likely to land well with most audience members today.

Just because a trope exists doesn't mean it is always appropriate or a good idea to write today.

That said, I would never say never to any writer who wants to tackle a potentially difficult, touchy, or fraught trope in a story. It's always possible to tell a fantastic story with sensitivity, grace, an ethical perspective, and profound meaning regardless of the subject matter. Just be careful and be aware as you choose your tropes of the possible pitfalls of some of them.

Beyond their potential to offend readers and viewers, it's also worth noting that tropes simply come into and go out of fashion. Indeed, in today's world of rapid streaming TV/film releases and eBooks that can go from idea to published story in a matter of weeks, these shifts can happen at light speed, rising and falling in popularity in a matter of months or a few years.

The good news is classic love stories have been around since the beginning of time, and they'll continue to stick around until the end of time. What is old becomes new over and over. The story of Cleopatra resurfaces as modern reverse harem stories. The Taming of the Shrew? It has been reborn as today's Grumpy-Sunshine trope.

Perhaps the most classic example of all is the tale of Romeo and Juliet, which has been told over and over through the centuries since Shakespeare penned his star-crossed-lovers tale (and in it, actually coined the phrase, "star-cross'd lovers").

But, let the record show the star-crossed-lovers stories of Orpheus and Eurydice, Tristan and Isolde, Hou Yi and Chang'e, Achilles and Patroclus, and Panganoran and Magayon, all pre-dated Romeo and Juliet...some of them by a lot. Even Shakespeare himself was borrowing classic tropes and re-adapting them to his own time and audiences.

Today's rapid rise and fall in the popularity of various tropes creates an interesting opportunity for story creators. Every time a new and trendy trope comes along, a dedicated fan base builds around that trope.

While the fans may get tired of binging on a particular trope, it's a good bet that in the long run a solid, core fanbase for that once-trendy trope will survive and thrive...even if that trope goes out of vogue as the hot new thing.

Indeed, various researchers have identified a cycle that book readers, in particular, tend to go through. In the first year of reading a particular type of fiction, they'll consume everything in sight. In the second year, they'll refine their tastes and start to be choosier about the stories they read...which is to say, they find their favorite tropes and begin to niche down more tightly in what they purchase to read. By the third year or so of being a dedicated book fan, readers know exactly what they like reading and they tend not to deviate from those types of stories for the long term.

I've never seen an academic study of how TV and film viewers choose their content, but I expect it's a similar arc of finding their favorite story types and sticking to them for the most part.

This tendency of tropes to come and go in popularity also means that, if you write fast and can bring your book or screenplay to market quickly, it's not a bad idea to write to the hot-trending tropes. (Assuming of course, that you don't have to write your trendy tale while trying all the while not to gag in disgust or break out laughing at the horrible implausibility of it.)

Readers and TV/film viewers are very perceptive and will spot in a second a project created by a writer who personally hates his or her subject matter. If you look closely, I suspect you'll be able to pick out which tropes in this book are not my cup of tea. I've done my best to disguise my personal biases, but we all have them.

The key in choosing a story that will resonate with readers or viewers and achieve popular success is to find the overlap between the stories you love and the ones the reading/viewing public currently loves.

If you find a trendy trope you love, but you happen to miss the big wave of its popularity, you can still write that trope and expect to find readers and viewers for it. You may have to wait for readers and viewers who are glutted on a certain story type to renew their hunger for that particular trope, but they *will* come back.

Tropes, once created, never really go away. They become an evergreen part of the collective consciousness of all people who consume stories in any format.

As you browse through this book, you'll see a definite pattern to how all romance tropes proceed. Readers and viewers also know that pattern. Even if they've never interacted with a specific trope before, they'll be pretty good at guessing where your story should go.

Almost without exception, all stories are built around a trope, or more often several tropes interwoven, that form the core structure of the story. We might even go so far as to say tropes are the individual vertebrae that form the backbones of all stories. They inform which scenes will be in your story and in what order they will happen. They are certainly the basis of the entire romance fiction industry.

At its most fundamental level, every love story ever written follows the trope of one sentient being meeting another sentient being, attraction forms, obstacles are overcome, and the beings end up together, usually happily ever after. Every single romance trope is some variation on that theme.

Tropes are one of the most important tools all writers use, knowingly or unknowingly, in constructing and delivering satisfying stories to their audience. And yet, they're little understood and often greatly misunderstood.

WHAT IS A TROPE?

Let's start at the beginning and talk about what a trope is.

The word trope originates from the ancient Greek work *trepein*, which means to turn, to direct, to alter, to change.

Trepein evolved into the later Greek word *tropos*, which means turn, direction, way. Sometime in the 1530s, the Latin word *tropus* was first used to mean a turn of speech or figure of speech.

It is worth noting from these early definitions that the concept of a trope includes turns of direction and change. There's movement to tropes, and they don't follow a straight line. They connote action. Travel from one point to another.

> **Tropes are a roadmap of where a story must go. They're a way of marking certain scenes a story must contain, and they're a way of breaking down the plot of a story into its core elements.**

Tropes are the universal, archetypal arcs that underlie *every* story.

If you pop over to a modern dictionary to look trope up, you'll find something along the lines of "a figurative or metaphorical use of a word or expression."

Secondarily, tropes are often defined as "a common or overused theme or device, a cliché." In fact, this may be the single most common understanding writers have of what a trope is. Many writers have been taught to believe tropes are bad things to be avoided at all costs.

Of course, clichés and overused themes are bad. But my entire argument is that tropes, in and of themselves, are not only good things, but absolutely necessary to stories that resonate with audiences.

So, what do people in the publishing industry or TV/film industry mean when they use this word?

KEY POINT: In the context of literary works and screenplays, the word trope means "a commonly recurring literary or rhetorical device, motif or cliché in creative works."

Let's unpack that a bit. A trope is a theme, arc, or plot device that runs throughout a story, and that is used repeatedly in many stories by many writers. Star crossed lovers, taming the bad boy, enemies to lovers, secret babies—they've been around since the very first stories were told in the distant mists of time and human speech.

How many ancient cavemen came back to their cave after a hard day of hunting and gathering, and by speech, sign language, or pantomime told the story, "There I was, taking a walk with my mate. And all of a sudden, a saber-toothed tiger jumped out of the bushes right in front of us. And then I..."

Or how many ancient cavewomen relayed to their friends, "I was out all day, hunting and gathering berries. And when I came back to the cave, you'll never guess who I caught Ogg messing around with on our skins. And then I..."

While I have no idea if primitive homo sapiens told these exact tales, you get the point. These stories, hero/heroine-in-jeopardy and cheating spouse, have been around as long as storytelling has existed, are universally related to and immediately understood by all people, and have reflected the human experience for as long as we've had the ability to share them.

Moreover, we tell these same classic, universal stories over and over, even today. Story tropes resonate down through history from

Ogg the caveman, to Greek theater, to Chaucer's Tales, to Shakespeare's plays, to the development of the fiction novel, right on down to modern commercial fiction in its many and varied forms of delivery to the consumer.

These recurring arcs and plot themes that shape a story are what make up that elusive thing called trope.

WHAT TROPE ISN'T

Writers often confuse story elements with tropes.

Take, for example a meet cute. I often see this described as a trope. While the hero and heroine meeting in a fun and creative way draws in the audience quickly and effectively, in and of itself, it doesn't tell the reader or viewer a single thing about where the story is going.

Will this be a secretary-boss romance? An opposites attract story? An other-side of-the -tracks or bad boy/girl reformed story?

The mere fact of two people meeting in a humorous or unusual way is not an entire story arc nor does it suggest a specific story arc. Ergo, it's not a trope.

The almost-left-behind hero/heroine, the big secret revealed, forgiveness granted, or sparks flying are all STORY elements but not tropes that suggest fully developed story arcs.

By themselves none of these elements tell the reader a thing about the type of story they're reading or where the story is going to end up.

Writers often confuse a character theme with a trope, as well.

A character theme is some attribute that describes a character. It often affects the story significantly, but it is not the source of twists, turns, and movement, the active plot if you will, of the story.

.   .   .

EXAMPLES:

- A widow is not a trope. A widow learning how to love again is.
- A shapeshifter is not a trope. A shapeshifter fated to love a human is.
- A bride is not a trope. A bride left at the altar and struggling to love again is.
- A cowboy is not a trope. A cowboy displaced to a big city and learning to fit in is.

Take the example of the cowboy. The fact that the hero is a cowboy may greatly color the mood and setting of your story, and the cowboy as hero comes with a ready-made set of props that the reader or viewer will absolutely expect to see.

Every historical cowboy must be accompanied by horses, and well, cows. Stetsons, spurs, six-shooters, saloons, and maybe a barmaid with a heart of gold would not be remiss. A modern cowboy may have traded in his horse for a pick-up truck or even a helicopter. Props aside, however, that essentially honorable, nature-loving, rough-around-the-edges loner remains.

And yet, for all the flavor a cowboy hero brings to any story, his existence alone does not give the story any movement or create any expectations for the reader of what conflicts and resolution lie ahead for our intrepid cowboy. That job belongs to the trope.

Will our cowboy have to fight off some threat to his ranch from a dastardly neighbor bent on stealing his herd or his land? Will our cowboy find a woman with no memory wandering on his land and take her in? Will our cowboy find himself stranded in a blizzard at the cabin of his attractive young widow neighbor? Will our cowboy be forced to move to a big city to build a new life?

The tropes in the previous paragraph—saving his home, amnesia, stranded with a stranger, and fish out of water—are what will give our cowboy's story movement, a problem to solve, and a logical, predictable story structure. These tropes will let our reader know what to expect from this cowboy's story.

Why do we care if the reader has any idea of what to expect from a story?

I'll say it again because it bears repeating.

> **One of the great paradoxes of fiction reading and TV/film viewing is that audience members don't want to be surprised, at least not in the large-scale movements that form the core of the story.**

When readers pick up a romance novel or viewers watch a romantic movie, they by golly expect the two main characters to end up together at the end of the story. Furthermore, they also expect a happily ever after unless you've specifically signaled to the reader/viewer up front that they're headed toward a more ambiguous happily for now ending.

If a reader picks up a mystery novel, he or she expects the mystery to be solved by the end of the story.

Spy thriller movie? The world must be saved before the final credits roll.

Crime thriller? Justice had better be served.

Likewise, readers and viewers have definite expectations of how the smaller arcs that form an overall story will progress and resolve.

If the cowboy's ranch is threatened, the reader/viewer absolutely expects that, after some scary threats and nearly losing the ranch, our cowboy hero will find a way to save his home.

If our cowboy gets stranded in a blizzard with a beautiful widow, the story consumer expects attraction to unfold as they're forced to get to know each other and work together to survive. Indeed, the reader/viewer also expects the storm to lift eventually and the cowboy and his widow to realize they want to stay together forever, even after life resumes its normal course.

> **KEY POINT: If you, the writer, don't deliver on the reader's or viewer's expectations of how a trope will unfold and resolve in your story, the reader/viewer will be outraged. Outraged readers and viewers have an unpleasant tendency to leave terrible reviews, tell everyone they know how awful your story was, and never buy another book or watch another TV show or film you've created.**

When you introduce any trope into a story, a specific set of problems is inevitably bound to occur as a result of that trope and require a specific resolution.

Returning to our cowboy, misplaced into a big city this time, he's out of his natural environment and must either learn to fit in or make his environment fit him.

Note that in this case, two possible outcomes are suggested. This particular trope is somewhat more flexible than some other tropes. But still, certain, specific conflicts and resolutions are required by this trope.

An important side note, the names that tropes are commonly given can be a bit confusing. Because they get discussed so often within the publishing and TV/film industries, there's a tendency to shorten the full descriptions of tropes into familiar nicknames.

EXAMPLE: Childhood sweethearts. In and of itself, the fact that two characters were once childhood sweethearts doesn't connote a classic story type or inevitable plot points. More accurately, we would call this trope, "childhood sweethearts reunite and fall in love as adults." But that's clumsy and a mouthful to say every time you mention it. Most people will refer to it simply as a childhood sweethearts trope. The rest of it is generally understood.

If you're confused as to whether something is a character theme or an actual trope, ask yourself, does the fact that a person has a specific characteristic or problem suggest an entire story arc?

If the answer is no, it's merely a character theme. If the answer is yes, it's a trope.

EXAMPLE: Your hero is a Scottish highlander. What has to happen because he's a highlander? We have no idea. Perhaps the English will seize his lands. Perhaps a feisty lass he grew up with will win over his heart. Perhaps he'll go raiding and kidnap himself a Sassenach bride. We have no idea where the story is headed, simply because the hero is a highlander. It only tells us he's likely to wear a kilt and speak with a brogue. So, highlander hero is not a trope.

WHY BOTHER WITH TROPES?

In the first place, you're not likely to avoid them altogether in any story you tell. Tropes are so baked into every book you've ever read, every television show or movie you've ever watched, even the casual verbal stories we share with other people, that you can hardly avoid them if you try.

> **We can even go so far as to say that our actual lives are a series of tropes, many of them universal to all human beings: growing up, falling in love, making a living, possibly raising a family or finding an intentional family, growing old, and dying.**

The many challenges common to all of us that form the conflicts, obstacles, tragedies, and triumphs of our lives are the stuff of tropes. We're all familiar with them. They resonate throughout all our lives.

One reason we read books and watch television and movies is to vicariously overcome these challenges as we live in the skin of the main characters of a story for a little while. We learn how to deal with the tropes of our own lives. We make peace with the tropes we've struggled through.

> **We learn from the hard lessons other (fictional or real) people have learned by reading about or watching them deal with the challenges posed by the tropes in their lives.**

Occasionally, authors brag that they've written books without tropes. I've even heard a publisher demand trope-free books or a producer ask for trope-free screenplays from time to time.

The truth is, writing without tropes is simply not possible if you expect to tell a story that sets up a dilemma or conflict of any kind and resolves it in the end.

Tropes are the beginnings, middles, and endings of story arcs, the predictable and logical progressions from a starting place to an ending place in a plot.

When a publisher or producer asks for a trope-free story, my guess is they're actually asking for a cliché-free plot. At a minimum, what they're asking for is a unique or rarely used trope, or perhaps a unique twist upon a traditional trope.

Let's face it. A romance is a trope all by itself. In its simplest form, boy meets girl (or some combination of interchangeable genders), there's attraction, there's conflict, there's happily ever after. Boom. A trope.

In publishers' and producers' defense, because tropes get used over and over by writers of all stripes across all genres and mediums of storytelling, it can be challenging to write a book or screenplay that feels new, fresh, and different from every other story that relies on the same tropes.

In fact, the word "trope" has come to be synonymous with cliché-laden writing. I would argue this has much more to do with tropes being written badly, packaged badly, and overused than with what tropes actually are.

The second reason to bother with tropes is that readers and viewers are trained to expect and look for tropes, and in fact, psychologists suggest that audiences crave the familiarity of tropes in their story-based entertainment. Why else would readers and viewers return to the same tropes over and over?

> **Lisa Cron puts it brilliantly in <u>Wired for Story</u> when she says, "We think in story. It's hardwired in our brain. It's how we make strategic sense of the otherwise overwhelming world around us."**

I would take that one-step further and propose that not only do we think in story, but more specifically, we also think in tropes.

Tropes are the building blocks of story, the sub-stories within the larger story that give our lives—and books, TV shows, and movies—shape and substance.

Tropes occur in an orderly fashion, and they show us the logical progression of events that must happen for a particular kind of story to reach a satisfying conclusion.

> **EXAMPLE:** A secretary falls in love with her boss. The only logical path forward for our beleaguered and ignored secretary to find happiness with her oh-so-attractive employer is for her to finally get the boss's attention, gain his romantic interest, overcome any obstacles presented by being his employee and by the work environment around them, and to persevere until that man puts a ring on her finger.

There's no other reasonable path forward to a positive conclusion for our secretary and her boss. In the absence of any of those steps, a happy outcome is thrown into serious doubt, and in fact, not likely to happen at all.

She never gains his attention? No way for romance to unfold. He's not interested when he does notice her? Not likely to move forward into a satisfying romance. Obstacles in the workplace can't be overcome? No way to ethically become a couple. No ring on the finger? Honey, that jerk is just taking advantage of you.

Tropes certainly have variations and can take differing paths to happily ever after. And of course, if your goal is to write a tragedy rather than a happy story, tropes can lead to a failed romance.

But at their core, these love stories *all* have a predictable beginning, middle, and end.

> **If you want to satisfy your audience, you must give them all the parts of each trope in your story.**

The third reason to bother learning about tropes and how to use them effectively is they are an incredibly powerful and useful tool for working writers.

- If you understand tropes thoroughly, your story's plot will unfold before you effortlessly (well, with somewhat less blood, sweat, and tears).
- Your characters will know what to do next when the sagging middle of your book is yawning before you like the Grand Canyon with the happy ending only a distant speck on the far side of the chasm.
- And best of all, you will deliver a deeply satisfying story to your audience.

OBLIGATORY SCENES

One of the great beauties—and pitfalls—of tropes is that they all require certain major scenes to happen, usually in a specific order, to tell that particular story motif.

If you're writing about a kidnapped heroine, she a) must be kidnapped, b) must be in danger of not being rescued, and c) be rescued. Leave any one of these elements out, and you don't have a satisfying story for your audience.

Sure, you could kidnap your heroine and leave her kidnapped forever...but how terrible an ending is that? How much more nervous about being kidnapped will every member of your audience be after seeing such an unhappy outcome?

If you're writing horror, go for it scaring your audience, but in any other genre of fiction, such a negative outcome will be deeply dissatisfying to your audience.

So, what's the moral of this story?

- **Every single trope has a logical starting point or inciting event.**
- **Every single trope has a logical middle that takes the form of an obstacle or conflict preventing its successful resolution.**
- **Every single trope has a specific black moment where all appears to be lost in a way unique to that particular trope.**
- **Every single trope has a logical and satisfying conclusion.**

When a writer creates a story, he or she enters into an unspoken contract with the reader or viewer. The writer agrees to deliver the story the reader/viewer expects. This contract also extends to the tropes the writer employs in the story.

If you break this contract with your reader/viewer, that consumer will not forgive you. Trust me. I've seen the hate mail and verbal attacks readers and viewers spew in fury at writers who break this contract.

> **KEY POINT: You must not fail to deliver the logical and satisfying conclusion your reader or viewer expects from the tropes in your story. Never, EVER, fail to deliver on the promise of the tropes you use.**

Filmmaker, Stanley Kubrick said, "Everything has already been done, every story has been told, every scene has been shot. It's our job to do it one better."

Every trope has been used thousands or even millions of times. But they continue to exist because we love them. Why do we love them so much? They're universally recognizable and familiar to all of us.

They're old friends; we grew up with them. We've listened to and learned these classic tropes since we could understand speech. They help us understand the world around us. And, in the case of romance tropes, they teach us logical ways to overcome universal, classic obstacles to love.

Another important reason we all love tropes is because they inevitably lead our hero and heroine—who are, of course, alter egos for the reader or viewer himself or herself—to achieve universally appealing dreams, wishes, or fantasies.

Who doesn't wish to be plucked from poverty and whisked into a life of wealth and ease?

Who doesn't wish to be waited on hand and foot?

Who doesn't want to be given a gift of great value, to be popular, to find one's tribe, or to be the one chosen to be loved out of all possible love interests?

Tropes *work* for the exact same reason we love them:

- We recognize them.
- We find them comforting and familiar.
- We have a deep-seated need to see each trope work out happily.

Your job as a writer, then, is to find a way to put into action what Kubrick said.

You must find a way to take what is old and make it new. You must tell your story in your own voice, with your own perspective, while remaining true to the time-honored tropes you choose to use.

I can't tell you how many times I've asked editors, or heard other writers ask producers, or even heard writers ask their fans, "What book/show/movie are you looking for, right now?"

The answer is always some version of, "I want the same story that has always worked before and that I've loved in the past, but new and fresh. Different but the same."

I also can't tell you how many times I've pulled out my own hair over that answer or listened to other writers wail in frustration over it. Different but the same? What the heck does that mean?

Let me translate for you.

**Editors, producers, readers, and viewers
want the classic tropes they've always
loved and that have always appealed to
them but told in a fresh, new way that
makes them enjoy the trope all over
again.**

One last piece of advice about using tropes: it is easy to write mechanically when focused solely on trope, marching grimly through the obligatory scenes of a trope, never varying, never embellishing, never reaching for anything more.

The most boring book or movie in the world is one that relies solely on tropes to define the story. However, the best book or movie in the world can also rely solely on tropes to define and tell a story.

Assuming all the requirements of a trope are met, quality of writing is not defined by using tropes or not using tropes, but rather how skillfully the writer uses them.

3

HOW TO USE THIS BOOK

This book covers external tropes that are universal to all sub-genres of romance, meaning they're adaptable to any type of romantic story, or even to a romantic sub-plot in a book or screenplay that's not primarily a romance. The entire romance fiction genre, which is very large, is usually divided into a series of sub-genres, including but by no means limited to:

- historical romance
- romantic suspense
- contemporary romance
- paranormal romance
- sweet romance
- romantic comedy
- small town romance
- inspirational romance
- and so on...

All the tropes analyzed in this book can be applied to stories in *any* of these genres.

There are many more tropes specific to individual sub-genres, of course. A forced marriage might work perfectly well in an historical romance, but it would struggle to translate well into a sweet, contemporary romance or a romantic comedy, for example.

I have not included those genre-specific tropes in these volumes relating specifically to universal romance tropes. (And yes, I promise to write a series of books dealing with genre-specific romance tropes.)

It is not uncommon to combine a romance trope with a trope(s) from another genre of fiction to create a crossover project. For example, a romantic thriller, fantasy romance, or a romantic mystery.

It's also entirely possible that these classic romance tropes can be borrowed by other genres of film and fiction and appear in young adult projects, science fiction projects, mysteries, and thrillers, to name a few. In fact, they can appear in any form of television/film/fiction/other story formats where two characters in the story fall in love after overcoming some sort of obstacle(s).

Overview of this Book

As you've seen, each trope description in this book includes:

- a definition of the trope
- adjacent tropes
- why readers/viewers love this particular trope
- a list of the obligatory scenes that form the beginning, middle, black moment, and end of the trope's arc
- any additional scenes that are key to doing this trope justice
- a list of questions to consider when writing this trope
- a list of potential hazards and pitfalls of writing this trope
- examples of movies and books that use this tropeAt the end of this book, I have included an appendix listing all

the universal romance tropes and which volume in the
Universal Romance Tropes series they appear in.

In some cases, several tropes may be closely related. They may
describe varying degrees of the same trait in a character, for example:
Reclusive Hero, Shy Hero, and Socially Awkward Hero. Or tropes
may be variations on the same idea, for example: Dangerous Secret,
Secret Baby, Secret Marriage, Secret Identity. Or tropes may contain
adjacent story elements or themes, for example: Love Triangle, Best
Friend's Sibling, Ménage, Harem.

In these cases when tropes overlap or descriptions of one may
help you develop another similar or related trope, feel free to refer to
similar tropes as you refine your primary trope or if you want to
expand beyond the strict confines of a specific trope.

At the end of this book, I have included an appendix listing all
the universal romance tropes and which volume in the Universal
Romance Tropes series they appear in.

If you already have some idea of the trope or tropes you'd like to
write about, you can go directly to those specific descriptions for
inspiration and thought-provoking questions as you plotters plan your
story or you pantsers ruminate on the possibilities you might like to
explore.

For those of you unfamiliar with the terms, plotters are those
writers who like to fully plan and outline a story before they
commence writing it. Pantsers are writers who prefer to sit down and
begin writing without planning much or any of the story in advance.
Rather, pantsers write by the seat of their pants, organically letting
the story unfold as the characters and story dictate in the moment.

Many writers are some combination of the two.

There is NO right or wrong way to write your story. Whatever
works for you is the best and right way for you to develop your story.
The good news is this book is designed to be useful to both plotters
and pantsers.

Plotters are likely to refer to this book during the planning process and before beginning to write as a tool for developing story, characters, and scenes. Pantsers may be more inclined to use this book as an idea generator either in the story development phase or when stuck on what to do next. Pantsers may also use this book to develop a very general idea of characters and/or where your story is going before sitting down to write.

All writers can use this book effectively during or after the drafting process to check their work against the expectations of the tropes that they've planned or that have emerged over the course of drafting their story.

If you've already drafted a story using particular tropes, you can go directly to those trope descriptions to get revision and editing ideas and to ensure you've delivered the kind of story your reader will expect...and more importantly, that your reader will LOVE.

If you've written a story and you're considering how to market it, you can also use this book as a guide to figure out which classic trope(s) your story best fits. You can check to make sure your marketing and advertising materials—title, logline, tagline, blurb, trailer, back cover copy—are properly tailored to signal your story's particular trope(s) to prospective consumers of your story.

HELPFUL HINT: The idea behind signaling in your marketing materials which tropes will be in your story is not to draw every reader or viewer to your story but rather to attract the readers and viewers who will absolutely love the tropes in your story. They'll get a satisfying experience, you'll get positive reviews, and you'll gain a loyal fan who trusts you to deliver the story you

promised. Most importantly, you'll gain a repeat customer.

If you're in the early planning stages of a story, or you're simply looking for an idea to spark a new story, this book is a useful tool for you as well.

HOW TO USE TROPE TO BUILD STORY

While plotting vs. pantsing describes how a writer develops story, what they think of first when developing story divides writers into two more categories.

In my experience, there are two kinds of writers in this world: character-driven writers who think in characters and develop characters first when creating a story, and plot-driven writers who think in events and action and develop plot first when creating a story.

As writers gain experience, over time and multiple projects, we all become more adept at thinking in terms of both character development and plot development as we prepare to write a new story. However, we all have a default setting that is our first, natural, and probably strongest skill in the story planning process.

Tropes can be one of, if not the most, powerful tools in *both* types of writers' story planning processes. Understanding tropes allows all writers to make sure they are creating fully realized plots *and* fully realized characters that will be satisfying to readers or viewers.

Many years ago, I participated in a continuity project at a major publishing house. Twelve authors were given a bible created by the publisher that described twelve linked stories, and each of us was assigned to write one novel in the series. It so happened that the heroine I was assigned was the sister of a heroine in another book in the series.

The author of the sister's book called me shortly after we all got to work on our books because she wanted to develop her heroine's back story and wanted to make sure the family and family issues she built for her heroine would also work as backstory for my heroine.

Now, I should confess here that I am naturally a plot-driven writer. It quickly became obvious that the other author I was speaking with was a character-driven writer. I opened the conversation by saying to her, "Tell me a little about the story you're thinking of writing."

She launched enthusiastically into a description of her heroine's hopes and dreams, fears and failures. She talked about wanting to write angst between the heroine and her father, and how hard it was going to be for the heroine to trust the hero because of that.

After about thirty seconds of her talking in this vein, I interrupted the author to ask, "Yes, but what does she *do*? What *happens* in your story?"

The lovely author went silent for a moment, obviously taken aback by the question, and finally said, "Tell me about your story."

I enthusiastically launched into telling her how my heroine stumbled across evidence of a plot to assassinate the president, went to a prison to question a terrorist where she got caught in the middle of a prison break, had to escape that, make her way to the White House, get a Secret Service agent to listen to her, try to find the bad guys—

And at about that point, the other author interrupted my tale of action, adventure, and danger to ask, "Yes, but how does she *feel*?"

I should probably add that my mind went completely blank and I had no idea how to answer that question. At that time in my career, I didn't typically figure out how my characters felt until I was actually writing (or sometimes, revising) the scene.

The moral of this story is that those two simple questions fully encompass both the plotting and character aspects of writing. You must answer *both* questions in the course of writing your story. Furthermore, in every major scene of your story, these same questions must be answered if you're to give your readers a satisfying experience.

. . .

Every single obligatory scene must answer these two questions:
   But what do they *do*?
   But how do they *feel*?

So, how can both character-driven writers and plot-driven writers use tropes to help plan and flesh out their story, and to be sure to answer these two vital questions?

DEVELOPING PLOT FROM TROPE

Often, writers have no trouble developing interesting, multi-layered characters with fascinating back stories and unique individual qualities. But once this fabulous cast of characters has taken shape, the writer must figure out what on earth to DO with them to carry an entire novel or screenplay.

Enter your friend the trope.

Take a look at the characters you've already played around with and browse through this book until you find several tropes that would challenge your wonderful and fascinating main characters and force them into either a personal transformation or into a relationship they must find a way to transform into a happily ever after.

ROMANTIC TRAGEDIES

Yes, I'm aware that not all love stories end in happily ever after. Many stories still classed as romances end more ambiguously in a happily for now or a sort-of happy. And of course, tragic love stories end in a failed relationship or worse. Cue the Romeo and Juliet theme music.

For the purposes of describing tropes in this series of books, I have chosen to describe a positive outcome to the love story built by each trope.

All that's necessary to convert any of these tropes to a negative outcome (a romantic tragedy) is simply to reverse the positive outcome of the 'ENDING' obligatory scene.

Interestingly enough, the rest of the obligatory scenes of the trope will usually remain pretty much the same. The characters will meet, fall in love, be faced with an obstacle or series of obstacles that become ever more challenging and difficult.

The lovers will arrive at a black moment where all appears to be lost...so far, we're tracking along pretty much exactly beside the lovers who get a positive outcome...but then, in the ENDING of the romantic tragedy, the lovers' climactic efforts to overcome the black moment fail. Boom. Tragedy complete.

In point of technical fact, I could title this series The Tropoholic's Guide to Universal Romance and Romantic Tragedy. But that's even longer and more of a mouthful than the current title, so I'll just stick with what I've got.

All plot in all types of romance stories, both happy and sad, is a journey of change—of two people starting in one place and ending up in another—a place that makes happily ever after not only possible but fully realized, makes their tragic failure to find love complete and devastating, or someplace somewhere in between the two extremes.

EXERCISE: FINDING PLOT FROM EXISTING CHARACTERS, USING TROPES

Divide a sheet of paper or your computer screen in half, vertically. Label the left-hand column, BEFORE. Label the right-hand column, AFTER. In the before column, write down a list of main qualities or beliefs your hero possesses, both good and bad, at the start of your story.

Now, beside each of those words, in the AFTER column write

down the opposite of each quality or belief. You have just mapped a very simple set of change arcs for your hero from the BEFORE quality to the AFTER quality.

Ask yourself the following questions about each pair of descriptive words:

1. What situation, crisis, or realization could cause the hero to shift from the BEFORE word to the AFTER word in a story?

2. Does the AFTER word represent a negative quality, which is to say a black moment (when the hero has lost everything, failed utterly, or fallen back into his worst, old ways)? Or does the AFTER word represent the hero's growth, change for the better, or overcoming his worst flaws, which is to say, a happy ending?

3. Now, keeping in mind your list of negative/black moment words in the AFTER column, browse through the trope descriptions in this book. Look for qualities in the black moments described in the book that match the black moment your hero might experience if he changes for the worse.

4. Likewise, look at your hero's AFTER words that represent growth and positive change, and browse through the endings of the various tropes in this book to find possible matches to your hero if he were to get his happily ever after.

5. You should now have a short list of possible tropes to use in your story that will illustrate your hero's change and growth over the course of your book.

6. Repeat this entire exercise for your heroine. See if any tropes in your two short lists match up to *both* your hero and heroine as you've designed them. Those tropes are obvious plot fits for the characters you've created. **It's**

fine, by the way, to write a separate trope for each of your main love interests in your story.

7. Tweak both your hero and heroine's main qualities as needed to find a trope or tropes that work for both of them.

8. Pick a trope that sounds fun to write and start plotting how the obligatory events of that trope will force your hero and heroine to change and grow until they finally find true love. Or pick a couple of tropes that sound fun to play with and commence torturing your hero and heroine!

It's worth pointing out that the above exercise is in no way mandatory. If you already know what trope(s) you want to write in your story, by all means, dive right in. This exercise is purely meant to help you narrow down possible tropes if you have a hero and heroine in mind and have no idea where to begin with creating a plot for them.

Once you've picked a trope or a few tropes that will work for your characters and that you would enjoy writing, it's time to take a look at the obligatory scenes of the tropes you've chosen. What would each of those scenes look like in a story containing your main characters, in the genre or sub-genre you're writing, in the setting you've chosen?

Next, you need to ask yourself what preparatory or lead-up scenes are necessary in your story to set up those big obligatory scenes?

If you're planning to use more than one trope in your story, you will have to include all the obligatory scenes from all those tropes in your story.

You may end up with anywhere from four to a dozen or more

beginning, middle, black moment, and ending scenes that *must* be in your book to set up and follow through on your chosen tropes.

As an aside, if you've chosen to use more than one closely related trope in your story, several of these obligatory scenes may actually overlap or end up being the same scene. All this means is you've got one less obligatory scene that has to be included in your book.

Of course, it's vital that, if you have an obligatory scene that's pulling double duty as a key scene for more than one trope, it still has to satisfy the requirements of *both* tropes.

Now, take a look at the list of obligatory scenes you've made and ask yourself the following questions:

1. What other scenes will be necessary to include in your story to set up each of these obligatory scenes? These lead-up scenes will share critical information with the reader, build tension that climaxes in one of your obligatory scenes, describe the events and actions that move your characters toward the next obligatory scene.

2. What additional scenes are necessary to explain to the reader how and why the main characters will evolve, and move, from one obligatory scene to the next?

3. What scenes are necessary to raise the stakes for both characters and make your readers/viewers care deeply about them as they move from one obligatory scene to the next?

4. What scenes are necessary to demonstrate how your characters feel about and react to the obligatory scene that just took place?

Once you've brainstormed through these questions for each set of obligatory scenes from each trope you've chosen, you should be getting close to having a complete major scene list for your entire story.

Now that you've got a list of major scenes, you can fill out the rest of your plot with the minor scenes that not only set up the major scenes, but also lend flavor, humor, emotion, context, romantic attraction, secondary characters, and key elements of the genre you're writing.

For example, if you're writing a steamy contemporary romance, not only will major scenes need to reflect this, but the minor scenes will also need to establish and support the steam heat and help raise the temperature level of the overall story. If you're writing a comedy, both the minor and major scenes will need to establish and support the humor.

At any rate, after listing out all of your obligatory scenes, major scenes, and minor scenes, you should have a fairly complete scene list for your entire story.

Because I see you running screaming from pre-plotting a book, my pantser colleagues, you still *must* include each and every obligatory scene from whatever trope your book ends up being built around. Whether you do that in your first draft or you have to go back and revise the obligatory scenes into your final project, you still have to get every obligatory scene of your trope(s) into your story.

While I would never wish to interfere in the organic pantsing process, there is value in at least having some idea of the major story points (the obligatory scenes) you should be aiming toward including in your project.

Many pantser-writers I know do go ahead and pick a specific trope or set of tropes before they begin writing their stories. They use the list of obligatory scenes included in this book as guideposts for their journey. They pants their way from the beginning to the middle, from the middle to the black moment, and from there to the ending, but always with the next obligatory scene in mind as a target to get to...by whatever circuitous route the characters and plot ulti-mately take to get there.

If even this minimal amount of pre-set plot is too much for you, by all means, go ahead and draft your entire story by the seat of your pants. But once you've got a draft in hand and have identified the trope(s) you ended up using in your story, you must go back in the revision and editing phase and make sure you have included all of the obligatory scenes required by your story's trope(s).

I've been told that adding in obligatory scenes to a completed draft can be a nightmare of epic proportions. It typically requires extensive rejiggering of the plot and can cause major direction changes for characters that force extensive rewrites.

Even if you're a pure pantser, as soon as you get some idea of what trope(s) you may be leaning toward as your story unfolds, it's worth taking a peek at that trope's description to give yourself some idea of where you might want to head with the story and what the obligatory scenes might look like.

DEVELOPING CHARACTERS FROM TROPE

If you're the kind of writer who develops plot first and then creates characters to fit the story you plan to tell, tropes are your friend, as well. You, however, are likely to start your story planning process with this book rather than end your revision process with it.

Browse this book and the other volumes in this series...my apolo-gies for the shameless plug...until you find one or several tropes that capture your imagination and sound like fun to build into a story.

Side note: I'm a big proponent of writers actually enjoying what they write. To quote the great Ann Maxwell, who wrote as Elizabeth Lowell, "It's very hard to write a wonderful story if you're typing with one hand and holding your nose with the other."

When you tell your story with joy and passion, it inevitably shows through in the words that end up on the page. Although I've given it a lot of thought over the years, and many of my students have asked me how to mechanically insert this sense of joy into a project of theirs, I can't give you a specific reason why it happens or describe how your passion comes through in the words you choose. But trust me. It does.

It's one of those mysteries of writing that ranks right up there with how a writer's voice comes across on the page. As far as I can tell, it has to do with the words you choose and the rhythms and cadences of the words you choose. But if you *love* the story you write, those who read your project *will* know it.

For my screenwriter colleagues, I realize you're at the mercy of directors and actors to share the same love of your story and ultimately to convey their passion and joy for your story to the viewing audience. But long before that happens, every agent, producer, studio scout/executive, investor, and creative person considering attaching to your project needs to feel your passion for your story.

You can't write a joyless, passionless screenplay and assume that someone along the way will inject passion for the project into your story. For that matter, you can't expect anyone to invest millions of dollars in your project in hopes that someone along the way in development will breathe life into your story. That's up to you.

Okay. So, you've found a few tropes that sound fun. Perhaps you already have a story premise in mind, maybe a hook that will start the story, or you've envisioned a big ending that would be fun to build up to. Maybe you have an entire plot developed already.

With all of these ideas in mind, browse the trope descriptions until you find several that will fit with the story you're planning to tell.

HELPFUL HINT: It's actually fine to choose tropes that don't seem to be a natural fit for the story you have in mind. Sometimes the unexpected trope creates a fascinating story with unusual

conflicts for the hero and heroine to overcome. Drop a secret baby into a spy thriller. Maybe a marriage of convenience collides with your gothic mystery. Strand a bride or groom at the altar in your sci-fi fantasy tale. The beauty of these universal romance tropes is they'll translate to any love story in any setting. That's what makes them universal.

Once you've chosen the tropes for your story, write down a list of the obligatory scenes required by your tropes. Add in any other scenes you already know you want to work into your story. Write down the major events you know have to be in your story and the other events that have to happen to set up each of those major events and obligatory scenes.

Now, you have to populate those scenes with human beings. Ask yourself the following questions:

1. What kind of hero/heroine would be **best** suited to do the all the things your rough plot outline requires of them? There's going to be a shootout? Do you need a police officer or an ex-soldier as your hero?
2. What kind of hero/heroine would be **worst** suited to do all the things your rough plot outline requires of them? Don't be afraid to throw your hero and heroine into situations way over their heads to handle. Force them to reach beyond what they think they're capable of. Force them to grow. Maybe that climactic shootout would be

more interesting with a pacifist or a scared-to-death-of-guns kindergarten teacher as your hero.

3. What are the emotional stakes baked into in each of the tropes you've chosen? What kind of character will find these emotional stakes difficult to embrace? Deeply meaningful? Painful? Challenging? Worth risking everything to achieve?

4. How will the hero and heroine change as a result of the tropes you've chosen? What is their beginning point and end point in the story based on these tropes? Will this be a journey of emotional transformation? Personal redemption? A change in understanding or attitude?

Once you've made a bunch of notes for yourself based on these questions, map out an arc for each main character where he or she moves from the starting points of the tropes you've chosen to the obligatory ending of each.

EXERCISE: FINDING CHARACTER ARC FROM TROPES

1. Once you have a list of the major scenes in your book, take a piece of paper and divide it in half vertically, or divide a computer screen vertically. Label the left-hand column, BEFORE, and label the right-hand column, AFTER.

2. You might want to number your scenes for convenience's sake. Now, for scene number one, write down in a few words or short phrases how your hero feels before the scene starts.

3. How does he feel about himself?

4. How does he feel about the heroine?

5. How does he feel about the situation in this scene before it starts?

6. How does he feel about this situation after this scene takes place?

7. What has going through this situation changed about the hero?

8. Repeat answering these questions for each major scene in your story. If you don't already know how the hero feels as he progresses through each of the major scenes, think in terms of progress, change, and growth toward a final lesson learned or a final and irrevocable change for the better in your hero that makes him able to love fully and completely.

9. Take a look at the hero's changes from major scene to major scene. Is there an overall arc of change? It's worth noting that there should be setbacks along the way, reversals of course, moments when he doubts himself, and moments when he rejects or refuses to take the next emotional step of change and growth. If you don't have the setbacks in his arc, build some in, now. Look at places in the plot where things can go badly for the hero and give him these setbacks.

10. Repeat this entire exercise for the heroine in the second column of your paper or screen.

11. By now, you have a list of how the events of the story affect your hero and heroine and drive their progress toward achieving their happily ever afters.

12. Now, ask yourself the question, how, as these events take place, can the heroine help along or actually cause the hero's change/growth/setback in that scene to take place? Vice versa, how can the hero cause the heroine's change/growth/setback in that scene to take place?

You should have a bunch of notes now about how the movement, the action if you will, of your story—the trope—shapes and defines your characters' growth and change throughout the story.

It's all well and good for the events of the plot to force the hero and heroine to grow and change. But at the end of the day, you're writing a love story (even if it's only a subordinate plotline in a larger, non-romantic story).

The hero and heroine themselves should also be drivers of teaching their partner the lessons and skills they need to become ideally suited for each other. Hence, the final question in the exercise above of how the hero and heroine affect and shape each other over the course of the story.

With that in mind, add into your plot-based scene list additional scenes that are needed to show your hero and heroine in conflict emotionally and beginning to address and resolve their emotional conflicts.

Then, go back one more time and add in any additional scenes needed to capture more emotional notes of tenderness, sadness, humor.

Add in whatever scenes you need to flesh out how they *feel*, to paint the heat level of their relationship, to add secondary characters who aid and abet or try to foil the hero and heroine's romance, and show the required elements of the genre you're writing in.

Helpful Hint: There is no right or wrong way to develop story. Use whatever method works best for you. Characters can shape the plot, or plot can shape the characters, or some combination of both. But in all cases, the glue that holds characters and plot together and makes sure they travel a logical path together to a satisfying

resolution is the story's trope(s). The plot is shaped by the tropes you choose, and those tropes will shape the emotional journeys taken by your characters.

LAYERING TROPES

In the shorter written romance story formats and in screenplays (particularly where the romance is a B plot), it's not uncommon to zero in on a single main trope to carry the entire story arc. In fact, it can make sense to stick to a single trope within the constraints of a smaller word count or page count.

The shorter the book or screenplay, the less room there is to interweave—and do justice to—multiple tropes. After all, for each additional trope you include in your story, the number of obligatory scenes goes up.

For some tropes, however, the obligatory scenes may overlap considerably. This can reduce the overall number of obligatory scenes enough to shorten the overall length of a novel or screenplay.

> **Example:** A left at the altar bride trope is layered with a redemption trope, and the groom who jilted her spends the story trying to earn back her trust.

In establishing why the groom left her at the altar in the first place, you're also establishing the starting point for your hero's redemption arc. Leaving his fiancée at the altar may be the very thing (or the outward symptom of the very thing) he's got to come back from.

The triumphant personal growth moment of the heroine finally moving on with her life is also the black moment for the hero as his attempt at redeeming himself in her eyes seems to have utterly failed.

The hero's triumphant personal moment of finally proving he's worthy to the heroine is also the obligatory resolution moment of the bride's left at the altar trope where she finally finds a man who will be steadfast and never, ever leave her.

Any number of universal romance tropes lend themselves to this heavy layering and intermingling of obligatory scenes.

Other combinations of tropes, however, will require distinct and separate resolutions of each trope before the happy ever after ending can be achieved.

The kidnapped heroine must be rescued before she can get her fairy tale wedding to her knight in shining armor.

The hero's devastating secret must be revealed before the burned-by love, distrusting heroine can take the leap of faith and agree to marry him.

Particularly in the case where a trope from another genre of fiction is blended with a romance trope, the need for distinct and separate endings often becomes more pronounced.

The evil empire must be defeated before the intrepid space cowboy gets the girl. The psychopathic murderer must be captured before the hero and heroine can relax enough to resolve their personal conflicts.

It's generally considered to be an especially elegant ending when all the tropes of a story can be brought to resolution in a single, cohesive climax.

But the practical reality is that this is simply not always possible. Often, a story needs two or more climactic scenes, one to resolve each major trope.

> **Helpful Hint: The general rule is to resolve the least important trope first and the most important trope last. In a story that's primarily a romance, the trope most likely to tear your hero and heroine apart will be the most important trope and resolved last.**

> **If you're combining a non-romance trope with a romance trope in a romance story, the romance trope will still usually resolve last.**

> **Vice versa, in a non-romance story, all else being equal, the romance would resolve first and the major trope of the primary story would resolve last.**

I stated earlier that I arbitrarily divided my master list of universal romance tropes into four categories: Internal Tropes, External Tropes, Backstory Tropes, and Hook Tropes.

In point of fact, however, each of these categories of tropes is a bit different from the others, and the tropes in each of these categories lean into one specific aspect of story more than the other aspects.

The internal tropes lean into the thoughts, feelings, and emotions of the hero and heroine. The external tropes emphasize the world the hero and heroine live in. The backstory trope focuses on past events in the hero and heroine's lives, and the hook trope focuses on how they meet.

A possible, and entirely plausible, way to layer tropes to form a complex and layered love story would be to choose one trope from each of these categories (which is to say, one trope from each of the four books in this series) and combine the four into a single story.

By choosing from these different categories, the tropes will generally tend not to compete against one another too violently for the characters', and hence the reader's or viewer's, attention. This is because each trope focuses on a conflict that pertains to a separate part of each character's personality, environment, past, and current situation.

Of course, you could also choose two tropes from one category and one trope from another category. Or one trope from each of three of the categories. Or four tropes from one category. And so on, and so on.

The number of possible combinations of tropes is astronomical. (For my fellow math nerds out there, there are over 8,500,000 possible combinations of tropes in my master list of 130 or so universal romance tropes.)

Another way to pick tropes would be to assign one to your hero and another to your heroine. In this case, you can pick complimentary tropes that work well together, or you can choose tropes that work strongly against each other.

Years ago, a literary agent told me about a demographic study my publisher had done that showed readers who liked books about sheikhs and kidnapped harem girls also tended to like stories about arranged marriages and artificial insemination babies. (I swear, I'm not making that up.) The publisher was looking for a story that combined all three tropes. The agent had an author client who struggled for months to come up with a story that included all three of those elements but had failed.

Tropoholic that I am, I took it as a personal challenge to come up with exactly that story. While I did end up substituting an adjacent trope—a secret pregnancy for the artificial insemination, I found I really enjoyed the challenge of combining several wildly unrelated tropes.

The book resulting from that exercise ended up winning several prestigious fiction awards and garnered many glowing reviews that inevitably mentioned how fresh, different, and exciting the story's twists and turns were.

It's also worth mentioning that, as the print publishing industry moves toward more online sales and away from rigid divisions of print fiction genres (historically driven by booksellers' need to know where in the store to shelve books), crossover fiction combining non-romance story elements with romantic story elements is becoming more and more common.

Romance writers are borrowing tropes from many other genres of fiction to enrich and broaden the types of stories they can tell. At the same time, many writers of other genres of fiction now feel free to pull romance tropes into their stories.

Likewise, with the advent of streaming television networks' willingness to experiment, and the sheer number of shows going into production, opportunity abounds to play with genre mash-up stories, layering multiple tropes in one project, and interesting or unexpected mixtures of tropes.

The bottom line: the number of possible combinations of universal romance tropes, genre-specific romance tropes, and tropes from other genres of storytelling is nearly endless, which is why it's still possible to write fresh, new, exciting stories out of the same tropes that every storyteller in history has used.

That said, let's dive into the tropes themselves...

4

ACROSS THE TRACKS/WRONG SIDE OF THE TRACKS

DEFINITION

A hero and heroine from very different economic, social, or cultural backgrounds have to overcome the differences in their upbringings/identities to fall in love. The core of this romance is rebellion. That rebellion takes the shape of confronting obstacles surrounding the couple. In fact, this trope doesn't depend on love as its main source of conflict. Rather, it depends on socio-economic and/or cultural clashes for its movement.

NOTE: Being from the wrong side of the tracks can be merely a character theme. The wrong side of the tracks TROPE relies on a character crossing over from the wrong side of the tracks background into a different world to seek love.

Typically, the obstacles facing characters falling in love from opposite sides of the tracks are external. Other people who object, lifestyle differences that must be resolved, misunderstandings that must be cleared up—these often form the core of the problem the hero and heroine must overcome.

The internal, emotional portion of this trope usually deals with how the hero and heroine resolve their own differences between them, how they feel and respond to the objections of others about their relationship, how they feel about each other in spite of their differences, and whether or not they're willing to sacrifice everything to be together. That "everything" might include wealth, privilege, comfort, and safety, but it also might include sacrificing family, friends, jobs, and social standing.

ADJACENT TROPES

--wrong side of the tracks

--cross-cultural/interethnic/interracial

--feuding families

--hidden wealth

WHY READERS/VIEWERS LOVE THIS TROPE

--being plucked out of poverty into wealth

--being carried away into a whole new world where all your old problems get left behind

--being waited on hand and foot, and possibly being given gifts of great value

--being the chosen one

--your lover is willing to sacrifice everything for you

--getting to cross over into the forbidden world

--breaking the rules

OBLIGATORY SCENES
THE BEGINNING:

The hero and heroine meet. While this might seem obvious, for this couple, the fact of their meeting is unusual for one or both of them. One or both of these characters is outside their normal environment and has crossed over to the other or "wrong" side of the tracks when they meet. This is usually a chance meeting but not necessarily.

The main characters have an immediate romantic spark. They may or may not know yet that theirs is a forbidden love.

The difference(s) between the hero and heroine's worlds must be established for the reader. These differences will pose the first obstacle to love for this couple.

THE MIDDLE:

The hero and heroine begin to fall in love. Again, an obvious development in a romance. However, for this pair, the act of falling in love is also an act of rebellion.

If they weren't already aware of it when they met, they figure out that they come from different sides of the tracks and that their relationship will be frowned upon or forbidden by others from their own sides of the tracks.

The hero and heroine may try to stay apart and fail. Or family, friends, and others around them may try to separate them. As the hero and heroine refuse to cooperate, pushback against their rebellion ensues from the people and forces trying to separate the hero and heroine.

This pushback probably constitutes a *major* obstacle for the hero and heroine. Societies are formed around the idea that everyone conforms to the same social values. Anyone who goes against those values threatens the very foundation of that society. The act of this couple falling in love will likely be perceived as a threat to both of their societies, and certainly as a threat to their families' places within those societies.

The tone of the story will be set by the types of people and forces that try to break up the hero and heroine and by the lovers' reactions. While this can be a comic or suspenseful story, it usually has a tragic element. This tragic subtext (or overt context) is based on the idea that all people are ultimately more alike than they're different and everybody should be allowed to love whom they please.

The hero and heroine encounter differences between the two of them that stem from their different backgrounds. These may take the form of beliefs, customs, behaviors, manners, and familiarity or unfamiliarity with various social, family, or work-related situations.

BLACK MOMENT:

The forces pulling the hero and heroine apart appear to have succeeded and the couple's chance at love appears destroyed.

The hero and heroine may choose to break up themselves because the threatened or actual consequences of them staying together have become too serious for them to continue on as a couple.

OR

External forces finally succeed in physically pulling them apart. For example, one or both will be disinherited, cut off from family and friends, or fired from a much-needed job. For this to rise to the level of being the black moment, not only have the hero and heroine been physically separated from each other, but the separation is insurmountable. The hero and heroine believe they will never be able to get back together again. They're finished as a couple, whether they like it or not.

OR

The hero and heroine's emotional or cultural differences are too great to overcome.

They may react fundamentally differently to the problems/obstacles facing them or have fundamentally different goals for their lives.

OR

Often, the black moment is the point at which the external obstacles to love and the internal obstacles to love come together in a crisis that's too much for the hero and heroine to resist or overcome.

THE END:

The hero and heroine overcome the forces pulling them apart to be together forever, anyway. Rebellion complete. Again, this sounds simple and obvious. But achieving this outcome may be anything but simple or obvious. Getting from the black moment to the end in this trope may require enormous sacrifices by one or both of our lovers.

One or both of them may have to leave behind everything and everyone they've ever known and loved to be with their true love. That's a really big sacrifice for any human being to make. If both must leave their side of the tracks, they will have to end up someplace new and different where the tracks they grew up across don't exist.

OR

The price becomes too high to pay for the external forces/opponents trying to keep them apart. The forces and people trying to foil their love must relent and let the lovers be together. The family, friends, and societal forces around them don't like the relationship, but will no longer stand in its way.

OR

Another possible outcome of this trope is that the hero and heroine will stand their ground, remain exactly where they started out, and the other people around them come to accept their relationship. Although this resolves the external obstacles thrown up by this trope, readers may find this ending less satisfying than the grand sacrifice for love that the first ending suggests.

In either case, the hero and heroine's rebellion is complete, and they have found and achieved the forbidden love they both reached for.

KEY SCENES

--the chance meeting

--realizing they come from opposite sides of the tracks

--being told he or she can't have the person they're falling for

--the first time each partner visits the other's side of the tracks, introduction to the other partner's friends and family

--introduction to the other partner's friends and family

--something terrible happens because of their stubborn insistence on being with their lover

--confrontation with the person(s) or force(s) keeping them apart

THINGS TO THINK ABOUT WHEN WRITING THIS TROPE

How do the hero and heroine meet? Is it an accident or not? Is the meeting machinated by one or the other? Is it a collision of their differing worlds or not?

Who has left their familiar world and crossed over into the unknown? What is his or her first impression of this new world? How will he or she later find out that those first impressions are exactly right or entirely wrong?

How are the hero and heroine's worlds different? Is it a physical difference? Financial? Cultural? Societal? Educational? Religious? This will largely define the external conflicts the couple has to overcome.

How do their different backgrounds make them different from each other? This will define some of the important internal conflict the couple has to overcome.

How do their worlds clash? How will you demonstrate that

clash? How can you make the clashing more intense? How about even MORE intense?

What do their worlds have in common? Do they deal with the shared problems in their worlds in the same way or differently?

Who, specifically, hates the idea of the hero and heroine getting together? Why?

Who supports them being together, either openly or in secret? Why?

Who and what from their opposing worlds will attempt to stop the hero and heroine's relationship from growing into love? Why do these people oppose the

relationship? NOTE: These may not be the same people who are willing to simply

tear the couple apart physically.

Are these objectors merely reacting to an incursion into their closed society? Do they see this relationship as a threat to the stability and good order of their society? Does the relationship pose an existential threat to the society that one lover is entering into as an outsider?

How do each partner's friends and family react to the interloper from across the tracks coming into their world and furthermore getting into a romantic relationship with their loved one? Do any of their friends/family support the relationship? Why? At what personal cost?

What parts of the new world will the hero/heroine be unfamiliar with? How will he/she/they react to these new elements? What will go wrong when first encountering these new elements?

What conflicts arise between the hero and heroine because of misunderstandings, opposing beliefs, and cultural differences between them? How will the couple resolve these?

To what lengths will those around the hero and heroine go to quash their rebellion? What's the most extreme thing these antagonists are willing to do to break up the couple? Can you push that extreme even further? What do these antagonists believe that justifies their efforts to stop the relationship? Why do they believe that?

Will the hero or heroine have to change his or her core beliefs to be with the other character? If so, what beliefs must change? Will they have to change their beliefs to live in whatever world the two of them end up in?

At what point will the price of staying together become too high for the hero and heroine? How do they react individually and to each other when this moment arrives?

If the people around them finally relent and agree to let them be together, what makes these people relent? If the hero and heroine decide to leave and start a new life elsewhere, where will they go, and why do they finally make the decision to leave everyone and everything they know and love behind?

How will the hero and heroine overcome the objections of those around them, the threats of those opposed to them, and any other obstacles that stand in their way to being together?

What do the hero and heroine each have to sacrifice to be with each other? Is there a way you can make these sacrifices bigger, grander, more dramatic, and more painful? Which is to say, the bigger the sacrifice, the bigger the love.

What does happily ever after look like for this couple (and they may each have different views of this) when they first fall in love? What does it look like by the end of the story? If it has changed, why has their view of happiness changed?

Where will the hero and heroine end up? Do they move fully into one of their worlds to live? Do they leave behind both of their known worlds and head for a brand-new world that is strange and new to both of them?

TROPE TRAPS

The character from the wealthier/more successful side of the tracks comes across as patronizing or having a savior complex.

The reason for the person reaching across to the "better" or "worse" side of the tracks is offensive to some reader groups.

Judgment of a "good" side of the tracks and a "bad" side of the tracks is easy to fall into when using this trope. This very notion may offend readers and poses a minefield that must be stepped through with care, delicacy, sensitivity, and respect if you don't want to get flamed by readers and reviewers.

Failing to resolve how these two people from very different worlds are going to live together happily and without ultimately falling into the same conflicts as already exist between their two sides of the tracks.

The act of rebelling is more important than the person the hero or heroine is allegedly falling in love with.

Failing to address how truly different their worlds are and how a person from one is going to adapt to the other world.

Assuming that anybody can casually fit into any other world. Failure to fully understand the differing values and experiences that lead to real and serious disconnects between the differing sides of the tracks these characters come from.

Making the characters and the sides of the track they come from so opposite that they could never realistically find enough common ground between them to fall in love.

Creating a hero and heroine whose core values are so fundamentally different and in such opposition that a happily ever after is entirely implausible to readers. The reality is that people rarely coexist happily in the long-term with someone whose core beliefs are very different from their own. A deeply honest person cannot live forever with someone who casually lies all the time. A person of profound faith rarely is happy with someone who is deeply cynical about faith in general and their partner's faith in particular. Negative people and optimistic people eventually rub each other the wrong way. People with diametrically opposed political beliefs will have to work *very* hard not to let those come between them.

Failing to resolve the opposition to their love in others in a believable way.

Failing to resolve the external problems that have arisen from their romance.

Failing to address the internal, emotional conflicts between the hero and heroine that have arisen from their differing backgrounds and circumstances.

ACROSS THE TRACKS/WRONG SIDE OF THE TRACKS TROPE IN ACTION
Movies:

- Maid in Manhattan
- Titanic
- Dirty Dancing
- The Notebook
- Moulin Rouge
- Inventing the Abbots

Books:

- Beauty and the Blacksmith by Tessa Dare
- Wuthering Heights by Emily Bronte
- Road to Desire by Piper Davenport
- Great Expectations by Charles Dickens
- Mackenzie's Mountain by Linda Howard
- Murphy's Law by Lori Foster
- Rett by Tess Oliver
- A Notorious Love by Sabrina Jeffries

5

BEST FRIEND'S SIBLING/SIBLING'S BEST FRIEND

DEFINITION

This trope is all about forbidden love, in this case a best friend's brother or sister or your brother or sister's best friend.

The sibling or best friend can be older or younger than you, older or younger than your sibling or best friend. Whatever the combination of age and gender, the hero or heroine falls for the sibling of his or her best friend or falls for their own brother or sister's best friend.

For the sake of clarity, the sibling or best friend who is fallen in love with by the hero or heroine will be referred to in this description as the love interest. The sibling or best friend of the hero/heroine who opposes a relationship between the hero/heroine and the love interest will be called the third wheel.

Correctly or incorrectly, the uber-attractive sibling/best friend is perceived by the hero/heroine and/or the third wheel as being off limits to the hero/heroine. The potential love interest may have entirely different ideas on the subject, however. This understanding of the love interest being off limits can be by explicit agreement between the hero/heroine and third wheel, or it can merely be unspoken and understood.

The hero/heroine may notice the love interest romantically first, or vice versa.

The love interest may have known the hero/heroine forever or may have just met the hero/heroine. Sometimes, it's both. The love interest knew the hero/heroine a long time ago and meets him or her again—and all of a sudden, what was platonic no longer is.

Both the love interest's relationship with the third wheel is affected by this new relationship, and hero/heroine's relationship with the third wheel is affected.

The result is an explicitly or implicitly understood to be forbidden love, and a potential disaster between best friends/siblings that may be the ruination of a close, long-time relationship.

ADJACENT TROPES

--Love Triangle (While in most cases the love between siblings will be platonic, the elements of a love triangle are otherwise all in place. Each of the members of the triangle are faced with an impossible choice between two people they love.)

--Childhood Sweethearts/Friends

--Friends to Lovers

WHY READERS/VIEWERS LOVE THIS TROPE

--there's something really naughty in falling for the one person you're not supposed to

--the danger and titillation of fooling around behind your best friend's and/or sibling's back and getting away with it.

--finally breaking free from a protective, interfering third wheel friend or relative to get what and who you want

--friendship (between friends or siblings) is stronger than ever now that we share love, in different ways of course, for the same person

--a good friend becomes family

. . .

OBLIGATORY SCENES
THE BEGINNING:

The hero/heroine and the love interest meet. This may be a first-time meeting or a reunion, but either way, sparks fly. The third wheel may or may not be aware of the attraction blossoming under his or her nose.

The forbidden nature of the relationship is established. The third wheel may forbid it, there may be a pact against dating friend's siblings or sibling's friends.

There may be some other reason altogether why the potential love interest is off limits. If this is the case, this reason is established up front.

The hero/heroine and love interest often resist the attraction initially, if for no other reason that out of respect for the third wheel, whom they both love.

THE MIDDLE:

The hero/heroine and love interest are thrown together—frequently by the external plot action of the story or by the third wheel. It's even possible the hero/heroine and love interest secretly sneak around to spend time together. It's a very good bet that in most cases, this couple will initially try to keep this forbidden or scandalous relationship secret.

The romance between them proceeds swimmingly...with one small fly in the ointment. What to do about sibling/best friend who doesn't know about the relationship and is going to blow his or her stack when they find out?

It's possible other characters catch on to the secret romance. These characters may or may not keep the secret and may or may not support or sabotage the relationship.

The lovers may wrestle with whether or not their relationship is truly wrong or if the third wheel is being unreasonable to keep them apart. The third wheel might or might not actually have a problem with the couple's relationship if he or she found out about it.

Tension mounts as the lovers try to keep their relationship secret. This gets more and more difficult to do. There are near misses with getting caught, the third wheel surely begins to suspect something's going on.

If there's a compelling plot reason why the lovers should not be together, it comes to a head as they fail to abide by the prohibition and finally get caught.

BLACK MOMENT:

The secret relationship between the hero/heroine and the love interest is revealed, especially to the third wheel. A blow-up ensues that destroys not only the secret relationship but also the long-time friendship and the sibling's trust for each other.

If there's a negative consequence from the external action of the story for these two having fallen in love, that consequence lands upon the lovers and takes effect.

Regardless of what the best friend thinks of the relationship, her or she is potentially furious or deeply disappointed that he or she has been lied to. The guilty hero/heroine and love interest both try and fail to make it all better,

The couple is tormented by grief and loss. They have not only lost their romantic partner but also their best friend/sibling—the one person who could help them process their grief and guilt, but who now will not.

THE END:

The external plot consequences of this illicit relationship are resolved and made right. This may or may not involve the third wheel but may involve apologies or reparations to other characters in the story.

The lovers also must sincerely apologize and make amends to the third wheel, who may set some kind of penance that the lovers must serve before the third wheel is appeased and can forgive them.

The third wheel must ultimately forgive the lovers' transgressions for this story to end fully happily. It may be that the third wheel would never have minded the romance between the lovers but was livid or disappointed at being lied to and not trusted to be mature about the relationship going on behind his or her back. Either way, the third wheel ultimately accepts that the lovers are a great couple and are meant to be together. The third wheel settles into being happy for the couple.

Romantic relationship, sibling trust, and long-term friendship are all restored. The lovers can be together and have the third wheels blessing to move into their long-term happily ever after.

KEY SCENES

--the current day first meeting of the hero/heroine and love interest

--nearly getting caught by the third wheel

--when the lovers give in to temptation the first time

--when guilt nearly destroys the romance from within

--the big apology is accepted by the third wheel

THINGS TO THINK ABOUT WHEN WRITING THIS TROPE

How does the third wheel initially feel about a relationship between the love interest and the hero/heroine? Does the third wheel hate the idea? Fear it? Why? Does he or she tell the truth about this to the hero/heroine and love interest?

How does the love interest think the third wheel feels about a romance between the hero/heroine and the love interest? Is this an accurate perception initially?

Has the hero/heroine not been honest about his or her feelings toward the love interest in the past? If so, how so? Why? To whom?

Is there a pact between the hero/heroine and third wheel regarding how off-limits the love interest is? If so, what is it? Why was it formed? When was it formed? How bound by it does the hero/heroine feel today?

Has the hero/heroine met the love interest before? Does he or she remember the love interest? What was his or her impression of the love interest in the past? What was the love interest's impression of the hero/heroine?

Did the hero/heroine have a crush on the love interest in the past?

If this is a first meeting of hero/heroine and future love interest, what is their first impression of each other?

What external plot actions of your story will throw the hero/heroine and love interest together over and over again?

Do any other characters know about the budding romance and agree to keep it secret from the third wheel?

What do near misses with getting caught by the third wheel look like?

Why does it get harder and harder to hide the relationship?

How does the relationship ultimately get revealed to the third wheel? To everyone else?

How do all three of the main characters feel when the secret romance is revealed?

Does the external plot action of the story have anything to do with how the relationship is uncovered? If so, how?

Is discovery inevitable for the lovers, or is there a mistake that accidentally reveals all?

Why do the lovers break up or separate when they get caught? Why not just brazen it out? What keeps them from doing this?

Why can't they just get back together when the third wheel calms down a little? What compelling reason(s) keep them apart once they separate?

Is there a conflict between the lovers themselves that must be resolved before they can be together again? If so, what is it? How will one or both of them resolve it?

What amends does love interest have to make to the third wheel to obtain forgiveness for falling for the hero/heroine? What amends does the hero/heroine have to make to the third wheel?

Does the third wheel have to forgive the lovers for falling in love? For lying to him or her? Both?

How does the restored friendship differ from the past friendship? How is it the same?

How does the restored sibling relationship differ from the previous one? How is it the same?

What causes the third wheel to finally become genuinely happy for the lovers?

TROPE TRAPS

Painting a third wheel who wouldn't mind the relationship at all if the lovers simply sat down and discussed it with him or her like adults. While this is the way real life should ideally proceed, there's not enough conflict in this story arc to sustain the backbone of a novel.

Failing to give hero/heroine and love interest guilt or remorse for going behind the third wheel's back.

Creating a love interest who doesn't seem ethical or moral for going after the hero/heroine (or vice versa), especially if they know darned good and well the other person is off limits to the third wheel, whom they both love.

Painting an unlikable hero/heroine the love interest wouldn't plausibly fall for, or vice versa, whom readers or viewers dislike.

Overdoing the whole, "hero/heroine (or love interest) is so gorgeous or so hot, and yet I never noticed you before now" schtick. Just how blind are your characters?

Failing to create a plausible reason why the love interest and hero/heroine didn't get together long before now if they're so attracted to each other now that they can't stay away from each other.

The lovers don't pay any price for their sneaking around or for lying to someone they both allegedly love.

The lovers' apologies don't come across as sincere.

The third wheel's forgiveness doesn't come across as sincere.

BEST FRIEND'S SIBLING/SIBLING'S BEST FRIEND TROPE IN ACTION
Movies:

- The Kissing Booth
- One Small Hitch
- Something Borrowed
- My Best Friend's Wedding
- You Again
- The Edge of Seventeen
- That Awkward Moment

Books:

- Twisted Love by Ana Huang
- Ugly Love by Colleen Hoover
- Fix Her Up by Tessa Bailey
- Bad Habit by Charleigh Rose
- Mr. Wrong Number by Lynn Painter
- To Love Jason Thorne by Ella Maise
- The Boy Who Sneaks In My Bedroom Window by Kirsty Moseley
- The Chase by Elle Kennedy
- The Unhoneymooners by Christina Lauren

6

BEST FRIEND'S/SIBLING'S EX

DEFINITION

In this trope, the main character falls in love with the ex-lover of either the main character's best friend or sibling. The entire tone of this trope is going to be set by two decisions you make—how "ex" is the ex, and how ugly was the break-up? The rest of your decisions in crafting this story will flow from those two.

At its core, this story is a love triangle. In this version, however, one leg of the triangle is broken or severed. For the main character and "ex" love interest's relationship to work and also have the best friend/sibling relationship with the main character survive, the exes must already have arrived or arrive at some sort of peaceful resolution to their break-up by the end of the story. Hence, the main character's happiness depends on the other two people in the love triangle working out their relationship because they both love the main character enough to gift him or her with happiness.

In this trope, the break-up between the best friend and the love interest can happen before the story begins, or it can happen during the story...which has potential to be a LOT more awkward for everyone involved and may call into doubt how honorable or thoughtful a friend your main character is. Who steals their best friend's partner, after all? The key to this main character remaining likable to your audience will be that he or she is in no way responsible for the breakup and only is responsible for picking up the pieces of both the best friend's broken heart and the love interest ex's broken heart.

The fact that the best friend and the love interest had a prior relationship may or may not be a secret. If it is secret, the revelation of that former relationship may be a nasty shock to the main character and will certainly pose questions as to why the pair has kept it secret from the main character.

If you're using a best friend in this story, the friendship between the main character and best friend may or may not survive this romance. If you're using a sibling's ex as the love interest, the relationship may or may not survive, but the stakes will be much higher if the sibling relationship is destroyed. If they can't stand the sight of each other in the future, one of them will not only have to sacrifice the sibling relationship but also participating in any family gatherings that include the other sibling. While the lovers may end up together, most audiences probably won't perceive having to sacrifice one's family for love to be a positive outcome to this story.

ADJACENT TROPES
--Love Triangle
--Forbidden Love
--Friends to Lovers
--Secret Crush
--Right Under Your Nose

WHY READERS/VIEWERS LOVE THIS TROPE
--someone who loves a person I admire and look up to thinks I'm worthy of love, too

--both my friend/sibling and lover love me enough to work out their issues

--who hasn't secretly fantasized about stealing the great person you'd love to have for yourself. And after all, they've broken up already

--finally being SEEN after spending the duration of the exes' previous relationship as the invisible best friend or sibling

--someone you've known as a friend becomes your lover

--he or she chose me over my best friend or sibling

OBLIGATORY SCENES
THE BEGINNING:

The main character and the love interest probably already know each other, at least in passing, through their relationships with the best friend or sibling.

If the best friend/sibling and the love interest haven't broken up before the story starts, they break up fairly early in the story so the real story of this trope can get rolling.

This trope actually begins when the main character and the ex first notice each other romantically. They may be thrown together in some sort of re-meet cute to start the story, or they have a chance encounter, or one of them asks to speak to the other. Regardless of how they come into physical proximity, romantic sparks fly. This may startle one or both of them.

The best friend/sibling may or may not be aware that these two have met and spoken or that the pair is romantically curious, if not overtly interested.

You'll probably need to create some sort of external plot that forces the main character and the ex into proximity for some or all of your story. Under any other circumstances and out of respect for the best friend/sibling, the two would probably otherwise never spend enough time together to fall in love. This external plot is launched in the beginning of your story.

· · ·

THE MIDDLE:

Complications ensue, based on how finished the best friend/sibling and the ex are, and how badly their breakup went.

Does the best friend/sibling consider reconciling with his or her ex at the same time the main character is falling in love with the love interest? Does the best friend/sibling warn off the main character, declaring that the love interest is no good or a terrible fit for the main character? Does the best friend/sibling think he or she and the ex were only on a break?

There are dozens more variations on the two questions I initially posed—how broken up do the best friend/sibling and the ex believe themselves to be and how ugly was their breakup—and how these serve to cause problems for the new couple.

The external plot moves forward, and whatever crisis or deadline you've built into it barrels forward, closing in on the new lovers.

The tensions and conflict of the broken love triangle also progress toward a crisis as the middle of your story concludes.

BLACK MOMENT:

The pressures and tensions of the broken love triangle finally explode into open conflict or the new couple breaks up because of their own problems, which puts even more pressure on the broken triangle, collapsing it entirely—meaning all three relationships implode. The best friend/sibling relationship breaks, the romantic relationship between the main character and the ex/love interest breaks, and any semblance of peace or truce between the former lovers (best friend/sibling and ex) breaks.

The external problem everyone has been trying to solve or stop fails utterly and the terrible thing they've all dreaded happens. It's worth noting that in all black moments, when "the worst" happens or all is lost, that leads to some even worse crisis or problem that must be dealt with in the story's climax.

. . .

THE END:

The three members of this love triangle each have to work out their conflicts, individually, and potentially as a group. In the worst case, you have four relationships to repair—each leg of the triangle and the group relationship of all three of them.

Through one last ditch effort, the big problem of the plot is finally fixed.

If there are going to be grand sacrifices or big apologies to resolve the relationship issues in this story, it may take two grand sacrifices at a minimum to put the triangle back together and set things right between all three characters. It's possible all three will have to learn a lesson and make a big gesture of some kind to restore the friendships and the one surviving romantic relationship.

As I discussed in the description of this trope, a happily ever after ending probably includes the best friends or siblings still being close to each other in addition to the main character and love interest ending up together.

KEY SCENES

--the moment the main character figures out the love interest is the best friend/sibling's ex in the case where this was kept secret

--the main character and love interest are almost caught together in a romantic situation by the best friend/sibling who's unaware of their new liaison

--the moment when the best friend/sibling finds out the main character and his or her ex are romantically involved

--the best friends or siblings compare notes on the love interest

--the best friend/sibling tells the ex he or she wants him or her back (may not apply to all stories)

--the moment the love interest has to choose one of the best friends/siblings over the other (may not apply to all stories, but maybe should)

THINGS TO THINK ABOUT WHEN WRITING THIS TROPE

How close are the main character and the best friend/sibling when your story begins? How open and honest is their relationship, really? After all, if they were mature adults and talked out the situation with compassion and frankness right up front, there would be no story for you to tell. What tensions exists within this relationship?

How does the best friend/sibling feel about his or her ex when the story begins? How does the ex feel about him or her when the story begins?

Why did the best friend/sibling and the ex break up? How civil or uncivil a breakup was it?

How much does the main character know about the former relationship? How much does he or she know about the breakup? Does the main character know all the gory details or has the main character never heard a word about this previous romance (and if not, why not)?

How will the main character and love interest be thrown together in your story? How will you justify multiple interactions between these two that are long enough or private enough to let the two of them get to know each other and see each other in a romantic light?

Did the main character or ex have a secret crush on the other one before they get together now? If so, when does he or she admit it?

How does the best friend/sibling find out these two are an item or may become an item?

Does the best friend/sibling support the new romance or despise it? Will he or she try to help it along or try to sabotage it? Is it possible he or she will do both?

What actions does the best friend/sibling take to help or hinder the romance between the main character and the love interest?

How do other people around this trio feel about the new romance?

What tensions will you introduce into the triangle of friends that ultimately break up the new couple? Are those tensions the same or different than the ones that broke up the old couple?

How does your external plot strain these three linked relationships to the breaking point?

Why do the main character and love interest break up? How does the best friend/sibling react to the breakup?

What will it take for all of these relationships to be repaired? How will addressing the big crisis at the end of the story help or hinder the repair of these relationships?

Who has to forgive whom? Who has to apologize to whom?

What does the relationship between the best friends/siblings look like at the end of your story?

TROPE TRAPS

Your main character is unlikable for having stolen the lover of his or her best friend/sibling before the former relationship was truly over and fully resolved.

The love interest is a scumbag for jumping out of a relationship with one best friend/sibling and into another one with the other best friend/sibling and audiences hate him or her for it.

The suddenness of the attraction between these two people who may already know each other fairly well seems forced or contrived. Were they really that blind to each other before now?

Failing to take the time to fully resolve, finish, and put to rest the former relationship between the best friend/sibling and his or her ex.

Creating no parallels between the former relationship and the new one. It would be strange for the love interest to manage to make totally new and different mistakes in each of these relationship.

Devolving into sophomoric antics by the three as they sabotage one another and wallow in the drama of it all, unless of course, you're writing middle school-aged characters.

Having the best friend/sibling come across as a wet sponge after forgiving the main character too easily for moving in on the ex, for keeping secrets, or for any other transgressions the main character has committed in the name of love.

Creating a main character who appears motivated to steal the ex by insecurity, jealousy, greed, or some other negative emotion that turns off the audience and makes it hate him or her. Even if you never overtly state these motives, if the audience catches even a whiff of any of these, they'll intensely dislike your main character.

Shortchanging or failing altogether to resolve each of the four relationships in the love triangle—the three legs of it and the group relationship as a whole.

The main character and/or ex showing little or no remorse at sacrificing a best friendship or a sibling relationship to be with the person they love. How selfish and uncaring is that?

BEST FRIEND'S/SIBLING'S EX TROPE IN ACTION
Movies:

- My Best Friend's Girl
- You & Me Forever
- In Her Shoes
- The Wicked Lady
- Kiss of the Damned
- Six Days, Six Nights

Books:

- The Sweetest Oblivion by Danielle Lori
- Fragile Longing by Cora Reilly
- Something In The Way by Jessica Hawkins
- My Darling Arrow by Saffron A. Kent
- My Best Friend's Ex by Meghan Quinn
- The Wrong Bride by Catharina Maura
- Something Borrowed by Emily Giffin

7

BEST FRIEND'S WIDOW/WIDOWER

DEFINITION

The hero or heroine has tragically lost a best friend and for some reason comes together to be with the widow or widower of the deceased best friend. These two grieving people comfort each other and end up falling in love.

You will have to decide how long it has been since the best friend/spouse has died, and this will be key to the tone of the rest of the story. There's a real risk in this trope of audiences not believing one character or the other isn't ready to move on to a new romantic relationship. There's also a risk of readers or viewers believing these two characters should not move on to a new romantic relationship.

In some ways, this trope is akin to a love triangle, but with one member of the triangle merely a specter of his or her former self. Nonetheless, the deceased member of the trio may, in fact, become a major character in this type of story.

ADJACENT TROPES
--Widowed Hero/Heroine
--Love Triangle

--Fresh Start

WHY READERS/VIEWERS LOVE THIS TROPE

--being plucked out of grief and loss into love and being cared for again

--being completely irresistible to someone

--being loved so much that your lover is willing to sacrifice what is proper for you

--being given a gift from Heaven (as the deceased spouse gifts you with their best friend)

OBLIGATORY SCENES
THE BEGINNING:

The best friend and the widow or widower meet. The attraction between them is established, and the properness or improperness, the timeliness or untimeliness, rightness, or wrongness of the attraction is established.

Typically, the way in which the deceased spouse/best friend died is also established. We may or may not see how the loss of the spouse affected the love interest or how the loss of the best friend affected the main character.

THE MIDDLE:

The best friend and widow/widower begin to fall in love. They may fight their developing feelings, or they may be grateful for those feelings. But either way, the act of falling in love causes problems for each of them individually and likely for them as a couple.

Both of these wounded souls probably have grieving to do and possibly baggage to work out after the death of their loved one. This may be a source of conflict between the lovers.

People around this pair may dislike the idea of a romance

between them. Other family members may think it is too soon, or disrespectful, or not what the deceased spouse might have wanted. Possibly, there's some sort of external reason why this pair should not be together. If so, that will unfold in the middle of the story.

BLACK MOMENT:

The forces pulling the hero and heroine apart, be it their internal feelings of guilt or wrongness, or external forces that do not approve of the relationship or that have a compelling reason to keep them apart, appear to win. The couple breaks away from each other and a happily ever after between them is impossible. All is truly lost, now. Not only have they each lost a spouse or best friend, but now they've lost each other as well.

THE END:

Whatever forces are pulling the widow/widower and best friend apart are finally defeated. External problems are solved in a way that allows the couple to be together. Their internal feelings are resolved, and they are at peace with moving on to a new love after grieving the lost spouse or friend.

The couple has permission from themselves to be together. They may never obtain permission from outsiders to be together, but in that case, the couple resolves to ignore what others think and do what's right in their hearts.

KEY SCENES

--the moment of first meeting between widow/widower and best friend

--the first moment of raw shared grief

--the moment of approval from the deceased spouse (this may be a metaphoric moment of approval, but at some point, the couple will need to feel as if they have the deceased spouse's approval

--going public as a couple

THINGS TO THINK ABOUT WHEN WRITING THIS TROPE

How did the deceased spouse die? Was it sudden? Was their warning that the spouse was dying? Was the spouse or best friend present at the moment of death?

Where did the spouse die?

How long ago did the spouse die? This will be a key decision that shapes the rest of the story.

If the spouse died recently, do the widow/widower and best friend go through the funeral and memorial observance process together or not?

When does attraction between the widow/widower and best friend first appear? Does it pre-date the death of the spouse, or is this a new development?

Did the widow/widower and best friend know each other before the spouse/best friend's death? If so, how long have they known each other? How well did they know each other? What was the nature of their relationship prior to the death of the spouse?

How do the surviving spouse and best friend feel about the idea of being attracted to each other? Guilty? Disloyal? Grateful? Relieved?

How complicated would it be if the pair gets together? How would other people react?

Does the widow/widower need help from the best friend? If so, with what or with whom?

Is there an external plot reason for the widow/widower and the best friend not to get together?

When in your story to the widow/widower and the best friend go public as a couple? How does that happen? Is it intentional or accidental?

How do other characters react when the couple goes public with being a couple?

What form does permission take from the deceased spouse to these two to be together? Is it discussed before his or her death? Is there a letter? Does the couple feel permission granted? Or do they both just know it would be okay with the deceased spouse?

How is disapproval or resistance by other characters overcome so the couple can ultimately be together?

TROPE TRAPS

The best friend moves in on the widow/widower too soon after the death and your audience finds it altogether squicky

The widow/widower is ready for a new relationship way too soon after his or her spouse passes away

Neither the widow/widower or the best friend feels any guilt or remorse about finding love together

Other people around the couple are unreasonably judgmental or resistant to a new relationship for the grieving widow/widower

The whole story and romance would work just fine if it was only set a year or two later, beyond the death, than it is

The external plot reason keeping them apart is hokey (like a will forbidding remarriage, for example)

BEST FRIEND'S WIDOW/WIDOWER TROPE IN ACTION
Movies:

- Random Hearts
- Yours, Mine, and Ours
- Fascination

- The Color of Rain
- Write Before Christmas

Books:

- Dream a Little Dream by Susan Elizabeth Phillips
- Mystery Man by Kristen Ashley
- The Raven Prince by Elizabeth Hoyt
- To Sir Phillip, With Love by Julia Quinn
- Jane Eyre by Charlotte Bronte
- The Air He Breathes by Brittainy C. Cherry
- Lover Reborn by J.R. Ward
- Virgin River by Robyn Carr
- Louder Than Love by Jessica Topper

8
CHILDHOOD SWEETHEARTS

DEFINITION

Two people who knew and liked each other in their childhood or youth, (may or may not have gone their separate ways), grown up, and have stayed or come back into each other's lives...only to fall in love as adults.

For the couple who met as children, liked each other, never fell out of touch, grew up together, and fell in love, there's generally not much by way of conflict to drive a story about them. Hence, the vast majority of Childhood Sweethearts stories involve the main characters having been in like or in love when they were younger, separating, and then coming back together when they're adults.

The source of conflict for the adult couple may be the thing that separated them as children.

OR

Their conflict may stem from changes in one or both of them that have happened during their years apart. In either case, the mere act of growing up will have changed each of them as people and will change the dynamic of the relationship they had as children/youths.

At its core, this is a reunion story. It's more about resolving an old conflict, solving a new problem that comes between them, or re-learning who someone is. This story is less about changing oneself or asking one's love interest to change so that a couple can be together happily.

While both main characters have changed in the interim years, their transformations are complete. The main problem for the couple now is to understand and reconcile with these transformations that are already a fait accompli.

ADJACENT TROPES
--Reunion
--Teenage Crush
--Unrequited Love
--Forgiveness
—A whole series of tropes that explain what broke up the sweethearts. To name a few:

- Love Triangle
- Burned by Love
- Across the Tracks
- Feuding Families
- Long Distance Romance
- Forgiveness

WHY READERS/VIEWERS LOVE THIS TROPE
--nobody forgets their first love. Everyone wonders what would have happened if they had made that first love work
--finding love again after the despair of losing love
--finding someone you have your whole life in common with...or at least a big chunk of it
--regaining the innocence and joy of childhood
--I've changed, but I'm still as lovable as I once was

. . .

OBLIGATORY SCENES
THE BEGINNING:

Some situation throws the hero and heroine together. They may or may not both recognize each other immediately. Depending on how they were separated in the past, they may or may not be glad to see each other.

Regardless, they react strongly and emotionally to seeing each other again—this may or may not involve a romantic spark.

Typically, these two characters meet when one of them returns to the town he or she left as a child and where the other main character has never left. It's also entirely possible for them to run into each other in some other geographical location entirely. In either case, the nature of their childhood relationship is established and probably how it ended.

THE MIDDLE:

Nostalgia affects both the hero and heroine. They remember the good times before they were separated. They remember good feelings, good times, and why they once liked or loved each other.

The reason they separated is remembered and rehashed.

The hero and heroine flirt around with the idea of getting back together romantically. Whatever situation has brought them back into proximity continues to throw them together in increasingly romantically fraught encounters.

The hero and heroine may fight the idea of getting back together. Or they may fling themselves into the idea, but old conflicts resurface. There's an ongoing push-pull between why they should get back together and why they shouldn't.

The ways the hero and heroine have changed in their years apart surface and become a source of problems and conflict. Can they accept the "new" version of the old person?

. . .

BLACK MOMENT:

Whatever conflict is coming between this pair is too much for one or both of them to deal with. They break up a second time...and this time for good. This break-up is all the more devastating after they've gotten their hopes up for having a second chance together, only to have their hopes dashed *again*.

THE END:

The hero and heroine are unhappy enough apart and love each other enough to fight through the crisis, overcome the conflict that seemed insurmountable between them, and reconcile. They regain not only the innocent and joyful friendship and love of their childhood romance, but now they have a richer, more complex, adult love to go with it.

KEY SCENES

--the meet-up where they see each other for the first time in a very long time

--the trip down memory lane together

--the old conflict rears its ugly head for the first time

--the first "adult" romantic or sexual scene

--the big break-up or separation scene from their youth repeated again as adults

--the big reconciliation scene

THINGS TO THINK ABOUT WHEN WRITING THIS TROPE

How old were the hero and heroine when they became sweethearts as children? How old were they when they separated?

Was it a physical separation that tore them apart? If so, did they control it or not? Did one's family leave town and take them away? Did one of them leave town to leave home, go to college, a job, or military service?

Or was it a conflict that broke them up? If so, what was it? Was it a disagreement just between the hero and heroine? If so, what was it over?

Or did interference by someone else break them up? Are the people involved with that aspect of the breakup still nearby? Will they surface in this story?

What did their family and friends back in the day think of their childhood romance? Did those people help or hinder the childhood romance? Are those people still around? What do they think of the adult do-over of that old childhood romance? Will they help or hinder the hero and heroine getting together now?

What situation brings these two characters back into proximity again? Is it a meet-cute, a meet-interesting, a meet-unwilling, or a meet-dangerous?

What have the hero and heroine done in the intervening years they've been apart? How have each of them changed and grown?

How have they grown in a similar direction or learned a similar life lesson? How have they changed and grown in different and conflicting directions? What are some conflicting life lessons they've learned that cause friction or disagreement between them?

What qualities did they have as children that still draw them to the other one?

What new qualities do they have that attract them more than ever, perhaps in a new and different way, to each other?

What battle scars from life do they bring to their adult relationship? How do those cause problems between them?

What fallout did they each experience when they separated the first time as children? Does any of that linger even today?

What do their childhood friends think of them getting back together? What do their new friends who don't know them from childhood think of them getting together? Do these friends help or hinder the relationship? Why?

What is going to tear them apart this time? Will it be an echo of what tore them apart the first time, or is it a new and different crisis... or both? Will one or both of them have to sacrifice something so they can be together?

If the first break-up was because of a loss of trust, that can plausibly be a holdover problem even after many years apart. Is there a trust issue now to overcome? If so, what is it?

How will the hero and heroine overcome this new crisis? What's required of each of them to overcome it? How can what they have to do or sacrifice be made even bigger or more difficult?

TROPE TRAPS

EVERYBODY seems to set up this trope as a coming home story. Either the hero or heroine comes back to his or her hometown, where the long-suffering childhood sweetheart left behind has languished all this time and is now in need of rescue from fill-in-the-blank ex-spouse or financial crisis. The trap is failing to do this in some even vaguely new, interesting, or creative way.

Failing to grow up the current-day characters.

Having the adult hero and heroine act in the relationship pretty much the same way they did as children or teens.

Whatever broke them up in their youths was something stupid or easily fixable if they'd only had an honest conversation with each other (unless you've set up someone who interfered to prevent it or some reason why they never were able to talk it out before).

Relying on a stalker-ex to be the big conflict or danger. It's fine to have one of these, but there has to be MORE to the issues in the relationship than just this person interfering.

Relying on the person who schemed or lied back in the day, broke up the hero and heroine, and then stole the hero/heroine to do the same thing this time around. Again, it's fine to have history repeat itself and have the scheming interloper try it again. But there needs to be MORE to the issues in the relationship than just this person interfering.

Failing to resolve whatever broke them up the first time.

Creating a black moment for the reunited adult sweethearts than can be solved with an honest, serious conversation between two adults.

Ignoring the events that have happened in the years they've been apart.

Not addressing the issues and emotional baggage they've each accrued in their time apart.

CHILDHOOD SWEETHEARTS TROPE IN ACTION
Movies:

- The Best of Me
- Forest Gump
- Love, Rosie
- Always Be My Maybe
- Love Me If You Dare

Books:

- It Ends With Us by Colleen Hoover
- Love and Other Words by Christina Lauren

- Dear Ava by Ilsa Madden-Mills
- Loving Mr. Daniels by Brittainny C. Cherry
- Unforgettable by Melanie Harlow
- Beneath the Stars by Emily McIntire
- The Player Next Door by K.A. Tucker

9

COUPLES' THERAPY

DEFINITION

As the title of this trope implies, a couple who is already together but having problems goes to some sort of therapy to try to save their relationship and regain their old happily ever after or find a new one.

However, this is one of those shorthanded trope titles that actually covers a broader group of stories wherein the hero and heroine, who are already a couple, undertake some project or activity together in an effort to resolve existing problems and save their relationship.

Implicit in this trope is the looming danger that, if the therapeutic activity together fails, the relationship will end. Also implicit is the fact that the relationship has *already* failed. If it was still a viable relationship, the characters wouldn't be in this pickle where they're seeking some external fix to a problem they cannot overcome on their own.

Also, the couple may or may not have entered into the joint activity voluntarily. Friends, family, or other outsiders may have coerced or tricked the couple into spending this time together. Or the hero and heroine may be thrown together accidentally.

At its core, this is a trope of forgiveness. Two people must reconcile and find a new beginning out of the ashes of a failed relationship.

The great challenge of this trope is to create a problem or conflict big enough to destroy a relationship but not so big as to be unforgivable. It's a fine line to walk between these two extremes and takes deft storytelling to navigate.

ADJACENT TROPES
--Reconciliation/Second Chance

--Forgiveness

--Redemption

--Fresh Start

WHY READERS/VIEWERS LOVE THIS TROPE
--a second chance at love

--a chance to forgive and forget old hurts, to reset a relationship, and move past the

accumulated mistakes and baggage

--still being lovable after all this time

--beneath that crusty, unaffectionate, or disengaged exterior, you really love me after all

OBLIGATORY SCENES
THE BEGINNING:
The hero and heroine are brought together to do some joint activity or project together. They may already be apart and only come together for this activity, or they may still live together but have obvious problems. In either case, the fact that they have serious problems or disconnects in their relationship must be made clear (although it's not necessary to spell out the details of the problem yet. In fact, it's probably a good idea to wait on that.)

. . .

THE MIDDLE:

That joint activity ensues. This project is a multi-step affair, and as each step happens, the hero and heroine's conflict comes into sharper and sharper focus. At the same time, the old attraction between them may also be coming into sharper and sharper relief.

The hero and heroine react to the joint activity and to the whole process of facing their core conflict. Old hurts, angers, and other feelings surface. Although they may both have volunteered to be here, we see them resist opening up and sharing their true feelings. The reader begins to see just how far apart they are emotionally from each other.

As the story unfolds, the layers and true depths of their alienation from each other are revealed. The core problem(s) between them is(are) revealed as the full story of why they're ready to break up is peeled back like an onion.

Other people around the couple react to their attempt to salvage the relationship, either by supporting the couple or attempting to sabotage them.

The hero and heroine may or may not "slip" and have one or more romantic interludes. (In some versions of this story, they don't physically get back together romantically until the very end when all their differences are finally solved, and this is the big emotional pay-off for readers.)

BLACK MOMENT:

The therapy, activity, project, or joint goal may be finished or achieved at this point in the story, and the hero/heroine realize that it has not solved their core problems and conflicts. It has clearly revealed those conflicts, but it hasn't led to the solution they both hoped for.

The problems and conflicts between the hero and heroine are too much for them to overcome. One of both of them cannot forgive the other. The last ditch, therapeutic activity has failed. All is lost. The relationship is over.

. . .

THE END:

In some versions of the story, if they haven't done so already, the hero and heroine will push through to finishing the project or activity, even though they've decided to end the relationship.

Only after losing each other do the hero and heroine realize just how unhappy they are without the other one. In light of how miserable they are now, alone and without each other, they finally find a way to overcome the previously insurmountable conflicts/problems.

With their core conflict resolved, they can finally resume their relationship with new understandings of themselves and each other. They have cleaned the slate and reset their love. And with what they know now, they'll be able to preserve their happily ever after this time.

KEY SCENES

--arriving at or getting thrown into the joint activity for the first time

--their first big fight

--revelation of the real problem at the heart of their alienation

--the final break-up

--the big forgiveness/reconciliation scene

THINGS TO THINK ABOUT WHEN WRITING THIS TROPE

What are the hero and heroine going to spend the entire story doing together? This choice will set the tone for the entire book. Is it light-hearted, wholesome, or fraught with danger?

Are the hero and heroine together voluntarily to pursue this joint project, or were they thrown together by other people, circumstances, or chance?

How does each step of the project provide a new and bigger opportunity to reveal the problem, reveal the spark between these characters, and/or advance the emotional arc of the characters? Which is to say, the project or activity should get progressively more difficult as the couple approaches finishing it.

How do they individually feel about doing this thing together? Will they tell the other partner how they really feel about it, or will they conceal their true feelings about it?

What's this couple's backstory? How did they meet, fall in love, and commit to a long-term relationship? How does all of this play into your story?

What's the big problem that's breaking them apart? How did it happen? Did one or both of them make a terrible mistake? Was it an outside event or external force that caused the problem?

Is their big problem based on a fundamental difference in their core values? If so, which one or both of them is going to have to make a VERY DIFFICULT personal change to save the relationship?

How will the romantic and sexual tension between them build during the story, and what will they do or not do about it?

Will the people around them support them getting back together or try to sabotage them reconciling? Why? How?

What events, memories, or activities will trigger nostalgia and the couple remembering at least temporarily why they fell in love in the first place?

What is the sticking point they can't get past that causes the black moment? What happens in the story to cause and to show the black moment?

How does each of them feel at the moment of accepting failure in their relationship? Do they share that with the other person or not?

When do they finish their project or activity? Does finishing it coincide with the black moment or with the resolution of the conflict and the ending?

What does each of them do after they break up and before they make up?

Is there a big crisis that throws the hero and heroine (back) together and forces them to work together in spite of their alienation and finally to face their biggest issue? What is that crisis?

How will they ultimately overcome or resolve the unresolvable conflict between them? Is this solution emotionally satisfying to readers and believable?

What do the hero and heroine finally learn individually and as a couple that allows them to move past their big conflict?

Do either or both of them have to change in some way to fix the problem? How hard is it going to be for that character to make that change permanent? Is it plausible that this character can stick by his or her resolve to change for the long term?

Will the new relationship at the end of the story look exactly like the one they had before their problems or will it be significantly different? If it's different, how so?

Does the power dynamic in the repaired relationship change from before or not?

How will they ensure they don't repeat the same mistake down the road?

How does their new happily ever after harken back to their first one, and how is it different?

TROPE TRAPS

Creating a couple who are so fundamentally different, particularly in their core values, that this conflict was inevitable.

Creating a couple so incompatible and prone to conflict or problems that readers think they shouldn't be together anyway, and don't root for them to get back together.

The conflict or problem between this couple isn't big enough to potentially break up a committed long-term relationship between two likable, decent, honorable, heroic characters.

The conflict between this couple is too big, too serious, or too severe to plausibly be forgiven and moved past. Or, if one of the characters does forgive this problem, conflict, or mistake, the reader loses all respect for that character for having done so.

Creating a conflict between this couple that could be talked out if they were only honest, open, mature, kind, and/or clear with each other.

Creating a story where one character has to do all the compromising and forgiving. Frequently, female characters are portrayed as doing all the forgiving and forgetting, which can come across as weak, gaslighted, or emotionally abused.

Forcing one or both characters to set aside their self-respect, self-esteem, or self-worth to reconcile.

Failing to portray forgiveness as an act of strength.

Asking a character and the reader to forgive something unforgivable. Not everything can or should be forgiven.

Creating a joint activity or project that's not sufficiently challenging to complete and doesn't push the hero and heroine into revealing their true feelings and problems.

Solving the core conflict in a lame way or stupid way. This seems obvious to say, I know. But big problems require hard work, sacrifices, changes, and real effort.

Solving the big conflict by having one or both characters promise to change in a way that no person, or very few people, can sustain in the long term.

If a character has agreed to make a major, fundamental change, failing to give him or her the outside support, watchdogs, and threatened penalties that will be necessary to make that change permanent.

Leaving the hero and heroine in a relationship exactly like the one that ran into trouble the first time.

COUPLES' THERAPY TROPE IN ACTION
Movies:

- Couples Retreat
- Did You Hear About the Morgans?
- The One I Love
- Hope Springs
- A Kid Like Jake

Books:

- My One and Only by Kristan Higgins
- The Snow Child by Eowyn Ivey
- Dane's Storm by Mia Sheridan
- Everyone is Beautiful by Katherine Center
- Private Arrangements by Sherry Thomas
- The Break by Marian Keyes
- After I Do by Taylor Jenkins Reid
- Love Her or Lose Her by Tessa Bailey

10

CROSS CULTURAL/INTERRACIAL

DEFINITION

A hero and heroine from different cultural, racial, or ethnic backgrounds have to overcome the differences in their upbringings/identities to fall in love and find their happily ever after.

Their differing origins, backgrounds, and identities will act as a source of external conflict throughout the story. The differences between the hero and heroine based on their differing upbringings and life experiences serve as a source of internal conflict throughout the story.

NOTE: Being from different cultural, racial, or ethnic backgrounds can be merely a character theme. It rises to the level of being a trope when these differences form the core of the conflicts the hero and heroine must overcome to find their true love and happily ever after.

At its core, this can be a story of personal transformation, growth, and/or learning, as one or both characters become familiar with a new and different world that is home to the other partner.

OR

At its core this may NOT be a story of character transformation. It may instead be a story of the lovers transforming the world around them to make space for their relationship.

While I would like to live in a world where this trope is no big deal and not subject to potential pitfalls, the truth is this is a trope to write with sensitivity and care. Do your homework if you're not from a world you're writing about, and beware of being perceived as dismissive, judgmental, patronizing, unaware, wrong, or even racist. Done well, this can be a trope of great and profound beauty, deeply satisfying to readers and viewers.

ADJACENT TROPES

--Across the Tracks/Wrong Side of the Tracks

--Opposites Attract

--Newcomer/Outsider/Stranger

--Fish Out of Water/Cowboy in the City

--Forbidden Love

--Feuding Families

WHY READERS/VIEWERS LOVE THIS TROPE

--love comes in many forms

--we're all not that different when everything else is peeled away —we all want to love and be loved

--being loved so much that your lover is willing to sacrifice everything (family, culture, background, upbringing) for you

--the allure of forbidden love

--breaking the rules

--standing up for what you believe in and want regardless of what others think

OBLIGATORY SCENES
THE BEGINNING:

The hero and heroine meet and a spark of attraction ignites. While this might seem obvious for this couple, their different and possibly conflicting cultures, races, or ethnicities may make this attraction unexpected or problematic.

We may be introduced to the hero and heroine's differing backgrounds right away, or that may not unfold until the middle of the story.

The hero and heroine may meet with a big, immediate clash of backgrounds and instant conflict...or they may meet innocently, develop an attraction, and only afterward realize there are issues of culture, race, or ethnic background to overcome.

THE MIDDLE:

The hero and heroine get to know each other and where they come from, and we see them falling in love. Again, an obvious development in a romance. However, for this pair, the act of falling in love is potentially a fraught or downright risky endeavor.

The main action of the story may revolve around some entirely separate plot device, and the cultural/racial/ethnic differences may come up primarily in relation to that story. Or their different backgrounds can take center stage in the story and be the main source of interactions, actions, and reactions that drive the story forward.

The hero and heroine are introduced to each other's worlds. They learn what they have in common and what is unique and different about each of their backgrounds. This may be a source of humor, stress, confusion, sadness, or any other number of emotions and reactions.

They meet family and friends from their partner's world and navigate the various reactions to their relationship. Various secondary characters may approve and others may disapprove of this budding romance, including family, friends, co-workers, and even total strangers. Someone may resent it, resist it, or sabotage it outright.

Pushback against the relationship grows toward a crisis that threatens the continued existence of the hero and heroine's relationship. This typically comes from people and forces surrounding the hero and heroine or from an unresolved conflict between them.

BLACK MOMENT:

The forces pulling the hero and heroine apart succeed and the couple's chance at love appears destroyed. Both the external forces trying to keep them apart and the internal conflicts that have been building between them have come to a head, and it's too much for the couple to withstand the pressure.

THE END:

The hero and heroine overcome the forces pulling them apart and they overcome their own internal conflicts to be together forever. They find a way to blend or ignore their backgrounds and create a relationship that is uniquely their own.

KEY SCENES

--the first introduction to each other's world of origin

--the hero and/or heroine assert to naysayers that everything will be fine

--the hero or heroine makes a big gaff while in the other character's world of origin

--the hero or heroine expresses their doubts or fears about what will happen if they continue pursuing this relationship

--something bad happens that's a warning shot across the bow, a harbinger of the larger crisis to come

--the first meeting of the hero and heroine after the black moment has exploded and ripped them apart

--the first declaration by the hero or heroine to their family/friends/community that he or she is going to be with this person, like it or not

--the final declaration by the hero or heroine to their family/friends/community that he or she is going to be with this person, like it or not

THINGS TO THINK ABOUT WHEN WRITING THIS TROPE

How do the hero and heroine meet? It is an accident or not? Is the meeting machinated by one or the other? Is it a collision of their differing worlds or not?

How are the hero and heroine's worlds different? This will define the external conflicts the couple has to overcome.

How do their different backgrounds make them different from each other? This will define much of the internal conflict the couple has to overcome.

Who and what from their opposing worlds will attempt to stop the hero and heroine's relationship from growing into love? Who and what will aid and abet their budding romance?

What parts of the new world will the hero/heroine be unfamiliar with? How will he/she/they react to these new elements? What will go wrong when first encountering these new elements?

What about the hero and heroine's two different worlds is exactly the same?

How will those around the hero and heroine attempt to quash their rebellion? What do these antagonists believe to justify their efforts to stop the relationship?

How will those around them react to the first public declaration of intent to be with their partner?

What genuinely, deeply draws these two people to each other

besides the rebellion and forbidden-ness of it all? What is the bedrock of their relationship?

What do the hero and heroine's doubts and fears about going ahead with this relationship look like? Do they ever express these fears to their partner? If so, when? How does the partner react?

What ultimately breaks them apart? Can you make it more wrenching? More devastating? More tragic?

How will the hero and heroine overcome the final crisis? What do they say to each other when they see each other again after the big break-up? What changes their minds?

Does one character make a grand sacrifice for the other character so they can be together? Which one? Is there a way to have both of them make a grand sacrifice to be together?

Will the hero or heroine have to change their core beliefs to be with the other character? If so, what beliefs must change?

Will the hero and heroine end up living fully in one of the worlds, creating some mixture of the two for themselves, or leaving behind both worlds in their entireties?

Is there a price for them to pay to be together that must be paid by the end of the story?

Do the people around them learn a lesson from the hero and heroine's journey? If so, what? If not, why not?

Does the story end with the hero and heroine at peace with the two worlds they've emerged from? Are they still at war? Have they achieved a truce?

Can the hero and heroine go home again someday if they want to?

TROPE TRAPS

They way these two people from different worlds meet is wildly implausible. Their worlds would never collide in such a way.

One or both of the characters bring offensive stereotypes to the relationship at first. Even if it's your plan to enlighten a bigoted character over the course of the story, readers or viewers aren't likely to stick around long enough to let you redeem a character who has already offended them deeply.

Your hero or heroine comes across as patronizing, judgmental, or belittling of the love interest's world of origin. It's okay for villains in your story to come across this way, but not the good guys.

Portraying one world as "good" and the other as "bad." Except in a few, unique cases, most cultures, races, religions, and ethnicities are mostly good and may have a little bad built into them. Remember, those living within the world of origin are probably there voluntarily. (It opens up a whole other can of plot worms if they're not in the world of origin voluntarily!)

Failing to address how truly different their worlds are and how a person from one is going to adapt to the other world.

Failing to resolve how these two people from very different worlds are going to live together happily. Which is to say, failing to resolve all the conflicts and friction points you've set up between them over the course of the story.

Failing to address what their world together will look like in the end.

Painting secondary characters who act unrealistically toward the relationship between the hero and heroine.

The act of rebelling by crossing over into an unfamiliar world is more important than the person the hero or heroine is allegedly falling in love with.

Assuming that anybody can casually fit into any other world, particularly without exerting real effort and change. Failure to fully understand the differing values and experiences that lead to real and serious disconnects between the differing worlds these characters come from.

Fetish-izing love interests of a particular race, ethnicity, or background. This is an ugly part of many countries' and cultures' histories and must be handled with care. Do your homework with regard to your story and don't accidentally step on a landmine.

Taking out a moral sledgehammer and bludgeoning your audience with it. It's all well and good to deliver themes and messages to readers or viewers, and it's fine to reflect and espouse your own beliefs, but nobody likes being clobbered over the head about anything. I'm not warning you about the content of the sledgehammer. Rather, I'm warning you about how hard you swing it at your audience.

CROSS CULTURAL/INTERETHNIC/INTERRACIAL TROPE IN ACTION
Movies:

- Maid in Manhattan
- Titanic
- Dirty Dancing
- The Notebook
- Moulin Rouge

Books:

- Beauty and the Blacksmith by Tessa Dare
- Wuthering Heights by Emily Bronte
- Road to Desire by Piper Davenport
- Great Expectations by Charles Dickens
- Mackenzie's Mountain by Linda Howard
- Murphy's Law by Lori Foster
- Rett by Tess Oliver
- A Notorious Love by Sabrina Jeffries

11

DIVIDED LOYALTIES

DEFINITION

A hero and heroine meet and are attracted to each other, but one or both of them also has some kind of existing commitment to someone or something else. This commitment usually takes the form of a promise that prohibits a relationship, for example:

- a debt that sucks all of the conflicted character's resources
- a commitment that takes a great deal of time, mental focus, and/or energy
- a relative or loved one who needs or demands a great deal of time, care, or attention
- a pledge to an organization or employer to put it first above all else
- anything that leaves the conflicted character with no capacity, resources, or time to sustain a long-term, serious, romantic relationship.

The conflicted character is almost always aware of the conflict right up front. He or she is wary of falling in love and concerned about committing to any romantic relationship and may be fully opposed to the idea from the beginning.

Some examples of things that could divide a character's loyalties include:

- a very demanding job that takes very long hours and/or huge mental effort, perhaps one that provides a great service, such as pediatric oncology or important research
- a military commitment, perhaps to serve in a remote location for an extended period of time or that will separate the lovers
- a debt owed that must be paid back—this can be financial, a time commitment, or some task that must be done or finished before the debt is cleared
- a child or parent whom a character is responsible for caring for and who takes a lot of time and energy
- an organization, employer, or family that demands complete loyalty to it first and foremost

However, the heart wants what the heart wants. Our conflicted character cannot deny the attraction to the love interest and is inexorably drawn deeper and deeper into a doomed romantic relationship. He or she may optimistically believe it's possible to juggle their first loyalty and a new love, but over the course of the story, and despite their best efforts, this proves impossible.

The character with divided loyalties must make an unbearable choice between two things or people that are incredibly important to him or her (possibly for completely different reasons). Making this choice will feel like being asked to cut off one's own arm and is a no-win dilemma.

The love interest may feel as if he or she is competing against the pre-existing thing or person their lover is already committed to. In this way, this trope can feel much like a love triangle, but with a debt, a promise, or a commitment of some kind acting as the third wheel.

This can leave the new love interest feeling very much like an interloper who must steal away the hero or heroine for themselves.

A character suffering from divided loyalties is typically a decent, honorable person or at least feels angst and conflict at the idea of breaking a promise. The greater the consequences of breaking that promise, the greater this character's angst will be. He or she never expected to be put into a dilemma of having to choose between two promises, but here he or she is, having to choose between true love and something/someone else vitally important to them.

This can be a trope of deception, or at least a trope of failing to be honest with oneself initially. It's a trope of false optimism clashing with harsh reality to create a doomed love.

At its core, the solution to this trope is one of compromise and accommodation as the lovers make room in their lives for both of the commitments the hero or heroine must make to have it all. Either the conflicted character or the love interest (or both of them) must make compromises or concessions to accommodate their lover's first loyalty so they can be together and have their happily ever after.

OR

At its core, this trope can force a very difficult or painful choice. The character with divided loyalties must eventually walk away from one thing or person they're loyal to or have true love and happily ever after with the love interest. Often there's a steep price to pay for walking away from an important promise or loyalty that makes choosing true love even more painful.

ADJACENT TROPES
--Love Triangle
--Feuding Families
--Forbidden Love
--Mafia Romance
--Boss-Employee
--Single Parent

WHY READERS/VIEWERS LOVE THIS TROPE
--being chosen over something very important to the hero or heroine

--who doesn't love a good, impossible choice and watching someone really squirm over choosing

--we all have to face choices like this at some point in our lives. We wonder if we chose or will choose correctly, and we vicariously make our own choice of what we would do if faced with the same dilemma the hero and heroine are faced with

--finding a way to have it all in the face of impossible odds

--finding or having the time and energy to fit everything and everyone into your life that you'd like to have in it

--someone makes a grand sacrifice for you or pays a high price to be with you

OBLIGATORY SCENES
THE BEGINNING:
The hero and heroine meet. One or both of them are interested, even attracted, but the conflicted character knows he or she has other commitments, debts, or promises to uphold that make a relationship with this person difficult or impossible.

The love interest may or may not be aware in the beginning of the conflicting interest, particularly if the hero or heroine with divided loyalties chooses to hide the conflicting interest while they try to have their cake and eat it too for just a little while.

The conflicted character is often shown right up front knowing that they can't have both their first loyalty and a new love. Thus, the impossibility of a happily ever after for this couple is established for your audience, if not for the love interest.

THE MIDDLE:

The thing or person to whom the conflicted hero/heroine is also loyal is revealed, and furthermore, begins to demand its due. The hero or heroine's divided loyalty is revealed, and the conflict and problems begin. The flavor of these problems will set the tone for your story. Are they funny? Absurd? Exasperating? Vaguely threatening? Deadly?

The love interest, who may or may not be aware of how doomed this relationship already is, falls in love with the conflicted character and commences competing for the hero/heroine's time, attention, and focus.

The conflicted character fights the growing attraction, fights the idea of falling in love and placing himself or herself in an impossible situation, and does his or her best to stop the relationship from evolving into full-blown love. He or she may bargain with themselves that they'll just indulge in a short-term relationship for now, not a long-term or forever relationship.

The middle typically ends with the conflicted character giving in to his or her feelings. The lovers get together, and we see how great they are together. The difficulty of the conflicted character's choice between his or her divided loyalties rises toward a crisis. We may see the lover interest demand that the conflicted character choose once and for all to whom his or her loyalty lays with

BLACK MOMENT:

The hero or heroine's competing commitment and his or her feelings of love clash horribly and explode into a crisis. He or she faces a stark either-or choice and can't avoid choosing any longer.

The conflicted character chooses the older, previous commitment over the new love.

The rejected lover is devastated. His or her gambit has failed. He or she has risked everything and lost.

THE END:

The conflicted hero or heroine reconsiders their choice, perhaps because someone urges them to. Perhaps they realize how unhappy they are in this old life of theirs. Perhaps the absence of the love interest makes the conflicted character realize how deeply unhappy they are now (and maybe always were) in their old life.

In any case, the conflicted character recants their decision to choose the old commitment, walks away from it completely, and instead chooses the love interest. He or she pays the price extracted from them for breaking their earlier commitment and betraying their original promise of loyalty.

OR

The conflicted character finds a way to honor both the old commitment, promise, debt, or person and to have the love interest. In this case, it may be the love interest who compromises in some way to make a happily ever after possible between them. Or, both characters may have to make sacrifices and compromise to meet in the middle.

KEY SCENES

--the moment the reader or viewer finds out that the conflicted character has hopelessly divided loyalties and this relationship is doomed before it hardly gets going

--the moment the love interest finds out about the first loyalty

--the person, organization, or thing to which the conflicted character owes loyalty reminds the conflicted character of it

--the conflicted character considers running away from all of it—from everyone and everything, including the love interest

--the love interest decides to fight for the person they love

--the moment when the conflicted character reverses course after choosing badly

--the reaction of the person, organization, or thing when it/they find out the conflicted character has abandoned them for good this time in favor of true love (or the moment when they find out a compromise solution has been reached)

--the previously conflicted character pays the price for his or her choice to walk away from the first person, organization, entity, thing

THINGS TO THINK ABOUT WHEN WRITING THIS TROPE

How do the hero and heroine react to meeting each other? What form does the conflicted character's strong attraction to the future love interest take?

What about the love interest is attractive and fascinating enough for the conflicted character to contemplate abandoning their previous commitments?

What about the conflicted character is attracting and fascinating enough for the love interest to fight through the conflicted character's initial reluctance to dive headlong into a serious relationship?

Does the conflicted character dive headlong into a serious relationship anyway, even knowing it's a terrible idea?

When will you reveal to your audience that this is a doomed relationship? Will it be at the same time you reveal it to the love interest or at a different time?

How is the relationship doomed? What about the conflicted character's first loyalty makes a happily ever after with the love interest impossible or nearly impossible?

What demands does the first commitment make on the conflicted character that cause problems for the couple? How does the conflicted character juggle these conflicts? Does he or she hide them from the love interest or not?

What is the tone of the problems? Do they cause ridiculous shenanigans to ensue? Threaten the life of the love interest? Make the conflicted character and/or love interest deeply uncomfortable?

How does the love interest feel and what do they think about the conflicted character's first loyalty? Do they find it honorable? Noble? Despicable? Stupid?

When does the love interest decide to fight to keep the conflicted character for himself or herself? Why does he or she make this decision? How does the conflicted character react to this decision? How does the entity holding the first loyalty react?

What crisis tied to the first commitment will force the conflicted character to step away from the love interest? How does the love interest react? What kind of tensions does it introduce into the relationship? This may be a harbinger of or lead up to the ultimate crisis yet to come.

When does the love interest figure out the relationship is doomed despite his or her best efforts to wrest the conflicted character away from his or her commitment? How does he or she react?

What crisis happens that's so significant it forces the conflicted character to walk away from his or her true love and still remain heroic in the eyes of your audience?

How will this impossible situation be resolved in a way the audience will buy into?

Who compromises? Who stands firm?

What price does the conflicted character or perhaps the couple pay for the conflicted character's decision?

TROPE TRAPS

Creating a thing or person the conflicted character is slavishly loyal to that the audience finds stupid or unworthy of such devotion.

Creating a wishy-washy conflicted character that's unlikable to your reader or viewer.

If the right choice for the conflicted character to make is obvious to the audience, yet he or she fails to make it, the audience will have no respect for this character and likely dislike him or her.

Failing to create a powerful enough dilemma between love and the thing or person to which the conflicted character is loyal.

The love interest coming across as selfish, cruel, immature, thoughtless, or narcissistic for trying to pull the conflicted character away from their first loyalty. Would Peggy Carter have been at all likable had she talked Captain America out of making a noble sacrifice for his country? I think not.

Creating a wimpy love interest who should fight harder to save the person they love from a terrible commitment that's damaging to the conflicted character.

Creating a love interest unwilling to compromise or sacrifice for love, even though he or she is asking the conflicted character to do exactly that.

Not putting sufficient thought into creating a plausible solution to this impossible situation.

Failing to exact any price upon the lovers for one or both of them walking away from a powerful commitment or promise. It's lazy writing to just let someone walk away from having given their word and made a promise and suffer no repercussions whatsoever.

Setting up a compromise solution to the dilemma that will lead to resentments and conflict down the road in this relationship. It's all well and good for now to ask a committed doctor to step away from their work, but when patients start dying, it's inevitable the doctor will feel a burning need to go back to those patients.

The love interest cannot extract promises from the conflicted character that he or she will bitterly regret later...at least not without setting up a relationship threatening conflict and a sequel story for this couple.

DIVIDED LOYALTIES TROPE IN ACTION
Movies:

- The Godfather (Michael and his wife's storyline)
- Indecent Proposal
- Captain America
- The Thornbirds
- Brideshead Revisited
- Les Misérables

Books:

- The Thornbirds by Colleen McCollough
- Everyone Wants to Know by Kelly Loy Gilbert
- Fragmented Loyalty by Tonya Burrows
- A Lethal Betrayal by Lori Matthews
- The Child I Never Had by Kate Hewitt
- Hello Stranger by Lisa Kleypas
- Kentucky Bride by Caryl McAdoo
- Gone With the Wind by Margaret Mitchell
- What's Left of Me by Amanda Maxlyn

12

EVERYONE ELSE CAN SEE IT

DEFINITION

Two people exist in close proximity to each other, perhaps as friends, co-workers, neighbors, or something else. The people around them—their friends, co-workers, neighbors, family, or others—clearly see the romantic potential between the pair. But the couple steadfastly refuses to acknowledge any potential for romance to develop between them...until it does.

This is a trope often combined with other tropes that kick in to provide obstacles to a happy ending after the couple themselves have seen the potential for romance and perhaps started to pursue a relationship.

It's possible that this notion of everyone else being able to see that these two people belong together is merely a plot device or premise for the story and not a trope. It can also describe an interfering mother, a busybody neighbor, or pushy best friend trying to throw two characters together romantically.

This becomes a trope when the potential couple makes fighting everyone around them over this idea—of the two of them falling in love—the entire focus of the story and the main conflict that must be overcome before these two stubborn, oblivious people finally give in and fall in love.

This is the ultimate external trope—people around the couple drive much of the tension of the story and push the relationship forward in spite of the hero and heroine and not because of them. In some ways, this story may be as much or more about the people around the lovers machinating to get them together than it is about the lovers themselves.

At its core, this is a story about stubborn refusal to acknowledge or explore one's feelings for someone else, and then experiencing a realization or epiphany that opens the hero and heroine's eyes to love with each other.

ADJACENT TROPES
--Oblivious to Love
--Friends to Lovers
--Commitment Phobia
--Right Under Your Nose

WHY READERS/VIEWERS LOVE THIS TROPE
--we all secretly love to engage in amateur matchmaking and/or to meddle in other people's lives
--most of us have secretly imagined what it would be like to fall in love with a friend, cute co-worker, hot neighbor
--being surprised by love where you least expect it
--love was always right in front of you. Love is close by if you only see it

OBLIGATORY SCENES
THE BEGINNING:

The proximity of the hero and heroine is established as is the nature of their relationship. It is definitely platonic. They may be old friends or co-workers who know each other well, or they may only be acquainted in passing, such as neighbors who pass in the hall, commuters who ride the same train, or people who share a club membership or mutual hobby that brings them together from time to time, to name a few.

We're probably introduced to the interfering friend(s), family member(s), co-worker(s) or other person who knows both the hero and heroine and who is going to stir up all the trouble by suggesting that the hero and heroine are perfect for each other and should pursue a romantic relationship. This person may be well-meaning but may also have some ulterior motive for stirring the romantic pot.

The reason the couple hasn't already become lovers or explored the possibility of a relationship may be established in the beginning or may be delayed until the middle of the book. One or both of them may be oblivious to romance, may be shy or insecure, distracted by other factors in their life, afraid of love, or a host of other reasons why one or both of these people hasn't taken a shot at a relationship before now. This may or may not end up being a major obstacle they must overcome in their story.

THE MIDDLE:

The shenanigans of the interfering character(s) ramp up considerably. This character not only says he or she thinks these two should get together, but the busybody typically begins to take action to throw the hero and heroine together. The busybody might recruit help from others and probably tells others that the hero and heroine should be together, too.

The machinations of the matchmaker start to cause problems. The type of problems and their severity will depend on how the hero and heroine know each other and the tone of your story. If two interfering mothers are throwing their two children together, they will likely keep their shenanigans confined to family situations. But, if a co-worker is trying to throw a couple together, the shenanigans might take place at work and start causing real problems for the hero and heroine professionally.

There's a wide spectrum of possible reactions from the hero and heroine. They may commiserate together. They may recoil from each other and not have anything to do with each other. They may be embarrassed or exasperated.

But odds are good that at some point, the hero and heroine start to push back against the manipulation and interference in their lives.

The hero and heroine privately start to consider the idea of entering into a romantic relationship with the other character. They may or may not confess this to a friend, but probably will not confess it to the main matchmaker. Which is not to say that the main matchmaker won't find out anyway. It will depend on how wide a net of conspiracy the matchmaker has cast around the couple, who and how many people around the couple have been enlisted to help throw them together.

The problems caused by the busybody(ies), external to the hero and heroine, in their jobs, lives, or other relationships get out of hand and become a crisis. At the same time, the pressure on the two of them to get together grows unbearable. This may be unbearable attraction they can no longer resist or can be unbearable desire to tell the matchmaker to back off and leave them alone.

It's possible that in the middle of the story, the hero and heroine actually do come together romantically. They may not want to tell the matchmaker and may want to take their first, tentative steps into romance privately and in secret.

It's also possible that the middle ends with the hero and heroine giving in and trying out the idea of a romantic relationship. This can be a date, a steamy night together, or even a simple conversation—

whatever's appropriate to your story's heat level and the characters you've drawn.

BLACK MOMENT:

The romantic encounter between the hero and heroine blows up in their faces. Something goes terribly, horribly, irrecoverably wrong. This thing can be a fatal relationship misstep by the hero or heroine. It can be the final straw of interference by the busybody matchmaker. It can be the external problem(s) caused by the matchmaker ruining one or both of their lives.

Regardless of how you tear them apart, the hero and heroine stagger back from the budding relationship and run screaming in the opposite direction from each other.

Typically, whatever relationship they had before this whole romantic fiasco is ruined as well. If they were friends, they've lost that friendship. If they were pleasant co-workers, they're now painfully uncomfortable working together and will try to separate their work lives. If they're neighbors, they'll assiduously avoid each other in the hallway. They'll take a different train, drop out of the club where they usually run into each other.

The relationship has utterly, completely failed. The matchmaker has also utterly, completely failed.

THE END:

Obviously, somebody has to do something to snatch another chance at love from the jaws of defeat. Perhaps the matchmaker comes up with one last gambit to throw the hero and heroine together so they can admit to each other that they're desperately unhappy being apart.

OR

Perhaps the matchmaker apologizes and swears to step back and never interfere again, thereby creating a safe space for the hero and heroine to talk things out without nosy busybodies interfering.

OR

Perhaps other friends, family, or co-workers step in to suggest to the lovers that they give it one more shot.

OR

Perhaps the lovers, finally relieved of all of the interference and shenanigans around them, realize on their own that they really miss each other and actually do want to give the relationship another try but completely on their own terms and in their own way this time.

No matter how they get back together, the hero and heroine realize they do actually care deeply for each other, they have what it takes to build a long-term romantic relationship with each other, and they commit to doing so.

KEY SCENES
—the first time the hero and heroine entertain the idea of being a couple and recoil from it
—the first time they go out in public or appear in front of friends and family as a couple
—each of them doubts that the relationship is a good idea
—something goes wrong that makes the question the relationship
—their first big fight
—an awkward romantic scene that they break off mid-moment

. . .

THINGS TO THINK ABOUT WHEN WRITING THIS TROPE

What kind of friends or acquaintances are your hero and heroine? How do they know each other and how well do they know each other?

Do they joke around a lot, are they confidantes, do they turn to each other when life kicks them in the teeth? Or are they two ships passing in the night? The less they know each other, the more important the matchmaker character(s) will be to pushing the hero and heroine together and driving the romance forward, particularly in the early stages of the relationship.

Why haven't they become lovers before now? What situation, taboo, agreement, or lack of awareness of some aspect of each other has prevented this relationship from progressing into a romance before now?

Is the reason they haven't become lovers before now an internal one within one or both of the main characters, or is it some sort of external prohibition from falling in love?

Does this obstacle to romance form a major obstacle now, or will there be some other obstacle that gets in the way of love between them?

Why has each of these characters not considered a romance, run away from romance, or perceived romance between them as forbidden or a bad idea?

Who is the main matchmaker?

Is whoever first sees these two together a single person or is it a widely held understanding in a group of people around the hero and heroine from the very beginning? Which is to say, does everyone in the office or family know these two belong together already, or does a single person plant the seed—in both the future lovers and in the other people around them?

Have this hero and heroine considered or tried a romantic relationship before? If so, how did it go? Why did they back off to being just friends or even less than that?

Why don't the hero and heroine just tell the meddling match-maker to shove off right from the start? What compelling reason stops them both from doing exactly this?

Are the hero and heroine already aware of each other as possible romantic interests, or will one or both of them discover this over the course of your story?

What do they see in the other person that changes their perception from friend to "potential lover"? How will they each see that thing? What situation are you going to throw this couple into that reveals this new, romantic potential?

What big thing changes in their world that jolts them into reevaluating their old friendship? Is it the interference of friends or busy-bodies or something else altogether?

Does the thing that jolts their relationship into romance also threaten the friendship aspect of their relationship? If so, how?

How does each character initially react to the idea of becoming lovers instead of friends? Is it hilarious? Embarrassing? Intriguing? Ridiculous? Why?

How does the hero's initial reaction make the heroine feel, and vice versa? Does it cause anger, hurt, friction, distance, emotional withdrawal, or something else?

How will their individual reactions to the changing nature of their relationship compare and contrast against each other in the story and cause friction and/or conflict?

Because these two characters start the story already acquainted to some extent and a matchmaker is shoving them at each other aggressively, the direction of the story is typically one of the hero and heroine resisting the pressure, pushing themselves apart as it were, while they gradually become attracted to each other and romantically aware of each other. What is the event or realization that causes them to question their efforts to push apart from each other?

What event or realization causes them to reverse direction and start (or consider starting) coming back toward each other romantically?

What are the external things—events, other people, doubts, fears, and conflicts that will work to separate them? What are the external things—events, other people, doubts, fears, and conflicts that will work to push them together?

Likewise, what are the internal thoughts, feelings, conflicts, trauma that work to push them apart and, conversely, to pull them together?

How do the hero and heroine feel about the matchmaker over the course of the story? Do their feelings toward this person change? If so, how? How does this meddling strengthen or weaken the relationship between the hero/heroine and the meddling busybody?

Why wouldn't the hero and heroine just stay friends? What compelling reason is there for them to take their relationship to the next level besides shutting up the meddling busybodies in their lives?

How does the implosion in their romance also destroy their friendship?

What event, confession, realization, crisis will finally draw these two characters back together? What event will pull them into physical proximity? What will pull them into emotional proximity?

Why do they forgive each other?

Do they forgive the matchmaker or not? What does that look like in the story?

What have they learned through this difficult journey to love *and* friendship?

What holds them apart or tears them apart until almost the end of the story?

If it only takes an honest conversation at the end to resolve their issues, why was this conversation impossible for them to have before? What has changed that allows them to work out their objections to being together now?

TROPE TRAPS

This couple should have realized a LONG time ago that they were in love. They come across as stupid or dense for not seeing it before now.

The reason they haven't gotten together before now is silly, weak, or boils down to laziness. None of those are likable.

Failing at all to answer the question of why the hero and heroine haven't gotten together before now.

The hero and heroine don't have a compelling reason that stops them both from telling the matchmaker to shove off, and they look stupid, weak or lazy for not standing up for themselves.

The meddling that jolts this friendship out of being "just friendship" and into something more isn't strong enough to do the jolting. If the matchmaker doesn't have to work hard at getting these two stubborn not-lovers together, it makes the hero and heroine look lazy and weak.

The hero and heroine are being forced out of a stable relationship into a wildly unstable one (at least until they achieve their happily ever after), and the reason for making this shift isn't big enough to justify all the chaos to follow.

Failing to put the friendship between the hero and heroine at serious risk.

Failing to put their relationship with the meddling matchmaker at serious risk.

The risk to these important friendships is a main source of tension, suspense, and danger that will pull the reader forward through the story. If it's a foregone conclusion that these two are such good friends and so perfectly in sync and so able to navigate problems together that they'll obviously end up together, there's not much reason to bother reading or watching your story.

The relationship between the hero and heroine lacks real conflict, both external and internal. In most relationships, this transition from friends to lovers is easy, flows naturally, and is the source of nothing but joy. But to be an interesting story, this couple has to have a MUCH harder time of it. Failing to do so—that is, relying *only* on their stubborn refusal to acknowledge the truth everyone around them sees—will bore your audience to death.

Failing to introduce complex new dynamics into the relationship as it transitions from simple friendship to something much more romantically complex.

Failing to justify why the hero and heroine ought to make this change in their otherwise fine relationship.

Relying solely on outside pressures or events to force this change from friends to lovers. At the end of the day, the hero and heroine both have to want this change, embrace it, and make it happen.

Failing to resolve the relationship with the matchmaker(s).

EVERYONE ELSE CAN SEE IT TROPE IN ACTION MOVIES:

- The Parent Trap
- Because I Said So
- Crossing Delancey
- Owl and the Sparrow
- Emma
- The Perfect Man
- Chance At Romance

BOOKS:

- Make It Sweet by Kristen Callihan
- Meant to Be Mine by Hannah Orenstein
- The Bride Test by Helen Hoang

- Accidentally Engaged by Farah Heron
- The Heir by Johanna Lindsey
- A Brush With Love by Mazey Eddings
- Because of Miss Bridgerton by Julia Quinn
- Ayesha At Last by Umza Jalaluddin

13

EVIL/DYSFUNCTIONAL FAMILY

DEFINITION

In this trope, we have a perfectly nice hero and/or heroine who happen to come from...you guessed it...an evil or dysfunctional family. As with many external tropes, having a terrible or damaged family doesn't necessarily constitute a trope, in and of itself. What turns this into a trope is when the hero and heroine must deal with the evil/dysfunctional family in some way to achieve their own happiness. They may have to break away from the family, overcome family interference, or in some way destroy the family or its influence over the hero or heroine.

This trope takes a meddling mama or raucous, interfering family and raises them to a whole new level of problem. The evil family that will do horrible, manipulative, hurtful, even cruel things to break up a budding relationship or force it to happen the way the family wants it to. The dysfunctional family will respond in painful, inappropriate, toxic ways to the budding romance between one of their own and an outsider.

It's worth pointing out that evil families are often dysfunctional as well, and vice versa. They may be elements of both evil and dysfunction for the lovers to deal with over the course of the story.

Part of what makes this trope interesting is the unspoken question of whether or not the hero or heroine from an evil family has inherited just a smidgin of his or her family's evil, or the hero/heroine from a dysfunctional family has inherited some portion of its dysfunction, also.

This taint can present itself by the hero or heroine doing something evil (but possibly out of character) back at his or her family to defend the new romantic relationship. Or it can be more subtle, a lingering darkness of spirit that the audience and love interest never quite know what to make of and whether or not to trust.

The odds are excellent that, in the absence of therapy or significant time away from their evil/dysfunctional family, the hero or heroine has picked up at least some emotional baggage over the years of living with their family.

Regardless of the taint of evil or dysfunction that your hero and/or heroine might have inherited, this trope is about dealing with the problems posed by the hero or heroine's family that block a path forward for the lovers to their happily ever after.

Obviously, no trope is complete without some good personal conflict, and this trope has plenty of that, not only between the hero/heroine and his or her awful family, but also for the love interest. It's often said you don't just marry the person—you marry the whole family. The love interest also is going to have to come to terms with the hero or heroine's family one way or another.

The lovers must find a way to overcome the challenge(s) presented by or caused by the evil/dysfunctional family before their happily ever after can be complete.

This trope is one that can very easily be turned into a tragedy simply by changing the ending to the evil or dysfunctional family winning. The hero/heroine ultimately chooses their evil/dysfunctional family over the person they love. As a side note: it's possible this choice is a noble one, a great sacrifice by the hero/heroine to save the life or well-being of the person they love.

· · ·

ADJACENT TROPES
--Feuding Families
--Forbidden Love
--Family Skeletons
--Dangerous Secret
--Mafia Romance

WHY READERS/VIEWERS LOVE THIS TROPE
--many of us have problems fitting into our new partner's family. We may fantasize about destroying our evil/dysfunctional in-laws or stealing away our loved one from their awful family forever

--the thrill and drama of saving or rescuing the one we love

--the satisfaction of fixing the person we love (I'm the first to admit this is pure fantasy. We rarely change anyone much, including those we love...not that this keeps us from trying.)

--being loved so much that your lover is willing to sacrifice his or her family for you

--it's titillating to imagine being swept into a powerful, dangerous family and becoming equally powerful and dangerous

--having a scary family (or slightly scary mate) means you'll always be safe...because nobody will mess with them or anyone they love

--escaping dysfunctional families of our own

--finding a healthy romantic relationship for ourselves in spite of our own dysfunctional families

OBLIGATORY SCENES
THE BEGINNING:
The hero and heroine meet. The innocent love interest and audience may not be made aware immediately of the evil or dysfunctional family lurking behind the hero or heroine. However, this trope doesn't really get moving until the problem of the evil/dysfunctional

family is introduced, so that typically happens in the beginning of the story.

What form of evil the family takes, how the hero or heroine responds to his or her family's evil, and how the love interest reacts to it will set the tone for your story. In the romantic comedy, the form of evil may be farcical in nature, and in the dark gothic, paranormal, or mafia romance, the family may be downright terrifying.

The love interest and audience may meet the evil family in the beginning of the story, or that may not happen until the middle of the story.

THE MIDDLE:

As the hero and heroine begin to fall in love, the problems posed by the evil/dysfunctional family begin to rear their ugly heads. If the hero/heroine is going to push back against his or her family, beginning to fight against their family to have the person they love, this typically begins in the middle of the story. What form this fight takes will also help set the tone for your story and may define much of its external conflict.

As the love interest learns more about the evilness or dysfunction of the family, conflict between him/her and the family begins to build. Conflict with the hero or heroine probably also builds.

The love interest's otherness or difference from the evil family ensures that he or she doesn't fit in and never will. The love interest may try to lure the hero/heroine away from his/her family. The love interest may try to take on and take down the evil family. Or the love interest may decide to find a way to fit into the family if that's the only way to have the hero/heroine.

The hero/heroine's dilemma builds toward a crisis as he or she is ultimately going to be forced to choose between love and family. The middle of the story inexorably forces the hero or heroine toward this crisis.

This choice can take many forms, ranging from staying with

their evil/dysfunctional family and forsaking the new love all the way to choosing to destroy their own family to clear the way for love.

BLACK MOMENT:

Faced with a choice between the person they love or their evil/dysfunctional family, the hero/heroine chooses family over love. The evil/dysfunctional family appears to win. Whatever external pull they've exerted or evil actions they've engaged in to break up the lovers has worked.

It's also possible that in the black moment the love interest chooses to walk away from the person they love rather that stay and continue having to deal with the evil/dysfunctional family. Again, the family has won by driving away the love interest.

Simultaneously, whatever internal conflict has been building between the hero and heroine over the evil family comes to a head. The love interest may give up on urging the hero/heroine to cut ties with the evil family. Or the lover's plan to destroy the family is sprung. It may or may not succeed, but either way it drives a spike of betrayal into the heart of the lover's relationship.

The hero/heroine has not successfully resolved his or her relationship with their evil/dysfunctional family and either chooses family over love or simply cannot do what is necessary to remove his or her family as an obstacle to love. Likewise, the love interest has had it and walks (or runs) away.

THE END:

The evil/dysfunctional family is vanquished and removed as an obstacle between the hero and heroine. What constitutes vanquished will be up to you, and there are many variations upon it. The hero/heroine may break away from the evil/dysfunctional family at long last and leave with the love interest, never to return. The love interest may break through the evil/dysfunctional family's resistance, earn its trust, and be welcomed into the family.

The evil or dysfunctional family may be utterly destroyed and no longer be a threat to the lovers. It's not unreasonable for key evil or particularly dysfunctional members of a family to die, clearing the way for the lovers to be together. Your imagination is the only limit to how the evil/dysfunctional family will be dealt with by the end of the story.

If you're hoping to write a sequel to this tale, you'll probably want to leave the evil/dysfunctional family defeated for now...with the promise of some or all of it rising again to be a threat to the lovers in later stories.

KEY SCENES

--the big reveal to the love interest of just what family or kind of family the hero/heroine belongs to and the love interest's reaction to that news

--a threat to the hero/heroine is leveled by a family member to dump the love interest or else

--the love interest meets the evil/dysfunctional family and it's a disaster

--the love interest is threatened by an evil or dysfunctional family member

--the love interest delivers an ultimatum to the hero/heroine—you must choose me or them

--the moment of wrong decision by the hero or heroine when faced with the ultimatum

--the love interest forgives the hero/heroine for their family's terrible actions and forgives the hero/heroine

THINGS TO THINK ABOUT WHEN WRITING THIS TROPE

What form will the family's evil or dysfunction take? What flavor is it—violent, dangerous, obnoxious, mentally ill, silly, or something else? This flavor can literally range from criminally insane to charmingly quirky.

Will all the members of the family be the same, or will some be better or worse than others on the scales of evil and dysfunction?

How affected and/or afflicted is the hero or heroine who grew up in this family? Why are they this little or this greatly affected?

Does the hero/heroine have an ally or two inside their family who will support them overtly or covertly?

Has the hero or heroine done any work to overcome the evil/dysfunction of his or her family? If so, what kind of work?

Has he or she had any professional counseling or therapy? Why or why not?

How does the love interest find out what kind of family the hero/heroine is from? Does he or she already know who the family is, or does he or she have to experience the evil or dysfunction firsthand?

How does the first meeting between the love interest and the family happen? How does it go...or rather how badly does it go?

Do the hero/heroine and love interest commiserate over the family and its issues?

Do the lovers form a plan of some kind to circumvent the family to spend time together? Does it work? If they get caught, how disastrously does that go?

Do the lovers form another, larger plan to escape the family's clutches permanently? What will escaping look like? How hard is it going to be to pull off this plan? How can you make it harder to pull off?

How can you raise the stakes...by a lot...for the lovers failing to pull off their plan? What catastrophe will happen if they fail to escape?

Is this escape an emotional one, a physical one, or both?

What does the love interest think of the evil/dysfunctional family? Does he or she tell the hero/heroine their real opinion from the start? Why or why not?

When does the love interest reveal what they think of the family? How does the hero/heroine take it? Is he or she relieved that someone else sees it too, or is the hero/heroine hurt, offended, or something else?

What does the family think of the hero/heroine and of the love interest individually and as a couple? Will the family tell either or both of the lovers their opinion? How do those conversations go?

What will the family do to interfere in the romance? How far is the family willing to go to prevent the lovers from being together?

How far is the hero/heroine willing to go to fight back and defend his or her right to love who they wish?

Does the love interest egg on the building hostilities between the hero/heroine and the family or try to diffuse the hostilities?

What triggers the crisis that forces the hero/heroine to choose between family and the love interest?

How does the love interest react and feel when the family wins? How does the hero/heroine react and feel?

How will the lovers reverse their fortunes and take one more shot at defeating the family so they can be together? Why do they think it's worth trying one more time?

Does the love interest find a place within the family—maybe not joining in on evil and dysfunctional things but tacitly not condemning them? Does he or she try to fix the family? How does that go?

Does the love interest fear the evil/dysfunctional family? Want nothing to do with it? Is he or she determined to pull the hero or heroine completely away from his or her family in a daring rescue?

How do things end up between the love interest and the family? How will the hero/heroine support this stance?

Will the hero/heroine have any relationship with his or her family by the end of the story? If so, what boundaries are now in place? If not, how will the lovers enforce that separation? While this may not seem germane to the story itself, it will give the audience confidence that this couple will be able to stay together for the long term—that the happily is going to be ever after.

TROPE TRAPS

Creating an evil or dysfunctional family that's so implausible the audience won't buy it. This can be a challenge for writers because reality can be so much worse than most people realize. If you're going for the gusto in creating a truly terrible family, you'll need to put extra work into making the characters from the evil/dysfunctional family seem entirely real to the audience.

Which leads to our next trap...creating caricatures of evil or dysfunctional villains rather than believable characters.

Not giving the hero/heroine any negative emotional baggage at all from having grown up in a toxic family.

Creating a hero/heroine who is so damaged from their toxic family that they're unlikable or perceived as unredeemable by the audience.

Failing to justify why the love interest falls for the (damaged) hero or heroine.

Failing to justify why the love interest sticks around after meeting the horrible family.

Creating a hero/heroine or love interest who is unlikable, unsympathetic, or uninteresting.

This trope typically calls for nuanced, complex characters, and failing to deliver on that need.

Not having the awful family actually do awful things to try to break up the lovers. If you say a family is violent killers and then they fail to try to violently kill the love interest, they won't be believable to your audience.

Failing to have any consequences for the evil/dysfunctional family's worst actions. Some behaviors are not only horrific, but criminal.

If you paint criminals doing crimes, you should seriously consider showing the criminals getting caught and facing justice. There may be some stories where this doesn't work, but you'd better explain why not to your audience or else expect to face some backlash.

The lovers staying in a relationship with the evil/dysfunctional family when the healthy and correct thing to do would be to walk away and never look back...or at least walk away and only interact from a very safe distance.

The lovers failing to seek outside help to deal with the family when it makes sense to do so and is available. (This could be police, mental health experts, or government family services, for example.)

Creating an implausible scenario of how the lovers get back together after the family has appeared to break them up.

Fixing the family. Very few people change very much once their personalities are fully formed. Bad people don't just have a sudden epiphany and become good guys. It takes hard work, desire, and perseverance to make any significant change to who one is.

Likewise, just fixing the hero or heroine who grew up in this terrible background. While it's a wonderful sentiment to suggest that the love of a good person makes all of one's baggage magically disappear, that's not how it works in reality. If you use nothing but love to fix everything for the hero/heroine in your story, the trap is failing to justify why and how love is going to do all this heavy lifting of emotional growth and psychological healing.

While love is vital in supporting someone's healing, get your wounded character(s) to professionals who can guide them in how to do the work. This is one of those ethical areas that has shifted in recent years. Mental health is a huge trigger issue, and destigmatizing both trauma and mental health care is important in the stories we tell one another.

EVIL/DYSFUNCTIONAL FAMILY TROPE IN ACTION
Movies:

- The Fockers
- Ella Enchanted
- The Godfather
- Cinderella
- The Uninvited
- Sweet Home Alabama

Books:

- A Kingdom of Dreams by Judith McNaught
- Texas Glory by Lorraine Heath
- The Unwanted Wife by Natasha Anders
- Very Bad Things by Ilsa Madden-Mills
- Just One Touch by Maya Banks
- Bad Blood by Cynthia Rayne (trigger warning for rape)
- Bound by Vengeance by Cora Reilly

14

FEUDING FAMILIES

DEFINITION

The hero and heroine come from two families who are at war with each other, either literally or metaphorically. These families can be blood relatives or they can be intentional families or family groupings, for example gangs, tribes, or some other type of close groupings to which the hero and heroine each belong.

Unlike in the evil/dysfunctional family trope, the members of the two families may not be evil, dysfunctional, or terrible in the normal course of events. But rightly or wrongly, they do have serious beef with the family that the other lover comes from.

The act of falling in love with the person the hero and heroine have chosen means they have fallen in love with the "enemy" in the eyes of their families. This is an act of huge betrayal to the respective families and is absolutely going to cause backlash.

In some cases, the romance between the hero and heroine ends up healing the rift between the two families. But in many cases, the romance does not heal anything and the lovers must find a way forward in spite of the intractable hostility between their families.

This trope is often paired with other tropes that explain the enmity between the two families—an interspecies romance, an interracial/interethnic/intercultural romance, their kingdoms are at war. In this trope, however, the differences between the families the lovers come from are raised to the level of open feuding.

Of course, feuding can take many forms. It can be as benign as two families competing financially over business assets or for market share, or it can be as savage as warring gangs, clans, nations, or races who kill one another on sight. This feud is often the source of external conflict over the course of your story.

Regardless, the hero and heroine are so attracted to each other that they overcome all the prejudices and misbeliefs they've been taught about their enemy to fall in love with a member of the enemy faction. This trope revolves around how the families react to this and how the lovers themselves react and create a space for themselves to be happy.

At its core, this is a trope of rebellion and possibly of reconciliation. It's also a trope of courage and standing one's ground in the face of great opposition.

ADJACENT TROPES
--Evil/Dysfunctional Families
--Forbidden Love
--Divided Loyalties
--No One Thinks It Will Work
--Rebellious Hero/Heroine

WHY READERS/VIEWERS LOVE THIS TROPE
--we all love to root for star-crossed lovers (side note: Will Shakespeare first coined the term, star cross'd lovers, in reference to Romeo and Juliet, who are unquestionably the most famous lovers from feuding families in all of literature.)
--the idea that great love heals great rifts is deeply appealing

--being loved so much that your lover is willing to sacrifice everything for you

--having someone see the good in you despite the bad things and people around you

--it's titillating to consider falling in love with the absolutely most forbidden, most off-limits person we can think of—this goes way beyond falling for a bad boy or girl. We're falling for the worst boy or girl possible

OBLIGATORY SCENES
THE BEGINNING:

The hero and heroine meet. While this might seem obvious, for this couple, the fact of their meeting is probably dangerous and definitely forbidden for both of them. The hero and heroine may or may not have any idea who the other one is at first. But since the core of this trope has to do with the feud between their families, that's usually established right up front, if not for the lovers, it's certainly made clear to the audience fairly quickly.

As soon as the families they're from are identified, the stakes must also be made clear. Just how bad is it going to be if their families find out who've they've met and are considering becoming involved with romantically?

THE MIDDLE:

If the identity of their families and the stakes hasn't been made clear already, it surely must be made clear heading into the middle of the story. This portion of the story is taken up by the hero and heroine evading their families to spend time together and falling in love.

Often the romance itself proceeds largely without a hitch. These two people will fall in love quickly, easily, and completely in most cases. The source of conflict in this scenario comes exclusively from trying to keep the romance secret and avoid the consequences of being found out.

OR

The lovers themselves are conflicted about falling in love with the enemy. The middle of the story in this case is made up of their own internal struggles to reconcile themselves with who they're attracted to, fighting their mutual attraction, and ultimately failing to resist the other person.

The lovers may enlist friends and allies to help them meet and move their romance forward. The lovers and their allies take increasing risks to be together, and with each risk taken, the stakes raise regarding getting caught. The more in love these two grow, the worse the consequences are going to be if they get caught.

The families may begin to suspect something. The families may lay a trap for the lovers, or someone may betray the lovers. Often, a crisis in the feud itself between the families occurs in the middle and grows toward an explosion of some kind.

BLACK MOMENT:

The lovers are caught and all hell breaks loose as both families are enraged and feel betrayed by their own young lover. All the consequences the hero and heroine have feared land upon their heads.

OR

The crisis in the feud explodes into open hostility, tearing the lovers apart. If they've been struggling with loyalty to their own families while falling in love with the enemy, this is the moment when they must choose between love of family or new love of the enemy.

Often both of these possible black moments happen in the same story. The feud provides an external crisis, while being discovered or torn apart by their own conflicted loyalties provides an internal crisis.

THE END:

The ending will be determined by the type of black moment you've chosen. In the case where the feud itself is not going to be resolved by the end of the story, the hero and heroine must each escape their families or find some way to reconcile their family to the idea of them loving one of the enemy.

In less severe versions of this trope, the family may reluctantly allow the hero or heroine to pursue their heart's true love. In the more severe versions of this trope, the families may each flatly refuse to accept the relationship and force a terrible choice upon the hero or heroine.

(Each family may react differently, by the way.)

In the case where the romance between the lovers is going to end the feud or unite the families, this must happen before the lovers can safely be together forever. You may choose to execute this in one climactic scene of reconciliation between the families at the same time you reconcile the hero and heroine, or you may choose to split this ending into two distinct scenes—one where the families reconcile and another where the lovers privately reconcile.

In either case, the hero and heroine are determined to end up together regardless of what their families think. If they've been struggling with a sense of divided loyalty between family and romantic love, that conflict must also be resolved before they can be together.

KEY SCENES

--the hero and heroine physically meet. Given that the families are feuding, the odds of these two ending up in the same place at the same time to meet are probably quite low.

--the hero and heroine react to finding out what family the other one is from

--the family declares or demonstrates the consequences to anyone who betrays the family

--the hero and heroine declare their love to each other—an act of great risk

--the hero and heroine are caught (this may be by a friend or ally, who now poses a risk of revealing the couple's secret, or it may be by a family member prepared to mete out punishment)

--the hero and heroine react to the crisis between the families

--the families take vengeance upon each other for one of their own being seduced away from them

THINGS TO THINK ABOUT WHEN WRITING THIS TROPE

How do the hero and heroine actually meet? It is an accident or an act of fate? Does someone else engineer the meeting, or is it purely chance? Does their meeting reflect the feud between their families or happen outside of the feud?

How are the hero and heroine's families different? Do these differences introduce conflict into their relationship? If so, how?

How are their families the same? Are they likely to convince their families to see the things they have in common? If so, how? If not, why not?

Who from their families will attempt to stop the hero and heroine's relationship from growing into love? This may be the hero and heroine's friends and allies—the family elders will likely react much more aggressively and immediately to break up the relationship if and when they find out about it.

Do the hero and heroine ever meet members of the other's family? If so, how does that go? Does it happen incognito? Is it a chance meeting or arranged? If it's arranged, by whom?

What are the consequences of the hero and heroine being caught together? How will you demonstrate these to the audience...and to the lovers? Can you make these consequences worse? Can you make them MUCH worse? Can you make them utterly devastating?

What escalates in the feud between the two families over the course of your story? What does a crisis in this escalation look like? Can you make this crisis worse...or much worse?

What triggers the escalation to turn into an acute crisis?

How does this escalation and ensuing crisis affect the hero and heroine? How do they deal separately and together with their conflicted loyalties?

What will break up the hero and heroine? Do the families catch them and rip them apart?

Do the hero and heroine separate voluntarily as the feud explodes into open warfare? Does the crisis itself separate them physically? If so, how?

Do the hero and heroine want to be apart when they break up? If not, how will they try to get back together?

If they initially choose to go back to their respective families, what changes for each of them to convince them they want to be back together?

How will the hero and heroine physically get back together?

What happens to the feud when these two reconcile? If it ends, how do the lovers end the feud? If it continues, how will the lovers extricate themselves from the feud to be together?

TROPE TRAPS

Failing to resolve how these two people from very different worlds are going to live together happily.

The act of rebelling is more important than the person the hero or heroine is allegedly falling in love with.

Failing to address how truly different their worlds are and how a person from one is going to adapt to the other world.

Assuming that anybody can casually fit into any other world.

Failure to fully understand the differing values and experiences that lead to real and serious disconnects between the differing sides of the tracks these characters come from.

FEUDING FAMILIES TROPE IN ACTION
Movies:

- Romeo and Juliet (duh)
- West Side Story
- Hatfields & McCoys
- The Big Country
- Jumping the Broom

Books:

- Romeo and Juliet by William Shakespeare (again, duh)
- Never Seduce a Scot by Maya Banks
- Condemned to Love by Siobahn Davis
- These Violent Delights by Chloe Gong
- The Rivals by Vi Keeland
- Captive Prince by C.S. Pacat
- The Secret by Julie Garwood

15

FISH OUT OF WATER/COWBOY IN THE CITY

DEFINITION

Either the hero or the heroine in this trope must move or has recently moved to a place deeply unfamiliar to him or her. After arriving in this very strange and new place, he or she meets someone to whom he or she is deeply attracted...and the shenanigans begin.

Although this is often a comic trope, it can just as easily be a completely serious trope of displacement and the struggle to make a place for oneself.

The fish out of water has two choices: he or she can change to adapt to the new environment, or our intrepid fish can change the environment to suit himself or herself. Often some combination of the two takes place in this type of story.

As for the love interest who falls for this strange duck, he or she also has two choices. The love interest can help the fish out of water adapt to the strange new place, or the love interest can learn about the fish's original world and adapt to that. Often some combination of the two takes place in this type of story.

This is not just a story of being unfamiliar with the physical trappings of life in a strange place. It's also a story of clashing values, customs, and traditions. The fish out of water typically hangs on to his or her "better" set of values in the cynical, depraved place into which they've been thrust. It's typically this oddball set of wonderful values that attract the love interest to the fish.

Part of the charm of this trope is the opportunity to mash-up two wildly disparate worlds into a hybrid of the two wherein the fish and the love interest can both feel comfortable and be happy together.

Because this trope compares and contrasts ways of life and value sets, it's important for you, the writer, not to come across as excessively critical or judgmental of one world or the other—even though the characters in your story may do exactly that!

If you have a character react sharply negatively to a way of life that any of your audience might actually be living, it's vital to make sure that character has an epiphany before the end of the story where he or she embraces the positive aspects of that way of life.

It's not necessary to make a utopia of any way of life, and you can certainly show the negatives of a "world" as made clear through the gaze of an outsider. But do think about how your audience will respond to your critique of what may be the norm in their lived experience.

At its core, this is a trope of transformation—either of self or of environment, and usually a bit of both.

WHY READERS/VIEWERS LOVE THIS TROPE

--we take a fresh look at the world we've always taken for granted

--this is a version of the rescued by a knight on a white horse story...and who doesn't love that

--being loved so much that your lover is willing to sacrifice everything he or she knows for you

--being swept out of your unhappy, mundane existence by someone who takes you away to an entirely new way of living, thinking, and being treated

--across time, distance, and the boundaries of very different worlds, there is one person out there who is *exactly* right for you

ADJACENT TROPES
--Newcomer/Outsider/Stranger
--Opposites Attract
--Socially Awkward Hero/Heroine
--Fresh Start
--Cross Cultural/Interethnic/Interracial Romance

OBLIGATORY SCENES
THE BEGINNING:

Meet-cutes are the norm for this trope. Of course, don't feel obligated to start your story with something silly if that's not the tone of the project.

The hero or heroine typically arrives in the new place with which they're completely unfamiliar, and it becomes clear immediately that he or she has no idea what to do or how to act in this wildly strange place. Which is to say, it usually goes very badly for the fish out of water.

Also typically, the hero/heroine meets the love interest fairly quickly. The love interest may rescue the floundering fish out of water or may simply show sympathy or kindness to this oddball who had dropped into their world.

A spark of attraction usually happens quickly but isn't mandatory for this trope. It's fine for the romance to unfold gradually in this type of story.

The fish out of water is usually distracted enough and fascinated enough by the new place he or she has arrived in not to immediately pursue returning home.

The fish out of water may have a "thing to accomplish" in this new place before he or she can contemplate leaving and returning home. If this is the case, this goal is usually established in the beginning of the story.

· · ·

THE MIDDLE:

The fish out of water explores, experiences, and interacts with the strange new world he or she has landed in. The love interest is taken along for this ride and gets an opportunity to see their familiar world through fresh eyes, as seen by the fish out of water. These explorations can take any number of tones—humorous, silly, wondrous, alarming, or downright dangerous—depending on the type of world the fish has landed in and how fraught with risks and hazards it is.

The two worlds begin to clash. The fun and games of exploration give way to conflicts in beliefs and values that cause dilemmas for both the fish out of water and the love interest. It's this conflict of beliefs and values that often leads to the main crisis between the lovers. Can they resolve the differences between them enough to find compromise that will let them be together?

At some point, the fish out of water begins to contemplate returning to his or her own fishbowl and leaving this new place to go home. This also may be a primary source of conflict between the hero and heroine. Will the fish stay or go...and will the love interest stay or go with the fish?

If the fish out of water has a goal of some kind, a task to do or a MacGuffin to find, he or she works toward accomplishing that. The middle of the story is where he or she will encounter obstacles along the journey and have to find ways to overcome them, often calling upon skills he or she learned back at home.

The love interest may use skills from the new world to help or hinder the fish out of water in achieving their goal, depending on what the love interest's personal agenda is. He or she may have a good reason to stop the fish from finding the MacGuffin or finishing the task, a reason he or she may or may not reveal to the fish.

The clash of differing values between the two worlds and between the hero and heroine becomes ever more pronounced and serious. Eventually, the lovers encounter a challenge where the fish out of water finally refuses to bend any further in the name of fitting in. He or she stands firm in their own beliefs to the vast frustration of the love interest. This provokes a crisis between them. The fish's stubborn stand may also provoke some sort of external crisis.

The search for the thing the fish is seeking comes to a head and a climactic obstacle is finally reached that will make or break the fish's search.

Throughout all of this exploring and seeking, the hero and heroine fall in love. They each see something in the other that their original world lacks, or they each see something familiar that they've each craved and not been able to find in their own worlds.

BLACK MOMENT:

The clash between the hero and heroine's values and worlds is too much for them to overcome. Neither of them is willing to bend in their beliefs, nor is either one of them willing to abandon their own way of life to embrace the way of life of the other one in the name of love.

The fish out of water's search for a thing/task to accomplish has failed. All is lost with regard to the external plot goal. The fish out of water may actually leave the new world, leaving behind the devastated love interest. All is lost with regard to their internal conflict. They have failed to resolve their differences and find a way to coexist or to blend their worlds into a shared space they can both be comfortable in.

THE END:

The lovers are miserable apart and make one last try at being together. The fish out of water may return to the new world. The love interest may follow the fish back to their home fishbowl. One or both of them make a heroic effort to find the thing the fish needed and accomplish his or her goal.

Lost without each other, the lovers finally resolve their difference in values. One of them embraces the other's values, or they both embrace some blend of shared values between them.

They settle in one or the other of their worlds...or they may leave and go someplace new to both of them. It's also possible that, whichever world they settle in, the fish to that world will inject some of his or her own fishbowl into the space they now share.

With their conflicts resolved and their goals accomplished, they can settle down to a glorious happily ever after.

KEY SCENES

--the fish out of water's moment of arrival in the strange new world

--the first time the love interest spies the fish floundering in the love interest's familiar world

--introduction of some aspect of the fish's world to the love interest (which is usually strangely appealing or seductive to the love interest)

--a demonstration of the clash of the lover's values

--introduction of the fish to friends and family of the love interest

--the fish's return to his or her own fishbowl

--the love interest's epiphanies—seeing his or her own world in a new light, realizing he or she cannot be happy with someone from their own world now, having met the fish out of water, who is "better"

THINGS TO THINK ABOUT WHEN WRITING THIS TROPE

Why does the fish out of water leave his or her own world to journey to this new one? Can you make his or her reason for making this move more compelling and urgent?

How does the fish get to the new world?

How does the fish arrive in the new world? What catastrophe strikes immediately, announcing that Dorothy is not in Kansas anymore?

When does the love interest first see the fish out of water? What's his or her initial reaction to this poor, floundering fish? Does he or she express that reaction to the fish or keep it to himself or herself?

How are the hero and heroine's worlds different? This will define some of the external conflicts the couple has to overcome.

How do their different backgrounds make them different from each other? This will define some of the internal conflict the couple has to overcome.

What about the hero and heroine's two different worlds is exactly the same?

What has the fish out of water come to this strange place to do? Is he or she looking for something? Does he or she have a goal to accomplish? Something to learn?

How hard would it be for the fish out of water to just pack up and go home? Can you make it harder for the fish to return home? Can you make it easier for the fish to return home? Which serves your story better—meaning, does it work better to create tension and conflict to have the fish utterly trapped in this new place, or does it cause more tension and conflict if the fish can leave at any time...and is tempted to do so?

Who and what from the new world will attempt to stop the hero and heroine's relationship from growing into love?

Will anyone or anything from the fish's old world show up in the story at some point? Will this thing or person try to pull the fish back home? Interfere with the budding romance? Reinforce the urgency of the fish accomplishing the thing they've come to this new place to do?

What parts of the new world will the fish be unfamiliar with? How will he or she react to these new elements? What will go wrong when first encountering these new elements?

How do the hero and heroine's values clash? How will you demonstrate this in the story?

What is the clash of values that will threaten to break them apart? What is the difference in beliefs that neither of them is willing to bend on, and which they cannot reconcile?

Will the hero or heroine have to change their core beliefs to be with the other character? If so, what beliefs must change? What will happen that causes this shift in beliefs?

Who ultimately changes to fit into the other one's world?

Which world do they end up in?

Will they both live fully in one world, or will they find a way to blend their two world?

TROPE TRAPS

Coming across as critical or negatively judgmental about one of the worlds you create in your story and offending audience members who come from that world (or a similar one).

Creating a clash of core beliefs that no two people could plausibly reconcile to be together. Keep in mind, people's core beliefs *rarely* change after they're fully formed. Also, almost nobody is willing to compromise on their core beliefs. These are the handful of things a person believes that define who they are, what they stand for, and what they want in life.

It typically takes a significant, life-changing event—usually a deeply traumatic one—to budge a person's core beliefs and values. The trap in this trope, then, is failing to create a significant enough crisis to provoke a change of values if, in fact, one or both characters is going to change at this fundamental a level.

Creating a fish out of water who's a jerk about the things they encounter in the new world that are unfamiliar or differ from things back home.

Painting two characters with so little in common that the audience doesn't buy that these two would ever fall in love.

Choosing a goal or thing the fish out of water is trying to accomplish/find that's not important enough for the fish to go through all this trouble and woe over.

Failing to explain why the fish doesn't just go home.

Failing to justify the overwhelming attraction between these two wildly different people.

FISH OUT OF WATER/COWBOY IN THE CITY TROPE IN ACTION

Movies:

- Kate and Leopold
- City Slickers (although this isn't actually a romance, it cleverly flips the cowboy in the city trope)
- Urban Cowboy
- Divergent
- Pretty Woman

Books:

- Radiance by Grace Draven
- Jane Eyre by Charlotte Brontë
- The Golden Dynasty by Kristen Ashley
- Lothaire by Kresley Cole
- Daughter of Smoke & Bone by Laini Taylor
- Virgin River by Robyn Carr
- Water for Elephants by Sara Gruen
- Twilight by Stephanie Meyer

- Under the Never Sky by Veronica Rossi
- Cry Wolf by Patricia Briggs

16

FOLLOWING YOUR HEART

DEFINITION

In its simplest form, following your heart means listening to one's instincts and emotions. It means figuring out how one feels and making decisions based on that. This is the guiding principle by which the main character in this trope lives.

This technique can apply to your main character's personal and relationship decisions, and it can also apply to broader career and life decisions. This trope could just as easily be called "I Want", "Making a Wish", or "Pursuing Your Dream".

It takes action to move a trope from beginning to middle to end, and merely making decisions based on your feelings is not necessarily enough to drive a trope. But the act of actively pursuing a dream or actively going after your heart's desire definitely can drive a trope.

This, then, is a story where the hero and/or heroine has a dream or deeply held desire that they listen to and actively pursue over the course of the story. This is a very broad trope that encompasses any number of things a person can do when he or she decides to make a change in their life and follow their heart.

The hero or heroine might move to a new place, find someone they once loved across the country, end a relationship, start a new one, change careers, start a business, or any number of other major, life-changing decisions. The only requirement is that the decision is driven by a passion for something or someone based on one's feelings or instincts.

The challenge to the love interest is to help along that dream (or hinder it) in the course of falling in love with the hero or heroine. The love interest may facilitate the hero or heroine following their heart, may represent a distraction from the desire of the hero or heroine's heart, or may derail the dream entirely.

This trope often revolves around the values of a feelings-driven person clashing with the values of a more logic-driven person.

At its core, this trope may not involve any internal transformation in the passion-driven hero or heroine. Instead, it may be more about learning a life lesson, or about compromise and learning to balance one's life to include both the dream and true love.

That said, at its core this trope absolutely can revolve around personal transformation. The person following his or her heart may take a journey of becoming self-aware as they learn what actually makes them happy. He or she may also learn self-love or self-care along the way and may completely reinvent himself or herself over the course of the story, whether or not the end wish or dream is ever fulfilled.

ADJACENT TROPES

--Fresh Start

--Forbidden Love

--Running Away From Home

--Quest/Search for the MacGuffin

WHY READERS/VIEWERS LOVE THIS TROPE

--who doesn't want to find and do the thing that makes us most happy

--we all crave deep satisfaction in our jobs, families, and relationships

--being able to completely scrap one's old life and build a new one that's perfect for us as we are now

--being someone's else's dream-come-true or biggest wish

OBLIGATORY SCENES
THE BEGINNING:

The hero or heroine may or may not have already identified their greatest desire, wish, or dream when the story begins. If not, he or she probably has an immediate crisis to open the story that leads to a realization that he or she is NOT pursuing their dream or following their heart. This leads to a crisis that leads to action. The hero or heroine physically or metaphorically leaves their old life behind to pursue a new life.

The love interest may already be in the hero or heroine's life when this crisis and new pursuit happens, or the love interest may enter the story only when the hero/heroine has begun pursuing their dream.

The love interest likely has opinions about the hero/heroine's rash plan to follow their dream and may or may not support the pursuit.

The hero or heroine may not be interested at all in being sidetracked in their dogged pursuit of their dream, may be reluctantly interested in the potential love interest, or the hero/heroine may see the potential love interest as the dream they're actually pursuing.

THE MIDDLE:

Obstacles to the hero/heroine's dream start popping up and must be overcome, one by one. These obstacles increase in difficulty or stakes as the story progresses. There may be fun and games with regard to pursuing the dream, or there may be great dangers to overcome, depending on the tone of your story.

The love interest's opinion of the dream the hero/heroine is pursuing becomes more complicated as the story progresses and becomes a source of conflict for the couple.

As the obstacles to achieving the dream mount, the hero/heroine may begin to doubt their dream or the wisdom of giving up everything to pursue it. People from the hero/heroine's past may try to draw this character back to their old life and may judge the hero/heroine for their brash choice...that's appearing more foolish by the day.

The pursuit of the dream builds toward a crisis where the hero/heroine is in real danger of failing utterly to achieve their dream. The love interest may be on the verge of walking away as the hero/heroine becomes more and more obsessed with their dream and less and less focused on a romantic relationship.

The hero/heroine feels as if *everything* depends on their succeeding. The pressure on the hero/heroine becomes unbearable, and something has to give, possibly catastrophically.

BLACK MOMENT:

The hero or heroine fails utterly and completely to achieve their dream. The whole project collapses in failure. As if that's not bad enough, they've lost the person they love in the process. They've been so focused on getting what they want that they've ignored or not noticed the person right in front of them who could've given them everything they really needed, or who at least could've made them happy.

The hero or heroine's obsession has ruined everything.

OR

The hero/heroine achieves their dream but realizes too late that it doesn't make them happy at all. They were wrong about what they wished for and have utterly blown up their life for a pipe dream or false wish.

OR

The hero/heroine can have their dream or the love interest but not both...and faced with that choice, chooses the dream over the romantic relationship. Even if they have the thing that makes them happy, they realize too late that there's still a gaping hole in their life and their heart in the absence of the person they love. Even having their wish come true doesn't make them happy if they have no one to share it with.

THE END:

The hero or heroine finds a way to reverse their failure to achieve their dream and turn it into a success. With the dream finally fulfilled, he or she can turn their attention to the love interest and find a way to repair the wrecked relationship and the damage their obsession has done to it. The hero/heroine has the life the love and the person they love. The risk was worth it and the journey has been a smashing success on all counts.

OR

The hero or heroine may modify the dream they were pursuing into a more achievable version of their dream that they can still be happy with, and that gives them the space in their lives to include the love interest. Having accomplished this, they return to the love interest, make amends, and commit themselves to a relationship with the person who truly makes them happy. The hero/heroine has it all—a life they love and a person they can share it with.

OR

The hero/heroine abandons the dream they've achieved and walks away from it without regret to pursue repairing the relationship with the love interest and making amends for their mistake. The hero/heroine has learned that the love of the right person is all they need to be genuinely, deeply happy. The hero/heroine may pursue a new dream after finding true love but will do it with the person of their dreams by their side, and it will likely be a shared dream they pursue together.

KEY SCENES
--the decision by the hero or heroine to go for it and pursue their dream

--the hero or heroine's "what have I done?" moment, when they second guess their decision or fully believe they've made a terrible mistake

--the argument between the lovers in which the hero/heroine's feelings-based decision is challenged by the love interest's sense of logic and reason...or at least questioning the hero/heroine's motivation and choice

--the moment wherein the love interest either embraces or reject's the hero/heroine's dream

THINGS TO THINK ABOUT WHEN WRITING THIS TROPE

What is the dream or wish your hero or heroine is going to pursue? What's so wrong with their old life to drive them in this new direction...or is this more about how deeply alluring the new dream is?

What event, big or small, provokes the moment of decision for your hero/heroine to go for it?

What does leaving his or her old life look like? Is it a physical departure from a place, an emotional departure, or something else?

When and where do the hero/heroine and love interest meet? Do they know each other from their old life? Is the love interest a holdover from the before times? Is the love interest part of the new life the hero/heroine hopes to step into? Is the love interest completely outside of the hero/heroine's dream world?

What does the love interest think of the hero/heroine's wish/dream/goal/desire?

Is the love interest going to support, sabotage, or interfere with the hero/heroine's goal? Why? What's his or her motive?

Is there a way to put the lovers in direct conflict regarding the dream? Something along the lines of, if the hero gets what he wants, then the heroine won't get what she wants? Or perhaps the hero needs something from the heroine to achieve his dream, and she doesn't want to give up that thing. Or the hero getting what he wants means he'll leave the heroine behind and never return. You get the idea.

Do friends, family, co-workers or others from the hero/heroine's old life show up in the midst of the new life to try to convince the hero/heroine to return to their old life? How does the hero/heroine react to that? How does the love interest react to that?

What are the obstacles that stand in the way of the hero/heroine achieving his or her dream? Do they increase in difficulty over the course of the story? Do they get big enough that the hero/heroine needs help from friends, allies, family, or the love interest to overcome them?

Does the love interest cause or control any of the obstacles to the hero/heroine achieving his or her dream? If so, which one(s)?

How obsessed is the hero/heroine with the dream? Do they ignore or overlook the love interest in pursuit of their dream? If this happens, how does this make the love interest feel?

What do the hero and heroine disagree strongly enough about (probably regarding the dream but can be separate) to threaten to break them up? Can you make this conflict have higher stakes for each of them? Will their conflict affect the outcome of the hero/heroine's dream? If so, how?

What about the hero/heroine utterly attracts the love interest? What utterly exasperates him or her about the hero/heroine?

How can you make the love interest not merely a passive supporter of the hero/heroine's dream? Is there a way to attach high stakes to the love interest regarding whether or not the dream comes to fruition or not?

What is the big crisis that threatens the dream? What's the big crisis that breaks up the lovers? Is it the same crisis? Two separate crises? If it's more than one crisis, is there a way you can tie them together or have one influence the other?

Which crisis (losing their dream or losing their lover) is more devastating to the hero/heroine? This may seem like it has an obvious answer...but don't knee jerk to the obvious answer for your hero/heroine. Consider the other answer and what that would look like, then ask yourself if your hero/heroine can be devastated in both ways.

What convinces both of your lovers to make one more mighty effort to save the relationship? What pulls them back together for a reconciliation?

Who compromises in the end? Is it primarily one character, or do they both compromise? If one character gives in more, how does he/she feel about it?

How will the dream/wish/goal turn out? Does the hero/heroine get exactly what they want, part of what they set out to get, or do they fail? How does the hero/heroine feel about this outcome? How does the love interest feel about this outcome?

Will friends, family, or co-workers from the old life be present to celebrate the new success, or are they left firmly in the past?

How does the outcome of following his or her heart shape, affect, or change the outcome of the romantic relationship with the love interest?

TROPE TRAPS

Giving the hero/heroine a dream that's not big enough to justify walking away from everything and everyone in pursuit of it.

Giving the hero/heroine a good enough old life that readers/viewers don't understand why anyone reasonable would walk away from it to pursue a dream. (While it might make sense to you and to your character, will it make sense to your audience?)

Creating a selfish or even narcissistic hero/heroine who's willing to hurt the people around him/her to get what they want.

Failing to create conflict between the lovers. It's all well and good for the hero/heroine to have a bunch of obstacles to overcome to achieve his or her dream, but where is the wrenching, emotional, angsty conflict between them?

Relying solely on external obstacles to the dream provided by the plot to move your story forward.

Creating a passive-bystander love interest who isn't engaging or particularly interesting to your audience.

If you're going to have your main character open an inn, bakery, or wedding business, for goodness' sake, do something interesting with the kind of business it's going to be, where it is, or who the clientele will be. Which is to say, beware of falling into a wildly clichéd story.

Failing to portray, or at least alluding to, the hard work that goes into achieving almost any dream worth having.

Painting a hero/heroine who has left a trail of destruction in their wake as they've callously up and left their old life to pursue a new one. What's to stop him or her from doing it again in a few years to the current love interest?

Failing to explain why this place, this job, this love, this life is enough for the hero/heroine to find peace, to put down roots, and to be happy forever.

Creating a love interest without agency or goals of their own—they serve merely as a prop for the hero/heroine's dream. While a devoted helpmate is a lovely person and may be a fine mate for your hero/heroine, they tend to make for a rather bland and boring story.

FOLLOWING YOUR HEART TROPE IN ACTION
Movies:

- Rock of Ages
- Amadeus
- The Devil Wears Prada
- Ratatouille
- A League of Their Own
- School of Rock
- Rocky

Books:

- Someday, Someday, Maybe by Lauren Graham
- A Week in Winter by Maeve Binchy
- The Absolutely True Diary of a Part-Time Indian by Sherman Alexie

- A Cuban Girl's Guide to Tea and Tomorrow by Laura Taylor Namey
- The Secret Billionaire by Erin Swann
- The Alchemist by Paul Coelho

17

FORBIDDEN LOVE

DEFINITION

This is a trope of two people who are, for some reason, forbidden to love each other. There may be an excellent or deeply entrenched reason why they're not supposed to be together, or it can be an altogether specious reason. Regardless, the act of ignoring this prohibition is fraught with danger and will exact a very high price upon the lovers if they are caught...which they inevitably will be in your story.

This story typically features distraught lovers, a great deal of drama, sneaking around, fear of getting caught, and angst galore. These people know they shouldn't love each other or be together, and yet they simply can't stop themselves. Their passion is too great to resist or even restrain.

It's also possible the lovers see some compelling reason why they should be together. They may think the reason they're forbidden from being together is stupid, ridiculous, outdated, or in need of reversal, and in this case, they may defiantly pursue their love and unconsciously—or consciously—hope to get caught. They may want to flaunt the rules and openly challenge them.

Either type of couple—the worried, secretive one or the openly defiantly one—is in for a rough road when they do finally get caught. They have their work cut out for them not coming to a tragic end.

At its core, this is a trope of rebellion and the price of that rebellion. The culture, system, or rules against which the hero and heroine are rebelling will set the tone for your story and its level of darkness, danger, fear, or its level of farce, silliness, and humor.

Unlike the Across the Tracks/Wrong Side of the Tracks or a Cross Cultural/Interracial/Interethnic tropes, in which the lovers *may* face strong disapproval, anger, and pushback, in the Forbidden Love trope, the lovers *will* face serious and inevitable legal consequences, punishment, or even death for disobeying a hard and fast rule, law, or taboo (along with the disapproval, disappointment, anger, and pushback of family and friends).

ADJACENT TROPES
--Following Your Heart
--Feuding Families
--Rebellious Hero/Heroine
--Dangerous Secret
--Across the Tracks/Wrong Side of the Tracks
--Cross Cultural/Interracial/Interethnic Romance

WHY READERS/VIEWERS LOVE THIS TROPE
--it's typically a highly charged trope that takes the audience on a roller coaster emotional journey

--we love to root for the underdog who's up against impossible odds

--your partner loves you enough to risk his/her *life* to be with you

--your partner will *die* for you

--we all like to think we would be heroic enough to defend our deepest values and/or true love with our lives

. . .

OBLIGATORY SCENES
THE BEGINNING:

The hero and heroine are introduced to the audience, possibly separately or just before their paths cross. They may need to start the story apart while the writer establishes the forbidden-ness of any potential relationship between these two people. In this scenario, when the hero and heroine do meet, they know up front that any relationship between them is a very, very bad idea. Hence, their decision to pursue a relationship is probably driven by overwhelming attraction and informed by a shared sense of understood risk.

OR

The hero and heroine may meet without understanding who the other person is or that a relationship between them would be a terrible idea. They may enter into the early stages of a relationship before they find out who the other person is and how forbidden continuing with the relationship would be.

In this scenario, the lovers have a terrible choice to make right away—a choice they will have to make over and over as the story progresses—of whether to continue on with the relationship or call it quits before they get caught.

The consequences of getting caught may be spelled out right up front such that the audience is fully aware of the risk, or these consequences may only be hinted at, creating a sense of questioning and suspense in your audience. Of course, it's possible the hero and heroine don't yet know the full consequences of their actions, in which case the audience may not find out right away, either.

The early stages of the relationship may happen completely in secret, or the couple may enlist the aid of a few trusted confidantes. These confidantes will undoubtedly advise strongly against continuing the relationship and serve to heighten the tension and sense of risk. If you choose to add confidantes as accomplices to your story, the stakes are raised as the hero and heroine put other peoples' lives in danger, too.

At its core, this is a trope of rebellion and the consequences of that rebellion...on steroids. This dramatic trope is usually defined by sky-high stakes.

THE MIDDLE:

The hero and heroine begin to fall in love. Much of the action of the story revolves around arranging and pulling off their trysts, and on scenes with the hero and heroine in their separate worlds, living a lie where they pretend not to be in love with the forbidden person.

If the consequences of the hero and heroine getting caught haven't been made clear before now, they definitely will be spelled out in the middle of the story.

The middle typically includes desperately romantic stolen moments, near misses with getting caught, and a rising sense of desperation in the hero and heroine the more they fall in love with each other.

It's not uncommon for lovers of this type to fall in love fast and for the relationship to move quickly. They probably have very limited time together for the relationship to develop, so each scene they're together in is likely a significant scene with substance and that moves the relationship forward. There won't be many or any scenes where they just hang out together casually. Every moment is stolen, and every moment counts for these two.

The middle is characterized by increasing emotion, increasing stakes, and increasing risk. As the lovers continue to get away with spending time together, they may be emboldened to go for something bigger—consummating the relationship, eloping, getting married in secret, or the like. This bigger goal they try to pull off is the one that will ultimately lead to a crisis and disaster.

. . .

BLACK MOMENT:

The lovers are caught. All is lost. They are pulled apart and the consequences of their ill-advised romance lands upon them (and possibly on anyone around them who helped them). Their gamble hasn't paid off. Not only have they lost their relationship, but they may now lose the person they love and face terrible repercussions themselves.

A black moment in this trope is bad. Really bad. As a writer, do not hold back on letting fly with all the terrible consequences you've promised earlier in the story. The devastation should be complete as you rake your characters and your audience over the coals.

THE END:

The hero and heroine are rescued, redeemed, or forgiven in the happy version of this trope. The lovers find a way to convince the authorities around them, those responsible for enforcing the rules, norms, customs, or taboos they've broken, to forgive them. The lovers snatch victory from the jaws of terrible defeat and are allowed to be together, after all.

This couple may be forced to leave their home and go into exile, or they may flee to a place where they're safe or where nobody knows them.

Even though they end up together, in this trope they usually pay a great price before the story is over. It can be a price paid as punishment for their transgression, or a price levied upon them in return for their freedom. Often it is both.

Remember: this couple did break the rules. Depending on what that rule is, your audience may be angry if the lovers don't pay a price of some kind for their rebellion or infraction. If it was an unjust rule, your audience may cheer if the lovers find a way not only to escape but also to avoid retribution or punishment for their transgression.

· · ·

KEY SCENES

--the moment when the hero and heroine realize that their love is forbidden

--the moment when the real penalties for getting caught are made clear to the lovers and to the audience

--the moment when the hero and heroine (maybe together or maybe individually) have a crisis of doubt about their decision to pursue this forbidden relationship

--the moment when a friend, family member, or other supporter finds out about the forbidden and secret relationship and that person's reaction

--the hero and heroine's last moment together before they're torn apart forever

--the hero and heroine's moment of reunion at the end

THINGS TO THINK ABOUT WHEN WRITING THIS TROPE

How do the hero and heroine meet? It is an accident or chance? Do they recognize each other immediately, or do they have no idea who the other one is?

Do the hero and heroine know a relationship between them is forbidden when they meet, or do they not learn that until later? If later, when and how?

Why is this relationship forbidden? Do the hero and heroine think this is a good, reasonable, or just reason *before* they meet each other? If so, how do they feel about the restriction on being in a relationship *after* they've met? Is it still a good rule?

Who enforces this prohibition on a relationship between the hero and heroine? Is this person the villain in your story? Is this person reasonable and right to enforce the prohibition? Does more or less everyone around this authority figure agree with the rule that makes the relationship forbidden? Are they right to agree or not?

What are the consequences to the lovers of being caught together in a relationship?

Who around them finds out about their relationship but keeps it secret or aids and abets the relationship? Why does this person help?

What will the consequences be to anyone who helps the lovers be together? Are the consequences less or the same as those faced by the lovers?

Who sends a warning shot across the bow to the hero and heroine that there will be bad consequences for anyone who breaks the rule(s) that the lovers are secretly flouting? How is this warning sent?

How will the hero and heroine sneak away for stolen moments and trysts together? They may use different tactics every time they meet, or they may repeat the same tactic.

How does each tryst get slightly more dangerous than the last one? What causes the stakes to go up each time?

Do the hero and heroine meet in a situation where they have to pretend not to know each other or to be in love with each other? How does that go? Does anyone around them pick up on something...off... between the lovers or get suspicious?

How far will they take their relationship in secret? Will they sleep together? Get married? Get pregnant?

What are they trying to do when they finally get caught? Is it just another tryst, or is this tryst special in some way?

How do the lovers get caught? Are they betrayed? Is it accidental? Do they make a mistake?

Who separates them, and how are they kept apart?

Are the full consequences promised earlier in the book leveled at the hero and heroine or not? If not, why not?

Are the consequences for the hero and heroine the same or different? Are they punished by the same person or by completely different people? For example, do their own individual families, clans, kingdoms, or governments punish them separately under different sets of rules? Or does the same official or person in authority punish them both under the same set of rules?

Does the hero or heroine own up to having done a bad thing by breaking the rules? Are they defiant about having broken the rules? Do they try to bargain with whoever's going to enforce their punishment?

Will the hero and heroine finish suffering the consequences before they get back together, or will they be pardoned, escape, or in some other way evade the full measure of the consequences? If they avoid some or all of their punishment, how do they do this? Do they do it together, or individually in separate pardons or escapes?

If the hero and heroine escape punishment, this may be the most difficult part of the story to pull off plausibly. Systems of control and punishment are typically designed to prevent escapes and are very hard to break free of. Also, your hero and heroine are probably separated, so two different escapes must be coordinated and timed simultaneously.

Where will they go after they're reunited? Can they stay home or will they have to leave? If they must leave, where do they go?

Are they known where they go or not?

What happens to their friends who helped them be together in secret? Are these people okay at the end of the story? How will the hero and heroine ensure these people are okay, assuming they're still alive?

TROPE TRAPS

Creating a hero and/or heroine who is more in love with the idea of love than their actual partner. Meaning, one or both of the characters gets so caught up in the tragic romance of it all that they lose sight of the very real risk and of the person they're actually in a relationship with.

Creating a couple that doesn't seem plausible for the long run. It may be all drama and danger now, but when all of that is gone, these two people are going to drive each other to distraction in a bad way and never survive as a couple for a happily ever after.

Creating a TSTL (too stupid to live) villain who enforces the rules even if they're silly or stupid rules. Bonus trope trap: the rule(s) the lovers are breaking need to make sense to the people enforcing them, even if they don't make sense to the lovers or the audience.

Not creating serious enough consequences for getting caught to sustain all the drama and secrecy the hero and heroine engage in. It's not enough for the hero and heroine to think the consequences would be horrible—the reader or viewer has to believe it, too.

Creating implausible situations where the hero and heroine get away with stealing a moment together but in which the audience knows they would normally be caught and should have been caught.

The lovers using the same tactics to be together over and over, when someone with an ounce of common sense around them would have caught on long ago to the tactic and caught them.

Not creating near enough misses with the lovers getting caught, which is to say, failing to keep your audience on the edge of its seats.

Creating a lame scenario in which the lovers are caught, or the lovers themselves creating a lame or overcomplicated plan that goes awry.

Failing to follow through on the consequences that were promised to the lovers and the audience at the beginning of the story.

Relying on a lame save to pull the hero and heroine out of the proverbial fire so they can be together at the end of the story.

Relying on an abrupt about face or change of heart in the person meting out punishment to relent and let the lovers be together out of the goodness of his or her heart.

I can't tell you how many of my Asian friends loved the movie, Crazy Rich Asians right up to the moment where the dragon mother sees her son unhappy, has a change of heart, and gives him her engagement ring so he can go get the girl. That's when my friends universally groaned and said something to the effect of, "No Asian dragon mother would ever back down after having successfully chased off the woman she doesn't like or approve of for her son!" While I'm sure that's not universally the case, don't create a villain who suddenly acts completely out of character for no good reason to let the lovers be together in the end.

FORBIDDEN LOVERS TROPE IN ACTION
Movies:

- Romeo and Juliet (the personification of the tragic version of this trope)
- The Thornbirds
- Dirty Dancing
- Titanic
- Guess Who's Coming to Dinner?
- Pride and Prejudice
- Clueless

Books:

- Birthday Girl by Penelope Douglas
- Twisted Games by Ana Huang
- Slammed by Colleen Hoover
- Matched by Allie Condy
- Daughter of Smoke & Bone by Laini Taylor
- Vampire Academy by Richelle Mead
- Delirium by Lauren Oliver
- The Sweetest Oblivion by Danielle Lori
- Red, White & Royal Blue by Casey McQuiston
- From Blood & Ash by Jennifer L. Armentrout
- City of Bones by Cassandra Clare
- Twilight by Stephanie Meyer

18

FRIENDS TO LOVERS

DEFINITION

Two friends become lovers over the course of the story. This seems like the simplest and most natural progression possible between a hero and heroine. However, this shift from friends to lovers can (and should) be fraught with obstacles and difficult challenges as the dynamic shifts between the hero and heroine from straightforward friendship to the complex and emotionally challenging relationship that is love. The challenge in writing this trope is *not* making the transition from friends to lovers easy and natural.

Something changes between the friends or their circumstances that acts as a catalyst for the change in relationship status. You're taking a stable relationship and completely destabilizing it in this trope. The couple's relationship is suddenly full of questions, what if's, and will we succeed or fail in this new kind of relationship? The friendship itself will be at risk before it's all said and done.

Friends, family, and co-workers around this pair may support or sabotage the change in relationship status, or the couple may change their relationship completely in secret. Shifting from friends to lovers may reframe much of what they thought they knew about each other. They will discover new elements of each other's personalities and may find new baggage, sounds, and secrets they never knew about each other.

Your challenge as the writer is to take an old relationship and make it new and different again, to find conflicts (possibly previously unknown) that threaten the success and survival of any relationship at all.

At its core, this is a deeply transformational trope. While on its surface it may be only the relationship that transforms, at a deeper level, both the hero and heroine will probably transform over the course of this story.

ADJACENT TROPES
--Commitment Phobia
--Oblivious to Love
--Right Under Your Nose
--Best Friend's Sibling/Ex/Widow
--Boy/Girl Next Door
--Secret Crush

WHY READERS/VIEWERS LOVE THIS TROPE
—who hasn't wondered what it would be like to get together romantically with a good friend?

—someone who knows you really well still thinks you're happily ever after material

—being whisked away from a life without romance into a whirlwind love

—finally being truly seen

—falling in love with someone familiar and safe

—your lover already "gets" you

OBLIGATORY SCENES
THE BEGINNING:

Clearly, the hero and heroine begin this story as friends. Their friendship (and the type of friendship it is) is established up front.

Something changes. An event, a trauma, a crisis, a bet—something sharply changes in their lives or their world to shake up the status quo and make them potentially more than friends. As a result of this crisis, or perhaps using it as an excuse, one or both of the lovers decides to make this relationship something more.

The friend(s) may announce that decision to the other partner, or the decision might be made in private. Either way, the audience definitely sees the shift in intent to become more than friends.

THE MIDDLE:

As their relationship changes, the hero and heroine's comfort level with each other is challenged. New situations these two have never encountered before crop up, and the couple and the people around them are faced with adapting to this new reality. This can be a source of awkward humor, deep discomfort, or outright panic and terror for the couple, which will set the tone for your story.

The new dynamic between the hero and heroine introduces new problems into their relationship. The type of problems can range from farcical to deadly depending on what's happening around this couple and why they've made the shift to more than friends.

These two may not realize immediately that they're in love. They may struggle to differentiate the love of friendship from romantic love. They may or may not intend to fall in love, and this will affect how quickly they identify that they're actually in love.

Emotional conflicts threaten to separate them. Guilt or even shame can rear their ugly heads, depending on why they changed from friends to something closer to lovers.

Every time the hero and heroine come together or almost come together in this new, romantic way, something has to pull them apart.

Think of this couple as a pair of magnets that are attracted to each other. Once they come together and stick, they're going to be very difficult to separate. This is because they already have most of the elements of a strong, inseparable relationship from their pre-existing friendship.

You, the writer, must prevent the two magnets from getting all the way together and "stuck" until approaching the end of your story, or you must devise a powerful crisis capable of tearing your two stuck magnets apart.

The middle of the story will build to this crisis that prevents them from coming together fully as a couple.

OR

The couple comes together as lovers in a newly formed romantic pairing until a crisis comes along that threatens to tear them apart in spite of how close they've become.

BLACK MOMENT:

The crisis tears the lovers apart. Not only does the romantic relationship fail, but the friendship is ruined as well. All is truly lost. This crisis may involve an external plot problem but will likely also involve some internal crisis between the lovers that they have failed to resolve.

Friends turned lovers have all the relationship and communication tools to overcome conflict between them...if they would only use those tools. Hence, it's easy to rely solely on an outside force or external plot device to break them up.

This crisis is your last hurrah in this story of keeping these two apart. Go ahead and dig for that one last, deepest, darkest, unresolved conflict left between these people who already know each other very well. It'll take the biggest unresolved conflict left between these two to drive a wedge between them and break these magnets apart.

. . .

THE END:

The hero and heroine finally overcome the final conflict and crisis keeping them apart and not only regain their friendship, but also find a deep and enduring love made all the stronger for the foundation of friendship upon which it was built.

The other aspects of their lives that have to change to accommodate their new relationship status change—housing, work situations, other friendships, family.

If overcoming this final conflict mostly involves having a serious, adult conversation with maturity and honesty, make sure this isn't a conversation they could have had one minute earlier in the story... otherwise, why didn't they have it then?

In this scenario, the crisis that broke them up has to be the thing that enables this conversation. Often the crisis provokes a realization of how one or both of them feel, or how they'll feel without the other one in their life (lives) at all.

KEY SCENES

--The event that jolts the friendship into something with the potential to be more between the hero and heroine

--the first kiss

--going public with their new relationship status

--the first love scene, if there is one

--the realization that they could lose their friendship if the romantic relationship fails

THINGS TO THINK ABOUT WHEN WRITING THIS TROPE

How did the hero and heroine meet? How old were they? Were they instant friends, enemies, frenemies, or something else?

Has the nature of their friendship remained constant over time or changed? If it has changed, what changed it?

What kind of friends are your hero and heroine now? Do they joke around a lot, are they confidantes, do they turn to each other when life kicks them in the teeth?

What has stopped the hero and heroine from becoming romantically involved before now? Have they tried a romance before? If so, how did it go? If not, why not?

Why now? What has changed that puts becoming more than friends on the table *now*?

How will each character react to the change in the relationship—with guilt, shame, or shock, for example? Do they think changing their relationship is a good idea, a bad idea, or a truly terrible idea?

How will their individual reactions to this change of relationship status compare and contrast against each other in the story and cause conflict between them?

How do the people around them react to this change in relationship status? Do they support it or oppose it?

What aspect(s) of their evolving relationship happen(s) as naturally as breathing? What about it feels completely awkward, unnatural, and strange to the hero and heroine?

Because these two characters start the book already together as a couple to some extent, much of the direction of the story revolves around pulling them apart before they can come back together. What are the things—external events, other people, doubts, fears, and conflicts that will work to separate them?

Why wouldn't they just stay friends? What compelling reason is there for them to take their relationship to the next level? What compelling reason is there for them *not* to take it to the next level?

What is that one last unresolved conflict between them that must be overcome before they can truly be together as a romantic couple? Is it a secret? An unresolved event in their past? A recent trauma that must be set aside? A character trait that has always driven their friend crazy?

How does the big external crisis at the end of the story highlight that last unresolved conflict between the couple and both mirror it and provoke it into becoming an emotional crisis between them?

How will they resolve their unresolved issue, which is the big, deep one that has actually been keeping them apart? Will one or both have a realization, compromise on something, overcome a fear, confess and be forgiven, or something else?

How does their new life as a couple differ from their old life as friends? How are they the same?

Who do they have to tell about their change in relationship? How does that go?

TROPE TRAPS

The thing that jolts this friendship into something more is too weak. The hero and heroine are being forced out of a stable relationship into a wildly unstable one (at least until they achieve their happily ever after), and the thing that forces this shift isn't big enough to justify all the chaos to follow.

The relationship lacks conflict. If they're so perfectly suited for each other and get along perfectly, why haven't these soulmates already gotten together, then?

Creating a hero and heroine who are both far too "nice." We tend to think of our friends as nice people. But if both of these people are too good, too kind, too thoughtful, too perfect, too lovable (all the qualities we tend to ascribe to our own good friends)—in effect, too nice—you will have zilch by way of real conflict between these two people to keep them apart or to drive them apart.

If you're relying on a past lack of romantic spark to have kept them just friends that "suddenly" changes, the characters look imperceptive, oblivious, perhaps shallow, and wholly unworthy of having the other character as their love interest.

If you're relying on some external reason for keeping them apart —it's forbidden at their place of employment or an important family member dislikes the friend, for example, the couple looks lazy for not overcoming that problem before now...particularly when they finally take action in your story to overcome that very problem, manage to do so, and end up with the love of their life. The audience asks itself, if they can overcome the obstacle now, why couldn't they overcome it before, and judges the couple stupid or lazy for not having done it sooner.

The hero and/or heroine look lazy or unlikable for not having pursued a romantic relationship before now. Which is to say, your answer to the question of why now, isn't strong enough.

Failing to introduce complex new dynamics into the relationship.

Letting this friendship proceed too naturally and easily into a romantic relationship in a story that's bland, boring, and dull.

Failing to justify why the hero and heroine ought to make this change in their otherwise fine relationship.

Relying solely on outside pressures or events to force this change. At the end of the day, the hero and heroine both have to want this change.

Creating an external crisis leading to the black moment that's not terrible enough to actually destroy the relationship entirely. Keep in mind that, not only do you have to blow apart the romantic relationship, but you have to blow apart the friendship, too.

Failing to tie an external plot crisis to an internal emotional crisis between the hero and heroine.

FRIENDS TO LOVERS TROPE IN ACTION
MOVIES:

- When Harry Met Sally
- Friends With Benefits
- Zack and Miri Make A Porno
- He's Just Not That Into You
- Love, Rosie
- Spiderman
- Clueless
- Sky High

BOOKS:

- Punk 57 by Penelope Douglas
- Playing for Keeps by R. L. Mathewson
- Hot Head by Damon Suede
- Josh and Hazel's Guide to Not Dating by Christina Lauren
- Lady Midnight by Cassandra Claire
- The Problem With Forever by Jennifer L. Armentrout
- Aristotle and Danté Discover the Secrets of the Universe by Benjamin Alire Sáenz
- The Mighty Storm by Samantha Towle
- Hopeless by Colleen Hoover
- People We Meet on Vacation by Emily Henry
- A Thousand Boy Kisses by Tillie Cole

19

GIRL/BOY NEXT DOOR

DEFINITION

In its simplest form, a boy and a girl live next door to each other, notice each other and fall in love. In reality, you're likely to write a story that's slightly more complex than that.

This hero and heroine might have grown up next door as children. They might have driven each other crazy, or one might have had a crush on the other. They might have grown up, moved away, and have now come back home.

They might not live next door now but may retain lots of friends, memories, and history in common with each other. He or she "was the kid next door" and now is something more. Much more.

Another variation of this trope is that two adult neighbors have lived next door to each other for some period of time, and for some reason notice each other now, approach each other or are drawn or forced together, and form a romantic relationship. They may or may not have known each other before coming together romantically, now.

A common aspect of this trope is the idea that the girl next door or the boy next door is someone good, kind, honest, and probably attractive whom the hero or heroine has known (or lived beside) for a long time but never taken notice of before now. They're a person in the hero/heroine's life who has always been there, always been nearby, and always been available romantically to them...but whom the hero or heroine has never noticed or never considered romantically before.

The boy-next door or girl-next-door is often portrayed as a long-suffering soul who has long had a crush on their oblivious neighbor and has waited patiently to be noticed by the glamour neighbor next door. In this scenario, the oblivious neighbor, who never romantically noticed our long-suffering boy or girl in the past, has left for some period of time, and the story begins when he or she returns "home" and this time notices the boy or girl next door.

Historically, a boy or girl next door is portrayed as pure, unsullied, squeaky clean, and for my American colleagues an "all-American kid". Think Superman, Wonder Woman or Captain America, a Girl Scout or Boy Scout, a person who volunteers at church or an animal shelter. While this isn't technically part of the trope, this image is so often tied to the phrase "boy next door" or "girl next door", particularly in American cultural iconography, that I would be remiss if I didn't mention it.

So. This trope, stripped down to its core, involves two people existing in close proximity now or in the past [they live(d) or work(ed) near each other, or in some other way bump into each other often], who've previously not both noticed each other (one may have noticed the other, but it wasn't reciprocated), who for some reason notice each other now, and form a romantic relationship.

ADJACENT TROPES
--Right Under Your Nose
--Oblivious Hero/Heroine
--Secret Crush
--Best Friend's Sibling
--Goody Two-Shoes

. . .

WHY READERS/VIEWERS LOVE THIS TROPE

-- the fantasy of going from being invisible to, not only to seen, but loved passionately

--looking back at people in our own lives and wondering what could've been

--your patience being rewarded as you've waited for someone to return to you or to notice you

--finding love where you least expected it

OBLIGATORY SCENES
THE BEGINNING:

The hero and heroine are established as living or working near each other. We may see them passing each other in a hallway or on a sidewalk, likely ignoring each other or perhaps only exchanging desultory greetings.

If one of them has a crush on the other, that is also typically established in the opening of the story. If this is the case, it is almost always established that the other character is oblivious to the crush, completely unaware of the person next door's interest.

Something happens or changes to bring the person next door sharply to the attention of the love interest. This trope allows you to pull out your best meet-cute idea and put it to use. The type of meeting and the situation around it will set the tone for the rest of your story.

If a total stranger breaks into the boy/girl next door's home and shoots it up, mistakenly believing the love interest lives there, that will set an entirely different tone than a box of cupcakes being delivered to the wrong address or a kitten getting stuck in a tree.

Having sharply noticed each other, they're now not able to un-notice each other.

The inciting incident of their meeting may throw them together going forward, or it may be an isolated incident that serves merely to get them talking, exchanging phone numbers, or the like.

THE MIDDLE:

In its most lighthearted form, this trope is primed for shenanigans to fill the middle of the story. Regardless of its tone, the middle of this trope is defined by a getting-to-know you period and the hero and heroine falling in love as they navigate a series of events.

The primary function of the plot of this story is to throw the hero and heroine together again and again in situations increasingly designed to force them to get ever closer emotionally and to know each other better.

While these characters may have known each other superficially for a very long time and have a great deal of common history, shared friends, and similar experiences, they are more or less strangers when the story begins. Although their shared addresses, workplaces, or hobby may provide a superficial common ground, the middle of the story is where they will find their differences, conflicts, and growing problems.

Because this is a trope of two people meeting and dating, as problems and conflicts arise between them, these two may not have a compelling reason to stick with this relationship. You, the writer will have to give consideration to why these two don't just walk away from their brief flirtation or relationship and look for someone more suited to them.

Your external plot may provide a compelling reason for the neighbors to stay together through a series of increasingly challenging problems, for example a shared threat, a common goal, a shared work project, or a loved one they both would hate to disappoint, for example.

If you're relying on the overwhelming attraction between these two to help them stick out the growing pains of their relationship, you will need to consider why they never noticed each other before now and what has changed in one or both of them to make all this sizzling attraction explode all of a sudden.

BLACK MOMENT:

The forces pulling the hero and heroine apart succeed. Either the problem that brought them together in the first place tears them apart, or some new conflict that has arisen as they've been getting to know each other breaks them apart.

This trope doesn't have to rely on high-stakes, high-concept drama to create a crisis that rip your lovers apart. This is a new relationship with people who don't know each other all that well. It's entirely possible one of them reveals some belief, trauma, fear, or character trait that causes the love interest to call it quits in the relationship.

Not only has the relationship failed, but now they must awkwardly and uncomfortably continue to live or work next door to each other. The misery is complete.

THE END:

The first question the ending must answer is why these two people don't just walk away and never look back. Something pulls them back together. Perhaps they miss each other more than they expected. Perhaps they learn something about the other one that explains something they didn't understand before. Perhaps the external crisis that has torn them apart is resolved.

Speaking of which, the second question the ending must answer is how the big conflict or crisis that ended the relationship is resolved and made to go away.

Last, the ending must answer the question of how the hero and heroine face the crisis, accept the explanation or apology, and decide to give their relationship another try. They obviously see something in the other person worth fighting for and with the potential to lead to a long-term relationship.

The last problems solved; the only question left is whose place they're going to live at.

KEY SCENES

--the hero and heroine encounter each other and don't notice each other

--the first time they talk

--the first time they got out on a date, touch romantically, and kiss

--the breakup scene

--the incredibly awkward post-breakup encounter

--the big apology or reconciliation

THINGS TO THINK ABOUT WHEN WRITING THIS TROPE

How do the hero and heroine come into proximity with each other? Are they physically neighbors? Do they work in the same place or on the same project? Do they share a health club, hobby, or commute that throws them into regular contact proximity?

Has one of them noticed the other one and perhaps had a secret crush? If so, what attracted them?

How oblivious is the oblivious character? Is he or she truly not noticing the boy/girl next door, or is it an act? If it's an act, why isn't he or she acknowledging any interest in the boy/girl next door?

Is there a reason these two people shouldn't get together? Is one of them already in a relationship? Is one of them a friend of a sibling who has declared them off limits? Is there a company policy against dating in house? Is there an ethical concern of some kind?

What event, inciting incident, or meet-cute brings these two to each other's notice?

What's the tone of this meeting?

Is this meeting or the circumstances around this event going to force the hero and heroine together again repeatedly over the course of the story? For example, are they going to work together daily until a project finishes, are they both in danger from the same threat that they must now work together to neutralize, or has one of them rescued a puppy that they will both need to care for daily?

If their meeting does *not* lead to ongoing interactions through your story, what will cause the hero and heroine to continue interacting with each other going forward? What shared interest, shared goal, or shared attraction causes them to pursue a relationship?

What conflicts arise between these two as they get to know each other? Are they external disagreements about how to deal with a situation, or are they internal conflicts of differing values, beliefs, personality, or ideas?

Is there a way to have the external and internal conflicts mirror each other?

What do these two discover that they have in common?

As the conflicts between them get worse, what is going to keep them from walking away from each other?

What about each character causes the other one to fall in love?

Why now? Why do they notice each other now, why is the time right for them to fall in love now? What has changed from the status quo of their existence before your story started to now that makes this change in their relationship not only possible but inevitable?

What crisis breaks them up?

What causes them to give the relationship another try after their break-up?

How will these two reconcile and what will it look like?

Given that they've already had a near miss with breaking up for good, what's going to keep this couple together permanently going forward? Have they learned something that makes forever possible? Do they get engaged or married?

.   .   .

TROPE TRAPS

Creating two gorgeous, dynamic human beings who would have no way missed noticing each other before now.

Making the way these neighbors ignore or don't notice each other implausibly oblivious. If these two are that blind to the person right beside them, maybe they don't deserve to have a romantic happily ever after.

Creating an unlikable boy/girl next door who, instead of coming across as patient and long-suffering comes across as wimpy, a wet blanket, having no self-esteem, and having no self-respect.

Creating so implausible a meet-cute that the audience doesn't buy it as being real, and the audience is unwilling to suspend their disbelief to go along with the mode of meeting.

Changing tone too much or too abruptly, mid-story. If these neighbors meet in a light-hearted way, beware of turning their story into a gritty run for their lives down the road...unless of course you walk your audience very deliberately from light to dark or vice versa. (Of course, no matter how dark a story is, you can always inject a note of humor to momentarily relieve tension. I'm talking about an overall change in the mood and tone of a story, here.)

Failing to create a compelling reason for this couple to stay together as their problems mount.

Failing to create a strong enough attraction/chemistry to pull them together and hold them together through the ups and downs of your story.

Not justifying why the hero and heroine get back together at the end and don't just go their separate ways after their black moment break-up.

Not showing your audience what these two have to fight for. Not creating a rich, complex, loving enough relationship to be worth fighting for.

THE TROPOHOLIC'S GUIDE TO EXTERNAL ROMANCE TROPES   221

GIRL/BOY NEXT DOOR TROPE IN ACTION
Movies:

- Superman
- Just Friends
- Eight Days a Week
- Captain America
- Growing Up Smith
- The Choice
- Eight Days a Week
- The Great Gatsby

Books:

- My Life Next Door by Huntley Fitzpatrick
- Playing for Keeps by R. L. Mathewson
- Anna and the French Kiss by Stephanie Perkins
- Obsidian by Jennifer L. Armentrout
- Wallbanger by Alice Clayton
- Mansfield Park by Jane Austen
- Everything, Everything by Nicola Yoon

20
HERO/HEROINE IN HIDING

DEFINITION

Either the hero or the heroine in this story starts the story in hiding. He or she is living a secret life, hiding his or her identity, or laying low in some way. He or she doesn't want to be found by whoever might be (or is) looking for them.

Implied in the fact of being in hiding is that the hero/heroine is in danger of some kind. While this might not be life-threatening danger, there's some compelling reason why this person doesn't want to be found, and usually it's because getting caught or found would be detrimental to the hero/heroine in some way.

In the midst of this person's secretive life, someone—the love interest—meets him or her.

The love interest may be a completely unrelated outsider to the world and people the hero/heroine is hiding from, or the love interest may, in fact, be one of the people looking for the hero/heroine.

This trope is often punctuated by fear and danger of discovery. An innocent outsider, the love interest, is sucked into the hero or heroine's need to hide and sucked into living a secretive life as well. The lovers may ultimately remain in hiding, but it's most typical in this trope for the hero/heroine in hiding to be found at some point and have to confront the persons or forces looking for him or her.

An honorable hero/heroine in hiding probably resists drawing an innocent bystander into their danger and secrecy, and this can be the source of much of the internal conflict for the hiding hero/heroine in the story.

Once the love interest becomes aware of the danger the hero/heroine is in, he or she must decide whether or not to stick with this person they're falling in love with or to bail out on the relationship in the name of self-preservation. This often provides much of the internal conflict for the love interest.

At its core, this is a trope of deception or secrets, uncovering these, and confronting them and their consequences.

ADJACENT TROPES
--Dangerous Secret
--Hero/Heroine in Disguise
--On the Run/Chase
--Fresh Start

WHY READERS/VIEWERS LOVE THIS TROPE
--being in on the secret
--being drawn into a secret world
--he/she loves you enough to risk everything, up to and including his or her life, to be with you
—he or she trusts you absolutely

OBLIGATORY SCENES
THE BEGINNING:

This story may or may not begin by establishing that the hero or heroine is in hiding. It will depend on whether or not you choose to let your audience in on this secret before or at the same time as the love interest.

At any rate, the hero and heroine meet. This may be a random or completely mundane encounter for the love interest. For the hero or heroine in hiding, however, every encounter with anyone is potentially dangerous, even this seemingly innocuous one with an interesting or attractive stranger.

One or both of them finds the other person interesting enough to seek out again or to meet again...maybe not by chance the second time. As their attractions grows, the romance begins.

You may or may not establish who the hero or heroine is hiding from in the beginning of your story, or you may leave that revelation for later. You also may not establish exactly how much danger the hero/heroine is in at the beginning. It's enough to hint at danger initially.

The hero/heroine in hiding may not be forthright with the love interest about his or her situation. He or she may wait until the love interest is inadvertently sucked into their dangerous world to reveal what's really going on. The hiding hero/heroine may temporarily pretend to live a normal life so as not to scare off the potential love interest.

As for the love interest, he or she is inexorably drawn to the hiding character. The love interest may be completely ignorant of the danger this attractive stranger is in, the love interest may sense the danger clinging to the hiding hero/heroine, or the love interest may find the danger and secrets fascinating when the character in hiding reveals his or her situation.

THE MIDDLE:

The hero and heroine begin to spend time together and to fall in love. This is a great risk on the part of the hero/heroine in hiding. The love interest may not initially realize how risky being with this person is, but somewhere in the middle of the story he or she will find out (or perhaps gradually become aware of the degree of danger) and will have to make some difficult choices regarding whether the hero/heroine in hiding is worth taking such a big risk for.

The persons or forces looking for the hero/heroine in hiding begin to close in on him or her. The risk rises with each minute, hour, and day the hero/heroine stays in this place with their love interest. Pressure builds on the hero/heroine in hiding to flee and leave behind the person they've fallen in love with.

The lure of the normal world the love interest lives in often grows stronger in the hiding hero/heroine. He or she may crave the stability of life with the love interest and may (foolishly, even disastrously) decide to try to blend into this normal world and live a normal life.

As the persons or forces the hero/heroine is hiding from close in on him or her, the situation builds toward a crisis. The hiding hero/heroine my try to send away the love interest. The love interest may refuse to leave. The danger that has been lurking close the whole time explodes into lethal risk.

BLACK MOMENT:

The persons or forces the hero/heroine is hiding from catch up with him or her. The consequences of being found are unleashed, and the lovers are torn apart. By now, the love interest may be fully as targeted as the hiding hero/heroine and may also experience devastating consequences of helping the hero/heroine hide. The lovers are separated and must face their respective fates alone, knowing they'll never see the person they love again.

. . .

THE END:

Exactly how the persons or forces pursuing the hero/heroine are appeased, called off, or otherwise neutralized as a threat to the lovers is up to your imagination. But in most cases, it has to happen somehow.

You also have the option of engineering some sort of escape for the hero and heroine wherein they both manage to free themselves and flee from the persons or forces that have been chasing the hiding hero/heroine. If you're planning a sequel to this story, you might want to choose this option or something similar, because it does leave the conflict between the hero/heroine in hiding and his or her pursuer(s) unresolved.

The lovers are back together. They are a team now, the two of them against the world. The love interest has voluntarily stepped into the same risk as the hiding hero/heroine. They are fully committed to each other and to facing whatever threats come their way.

You may choose to let them have a normal life when the dust settles, and it's not uncommon to add an epilogue or denouement that gives the audience a brief glimpse of our lovers finally settled into their ever so normal life together.

KEY SCENES

--the risk to the hero/heroine in hiding of seeing the potential love interest again is made crystal clear to the audience

--the hero/heroine in hiding decides to take the risk of getting to know the love interest

--the love interest learns the full extent of the danger surrounding the hiding hero/heroine...and decides to stay anyway. (This may be one scene or broken into two scenes.)

--the lovers barely escape the people searching for the hiding hero/heroine

--before the lovers are torn apart, they have a last, tragic moment of farewell

. . .

THINGS TO THINK ABOUT WHEN WRITING THIS TROPE

Who is the hero/heroine in hiding actually hiding from? Why? What will happen to him or her if he/she is found?

Will your hero/heroine in hiding up and leave his or her current location if he or she thinks someone might have an idea of where he/she is?

Will you show the audience the danger to the hero/heroine in hiding before you show the love interest or not?

How do the hero and heroine meet? How dangerous is it for the hero/heroine to have even a casual, random meeting with anyone? How will you demonstrate that danger to your audience?

Will the love interest be aware of the danger surrounding this seemingly mundane, normal meeting with a stranger?

If the love interest is blissfully unaware of the danger around this attractive stranger, how long will you keep him or her in ignorance of the truth?

How will the love interest learn of the danger? Will the hiding hero/heroine tell the love interest, or will the love interest find out some other way? If it's some other way, how?

How does the love interest react to the revelation that the person they're falling for, or have fallen for, is in hiding?

What does the closing of the net look like as the persons or forces close in on the hiding hero/heroine?

Will the lovers have close calls with getting caught? What do those look like?

At what point does the hiding hero/heroine begin to seriously doubt his or her decision to be with the love interest or doubt his/her ability to keep the love interest safe?

At what point does the love interest seriously question his or her decision to stay with and stand by the hiding hero/heroine as the danger gets progressively worse?

How will the love interest help hide the hero/heroine? Does doing this get him or her into legal trouble? Does it draw the ire of the persons or forces searching for the hero/heroine in hiding?

Do friends, family, or coworkers of the very normal love interest know about the hiding hero/heroine's existence? If so, do they have any idea of the danger surrounding this new romantic partner? If so, how do these people react to the risk the love interest is taking?

Do the hiding hero/heroine and/or lover interest have friends or allies who help them? If so, what kind of help do they offer?

How will the persons or forces searching for the hero/heroine look for him or her? Find him or her? Close in on him or her? Capture him or her?

Is the love interest in league with the persons or forces searching for the hero/heroine? If so, how will the hiding hero/heroine react to this betrayal? How will the love interest prove his or her feelings are real, after all? What consequences will the love interest face for betraying his or her loyalty to the person or forces they're supposed to be working for?

Are there any near misses with getting caught or found? What do those look like?

If they flee "captors," how do the separated lovers pull off dual escapes and time them to happen together? Does someone help plan the escapes, communicate between the lovers, or help execute the escape plan(s)?

Is the conflict resolved between the hiding hero/heroine and his or her pursuers? If so, how? Can the lovers live in the open and assume a normal life after the conflict is resolved?

If the conflict isn't resolved, how will the lovers disappear from their pursuers? What will their life together look like now?

TROPE TRAPS

The persons or forces the hero/heroine is hiding from aren't scary or dangerous enough.

The hero/heroine's reasons for hiding are lame or not reasonable.

The hero/heroine in hiding is living way too normal a life for the degree of risk he or she actually faces.

The hero/heroine doesn't seriously consider (or try) running when the people pursuing him or her start to close in. It's all well and good to be attracted to someone new and maybe be falling for them, but hardheaded survival often dictates leaving everything and everyone behind...fast...when one's pursuers find you.

The love interest never seriously considers getting away from the danger surrounding the hero/heroine or never tries to leave.

There's no warning that the pursuer is closing in until, all of a sudden, he or she shows up out of nowhere, which is to say, you rely purely on surprise in this story instead of building suspense.

The person searching for the hiding hero/heroine isn't smart enough or equipped enough to pose a real and serious threat to the hiding hero/heroine. Or the reason he or she is searching for the hero/heroine can be cleared up too easily.

Creating a situation where the hiding hero/heroine would never take along the love interest if he or she were ethical.

Failing to create or levy any consequences for the love interest having helped the hero/heroine hide all this time.

Making it too easy or uncomplicated for the love interest to up and leave his or her regular life to run away with the hiding character.

HERO/HEROINE IN HIDING TROPE IN ACTION
Movies:

- The Fugitive
- Sleeping With the Enemy
- The Net

- My Blue Heaven
- Enemy of the State

Books:

- The Witness by Nora Roberts
- River Wild by Samantha Towle
- Darling Beast by Elizabeth Hoyt
- She Can Run by Melinda Leigh
- Sweet Revenge by Rebecca Zanetti
- Written in Red by Anne Bishop
- The Bourne Identity by Robert Ludlum

21
HIDDEN/SECRET WEALTH

DEFINITION

A hero and heroine meet and fall in love, and one of them is hiding the fact that he or she is very wealthy. It's not necessary that the love interest be desperately poor, but it is a common device to pair the secretly wealthy hero or heroine with someone who has a serious financial need or crisis to deal with. In this version of the story, people from different worlds come together to find love in spite of their wildly differing financial circumstances. It's also a common device for the character who is hiding his or her wealth to be a fish out of water in the "regular" world, which is to say not wealthy world, and have to learn to function in new and strange circumstances.

Implicit in this trope is the assumption that the love interest of the character hiding wealth has much less wealth than the character hiding his or hers. Otherwise, it would be no big deal for the wealthy character to reveal his or her wealth, and there would be no conflict upon which to hang a love story, other than the fact that one character lied to the other. (If both characters are wealthy, one of them lying about it wouldn't even be a big enough lie to carry a story arc as a lie.)

This is a trope many readers will find highly aspirational. Who doesn't love the idea of being swept off your feet by your true love, who also happens to be able to offer you a life of beauty, comfort, and ease?

But is it really that easy? How will the character of greater wealth ever know for sure that he or she is loved for himself and not for his wealth? How will the less wealthy partner learn to handle wealth? One of them is going to have to enter a foreign and uncomfortable socio-economic space for the sake of love.

It's when the hidden wealth is revealed that the real trouble begins for this pair. The core of this trope is a deception, or at least a misrepresentation, and the consequences of that. Can this couple overcome the deception to find forgiveness and true love?

It's worth noting that wealth, although usually financial, is not always measured in money. Someone could possess something tangible or intangible of great value that the love interest doesn't have but covets. For example: knowledge, a noble title, or a collection of something physical like art, or say, horses.

ADJACENT TROPES
--Billionaire Romance
--Across the Tracks
--Rags to Riches
--Riches to Rags
--Secret Identity

WHY READERS/VIEWERS LOVE THIS TROPE:
--being swept into a world of wealth and ease
--being waited on hand and foot
--physically transforming oneself to fit into a different world
--being in on the secret
--a (rich, privileged) person who could have had anyone chose you

--there's something special about you that the wealthy hero or heroine saw in spite of your lack of the trappings of wealth

--being "discovered" and rescued from or lifted out of a bad situation

OBLIGATORY SCENES
THE BEGINNING:

The average (or impoverished) character is introduced living in his or her world. Into this world, the character with hidden wealth enters. The hero and heroine meet and attraction ensues.

The world the wealthy character comes from must be glimpsed in some way or made known to the reader if you want to let the reader in on the secret from the beginning. You may choose to keep the reader in the dark initially, along with the non-wealthy love interest. In this case, though, you might want to consider dropping clues to the reader that all is not as it seems with the character hiding his or her wealth. For the sake of this entry, however, we'll speak of wealth only in terms of money.

THE MIDDLE:

The hero and heroine fall in love, all while the wealthy partner continues not to reveal his or her wealth. The wealthy partner has to learn to live in the love interest's world, which is impoverished relative to what that character is accustomed to. Shenanigans, misunderstandings, or conflict may ensue from this aspect of the wealthy character's ignorance.

At some point in the story, the reader must be let in on the secret. And, at some point, the love interest either figures out the secret or has to be let in on it, too. You can let the reader in on it before or at the same time as the love interest.

Regardless, when the love interest finds out, it will definitely provoke conflict between the main characters—even if the love interest is delighted to find out that his or her money issues may be over forever, he or she has also been lied to and deceived and shouldn't appreciate it.

A pressing need for money (or whatever the form of "wealth" takes), by one or both partners, may arise. The wealthy character is increasing conflicted about not revealing his or her wealth and accessing it to make life easier, solve a problem, or present the love interest with lavish gifts.

The love interest may be increasingly frustrated with the wealthy character's belief that money solves all problems or that money and financial considerations aren't important at all. If the love interest is already aware of the hidden wealth, he or she may demand that the wealthy character NOT access his or her wealth and learn to solve his or her problems the way non-wealthy people do.

BLACK MOMENT:

The wealth is revealed and the lie and/or the wealth itself ruin the relationship. The non-wealthy love interest walks away.

OR

The wealthy character can't resist accessing his or her wealth to solve a problem. In so doing, the love interest is alienated by the wealthy character's lack of, well, character, and his or her reliance on money.

OR

The non-wealthy character has had enough and walks away. Perhaps he or she can't reconcile himself or herself to having been lied to. Perhaps this character feels used, doesn't appreciate being the object of a slumming adventure, or may dislike the world of wealth the wealthy character comes from and plans to return to.

. . .

THE END:

Both partners in this scenario must make their peace with the wealthy partner's wealth—what that looks like is completely up to you, and there are many options for it. The lovers can move into the world of wealth, move completely out of the world of wealth, or find some compromise in the middle. One or both character's relationship to money and wealth may change a little or a lot.

The one constant in the ending is that the lie—that is the act of hiding wealth—is forgiven. The main characters both have learned that love is more important than money, and they have reached a solution that allows them to be together to live happily ever after.

For Example:

The wealthy character withdraws the financial bailout and resolves the problem without relying on money, thereby proving his or her choice of love over money. By doing so, he or she earns the love interest's forgiveness and true love in exchange.

OR

The wealthy character is willing to give away his or her wealth entirely and chooses love over money. This gesture convinces the love interest that money is not a crutch for the wealthy character and that the wealthy partner has truly learned to value love (and other things like hard work, frugality, family) over money.

OR

The love interest moves into the wealthy character's world and life of wealth and is happy and comfortable in it.

KEY SCENES

--the wealthy character's first encounter with a dilemma he or she would normally resolve by spending money, but now can't

--the non-wealthy character's first suspicion that all is not as it seems with the character pretending not to be wealthy

--the big reveal of wealth

--the big backlash to the wealth by the non-wealthy character

--the apology by the wealthy character for the deception

--acceptance of the apology, which may or may not result in reconciliation

--the grand gesture of love by the wealthy person

THINGS TO THINK ABOUT WHEN WRITING THIS TROPE

What form does your wealthy character's wealth take? In most stories, it's financial wealth. But now and then, it may take some other form.

Why is the wealthy hero or heroine hiding their wealth? Does it start out as a joke, slumming, or is there a more compelling or threatening reason for the wealthy character hiding his or her wealth? (This choice will set the tone of your entire story—comic versus suspenseful, dark versus lighthearted)

Is the reason the wealthy character is hiding his or her wealth a personal one or an external one? For example, does the wealthy character want to meet someone who doesn't like him or her just for the money, or would the wealthy character be in danger if the people around him or her realize how wealthy he or she is?

Does the wealthy character fit in easily to the "commoner" world or not? Is this a source of danger, friction, humor, or stress to the hero and/or heroine? Is this fish-out-of-water element a key source of plot in your story or not?

Will you let the reader in on the secret from the beginning or string the reader along with the love interest?

When and how will you reveal the wealth? Why then? What makes that moment special and necessary for the reveal? What changes the wealthy character's mind about hiding his or her wealth?

How is the non-wealthy partner going to react to the revelation of wealth?

What is the non-wealthy partner's opinion about wealth—both their expressed opinion and their real opinion? Are these a source of conflict within that character and/or with the wealthy character?

What manifestation of this wealth is most appealing/tempting to the non-wealthy character and what is most off-putting about wealth to him or her?

When in your story will the most appealing thing be dangled as a temptation or gifted to the non-wealthy character? Conversely, when will the non-wealthy character be exposed to the most off-putting aspect or manifestation of wealth? How will he or she react in both cases?

If the wealth is revealed to solve a major problem the non-wealthy character had encountered, why won't the non-wealthy character just react with gratitude? What aspect of the revealed wealth will cause new and greater conflict between the lovers?

How will the non-wealthy character react to having been deceived or lied to, even if it is only by omission?

How will the wealthy character make amends to the non-wealthy character for the deception?

What grand gesture will it take to regain the non-wealthy character's trust and love?

Which world will the hero and heroine choose to live in permanently? The world of wealth or the non-wealthy existence? How easily or not easily will the non-wealthy partner fit into the wealthy partner's world in the end, or vice versa?

What lesson has been learned by the character who hid his or her wealth?

Has the non-wealthy character learned anything? If so, what?

· · ·

TROPE TRAPS

Relying only or too heavily on the wildly overused cliché of this trope—that the wealthy partner hides their wealth because he/she wants to be sure that whoever falls in love with them doesn't do so just because of their wealth. It's fine to use this, of course, but you'll have to justify and really sell it as a legitimate concern for the wealthy character.

The non-wealthy partner's reaction to the revelation of the wealth's existence is one-dimensional and consists solely of total delight.

Creating a character who comes across as obnoxious because they're merely playing at being poor without having to actually deal with the difficulties and struggles of actual lack of wealth or real poverty.

Failing to resolve how these two people from very different worlds are going to live together happily in some shared world, or in one partner's world totally removed from the other partner's life.

Failing to address that the wealthy partner lied to the one he or she loves.

Failing to (convincingly) convince the wealthy character (and the reader) that the impoverished character truly loves the wealthy one for himself or herself.

Failing to address how truly different their worlds are and how a person from one is going to adapt to the other world.

SIDE NOTE: In reality, people who have never been around much money have a great deal to learn about how to manage money, what certain luxuries really cost, how to spend money wisely, how to save and invest it, when and how to flaunt and NOT flaunt it, and more.

The trap, then, is when the character with less experience with wealth ridiculously unrealistically moves into comfort and ease with handling wealth. Vice versa, when the character with hidden wealth unrealistically easily adapts to a world of less—or a world of outright poverty.

I get a lot of pushback on this one, so I'm going to give you a contemporary, real-life example. My child went to school with the children of a billionaire, whose wife I got to know slightly.

The kids came to school every day with no-kidding armed bodyguards who monitored them on cameras all day long at school, for fear of the kids being kidnapped.

The wife also had full-time bodyguards. The whole family had to understand how to work with and around professional security teams, which is not as simple as having someone trail around behind you.

The mom and dad take separate flights (whether commercial or private jets) everywhere they travel because the repercussions to their companies and charities if both died at once would be so devastating.

The wife manages a massive estate with multiple employees, including the finances of the house and staff. She plans elaborate, complicated parties, and is expected to host them smoothly. She has to understand the workings of large charitable organizations.

The list of things to know about how to live "rich" goes on and on.

The same holds true of historical characters managing wealth.

It's a highly specialized skill set that can't be learned overnight and would be disastrous if not mastered. Ask any of the 70% of lottery winners who go bankrupt within a few years of hitting the jackpot.

HIDDEN WEALTH TROPE IN ACTION
Movies:

- Rich in Love
- Crazy Rich Asians
- Dances With Dragon
- Coming to America
- How to Marry A Millionaire

. . .

Books:

- The Undomestic Goddess by Sophie Kinsella
- The Neighbor's Secret by Kimberly Montpetit
- Falling for the Secret Princess by Kandy Shepherd
- Falling for the Secret Millionaire by Kate Hardy
- The Secret Billionaire by Erin Swann

22

HOME FOR THE HOLIDAY/VACATION FLING

DEFINITION

In this trope, either the hero or heroine comes "home" for a visit, with the intention of leaving again in a fixed period of time. During this visit, he or she meets someone and falls for him or her. Conflict ensues.

Although the name of this trope specifies it's a holiday or vacation causing the hero or heroine to go someplace, it could just as easily be a short-term work assignment, taking care of a dying relative, or any other reason you can imagine for going to a place, staying for a short time, and then leaving.

The point of this trope is that there's a time lock on the relationship. Two classic methods of drawing a story to a close are an option lock or a time lock. In the option lock, the character(s) gradually run out of options until only one path forward to solving the story problem is left. In a time lock, the character(s) run out of time to solve the problem of the story.

Because the hero/heroine is only in town for a fixed amount of time in this story type, the lovers are going to run out of time to develop their relationship and figure out what to do about it. That countdown timer is always ticking away in the background, providing tension and urgency in this trope.

To have plenty of conflict in this story, the love interest typically cannot up and leave everything behind at the drop of a hat to follow their new love back to his or her home. The hero/heroine must leave, the love interest must stay.

At its core, this is a trope of competing responsibilities and needs. One partner must give up his or her life and home, or the couple must somehow compromise between their competing lives. Bargaining and negotiation will feature prominently in this type of story.

ADJACENT TROPES
--Coming Home
--Childhood Sweethearts/Friends
--Reunion
--Newcomer/Stranger/Outsider

WHY READERS/VIEWERS LOVE THIS TROPE
--a mysterious stranger comes to town and sweeps you away from your mundane, boring life and into a new, exciting world

--the one who got away and left you behind comes back to claim you

--being loved so much that your lover is willing to sacrifice their home, career, friends to stay with you

--going back home and fitting in this time, being embraced by family and old friends

--going back home and being able to show off your success, accomplishment, wealth, adult attractiveness

OBLIGATORY SCENES
THE BEGINNING:

The hero or heroine arrives back home for the holiday or at a vacation or work destination. Shortly thereafter, he or she meets the potential love interest and sparks of attraction fly. Both the visiting hero/heroine and potential love interest may think initially of it as a short-term fling and may not be prepared to envision their relationship in more permanent terms.

There may be a conflict of expectations from this new relationship right off the bat. The potential love interest may not be aware initially that the visiting hero/heroine plans to leave town in the near future. He or she may be prepared to dive into a long-term relationship and think this one is it, whereas the visiting hero/heroine knows full well there's an expiration date on this romance.

The relationship probably starts out casual and fun. It may involve friends, family, celebrations, or light-hearted interactions.

THE MIDDLE:

The hero and heroine begin to fall in love. The visiting hero/heroine absolutely knows this is a problem for him or her as he or she has no plans to stay in town permanently.

Depending on how aware the love interest is of the looming expiration date on their relationship, he or she may or may not understand how big a problem it is to fall in love.

As the fun and games, parties, dates, and vacation-style activities continue, a darker note enters the relationship. Not only is the clock ticking louder with every passing moment, but conflicts start to arise from the growing seriousness of the relationship. Who will give up his or her life to stay here or move away from their current life?

The love interest's life and responsibilities in this town make it hard or even impossible to contemplate dropping everything and moving away to be with the visiting hero/heroine. Vice versa, the visiting hero/heroine has a fully realized life somewhere else, a life he or she both wants and needs to return to.

The lovers may contemplate trying a long-distance relationship, but in this trope there's a compelling reason why that's not going to work for them. If it did, there would be no time-lock, they could easily pursue a long-term relationship, and there would be no conflict to move your story forward.

As they run out of time, the lovers head for a crisis of whose life will give way to the other's. Their separate lives may each be making some specific demand on them that grows toward a crisis in its own right, pulling them both back toward their own lives with ever increasing urgency.

BLACK MOMENT:

The hero or heroine must return to his or her own life, and the love interest must stay put at home to deal with his or her own responsibilities. If some crisis has been building in one or both of their lives that requires their presence where they currently live, that crisis explodes.

The lovers haven't found a way to be together. Their lives are too different to combine, neither of them can change their life enough to be with the other person, and regardless of how much they love each other, they see no way to be together romantically.

All is lost. As much as they love each other, the timing and geography are all wrong, and their relationship is doomed.

THE END:

After being apart and totally miserable, the hero and heroine realize they must find a way to be together. They're not willing to give up their relationship for the other factors in their lives that have torn them apart. One or both of them gives up some aspect of their life (a job, a home, friends, proximity to family) to be with the person they love.

Their priorities have changed, and they have realized their love for each other is more important than everything else in their lives. They are reunited in their new life together and can now have their happily ever after.

KEY SCENES

--the meet-cute...with the caveat that as much as audiences love cute meetings, not all meetings have to be "cute". But they probably do need to be memorable or interesting

--the local love interest introduces the visiting hero/heroine to his or her world right here

--the visiting hero/heroine introduces the local love interest to his or her world elsewhere, either physically or virtually

--the first argument over who's moving where

--the grand farewell—often a love scene but always poignant or bittersweet—in the last moments before the clock on the visit runs out

THINGS TO THINK ABOUT WHEN WRITING THIS TROPE

Where do the hero and heroine normally live?

What brings the visiting hero/heroine to this place at this time?

How long is the hero/heroine visiting for? Why must he or she go home when he or she is scheduled to?

Do the hero/heroine and love interest already know each other or not?

How do the hero/heroine and love interest meet? What do they think of each other upon first meeting? Is the attraction instant or will it develop over the course of your story?

How will the hero and heroine keep meeting each other? Do they start dating immediately, or is there some other plot device that keeps bringing them into close proximity or that forces them to interact?

What person, job, responsibility, or need in the love interest's life keeps him or her firmly planted in this place? Why can't he or she leave town or move away permanently?

What are the type and tone of the dates/encounters/interactions these two people have as they get to know each other? How do they become increasingly romantic and serious?

At what point does the love interest find out that the visiting hero/heroine is leaving town and when?

How long before the visiting character has to leave does the panic, negotiation, debate, argument set in over what they're going to do? Does it happen early on, or does it wait until the clock is ticking very loudly? Do the lovers avoid or put off this discussion? For how long?

At what point are the lovers forced to face the time lock and how contentious is it?

Does one of them (wrongly) just assume the other one is going to stay in town or follow him/her home? Or do they understand from the beginning that there's no way either of them can change their lives for each other?

Do they discuss a long-distance relationship? Why won't that work for this couple?

Do friends, family, or co-workers warn these two not to fall in love?

Is there some external crisis building in each of their separate worlds that calls them each back to their own lives? Does this external crisis in some way mirror their relationship? Is this emergency job related, family related, personal—realizing that whatever part of each character's life is most important to him or her is where this crisis should occur?

Why does each character prioritize this other responsibility over love or their own personal happiness? Does the other partner respect and agree with this prioritizing or not?

What does the grand farewell look like as time runs out on them?

Will both of them make a grand sacrifice to be with the person they love, or will just one of them do it? What are these sacrifices?

While it is sufficient to say that the hero or heroine is willing to sacrifice something very important to him or her in the name of true love, is there some other compelling reason the hero/heroine or love interest arrives at the decision to walk away from their life to be with their true love?

Why can't the lovers make these sacrifices to be together much sooner in the story? Why did they have to wait until after the black moment and after their painful separation to change their lives and/or priorities to be together?

What does their new life together look like?

TROPE TRAPS

The visiting hero/heroine is unlikable because he or she should've known better than to fall for someone local. The hero/heroine never should have led on the love interest about his or her ability to engage in a long-term relationship.

The love interest seems stupid to have fallen in love when he or she should've known not to fall for someone who's only in town for a short time.

The attraction and later, love, between the lovers isn't portrayed as deep and passionate enough to justify one or both of them upending their lives for each other.

Failing to give the visiting hero/heroine a compelling enough reason to go back home.

Failing to give the love interest a compelling enough reason to stay home and not follow the visiting hero/heroine back to his or her home.

When the lovers finally do find a compromise solution, failing to justify why they couldn't have arrived at that decision earlier and saved themselves a lot of suffering.

The lovers are selfish or unheroic for leaving other people in the lurch so the two of them can be together, which is to say, failing to sew up the loose threads left in their lives when one or both of them leaves their old life to be with their true love.

HOME FOR THE HOLIDAY/VACATION FLING TROPE IN ACTION
Movies:

- Sweet Home Alabama
- Home for the Holidays
- The Noel Diary
- Serendipity
- Before Sunrise
- Call Me By Your Name
- The Notebook
- Dirty Dancing
- Roman Holiday

Books:

- In a Holidaze by Christina Lauren
- A Merry Little Meet Cute by Julie Murphy and Sierra Simone
- It Happened One Wedding by Julie James
- Master of the Mountain by Cherise Sinclair
- Honeymoon for One by Chris Keniston
- Return to You by Kate Perry

23

LONG DISTANCE ROMANCE

DEFINITION

In and of itself, the fact that a romance is long-distance does not make it a trope. The challenge of having to find a way to be together or of trying to sustain a romance long-distance is what turns it into a trope.

In this trope, two people are either living far apart when they meet and develop a relationship from afar, or they have a pre-existing relationship and then one partner must go far away for some period of time or permanently. Either way, the challenge is to maintain and grow the relationship and eventually to find a way to be together.

In some stories, the couple is going to be apart for a finite amount of time—say, because one partner has been deployed by the military and will be away for a fixed length of time, or because one partner has taken a job with a fixed duration or until completion of a project. In this version of the story, the challenge is to keep the relationship alive until the traveling partner returns home.

Sometimes conflicts, temptations if you will, tempt one partner to leave the relationship. In other cases, a conflict arises between the partners that threatens to destroy their relationship. A situation, like a war, may separate two people for an unknown amount of time, and the uncertainty of this separation can be the main threat to the relationship.

It's common that two people grow apart or grow in different directions when they're separated from each other for a long time. This, too, is a plausible challenge or destroyer of a long-distance relationship. Whatever challenges or conflicts you choose for your separated lovers, the pair will have to overcome both those and the distance between them to be together and have their happily ever after.

I have seen a few stories over the years where the lovers never overcome the distance between them but nonetheless sustain a deeply romantic relationship over a long period of time. Which is to say, for every rule in writing, there is always an exception.

Letters, phone or video calls, etc. are the typically means of moving the relationship forward. Because there's no possibility of this couple physically being together during much of the story, this trope relies heavily—almost exclusively—on communication and feelings and tends to be intensely romantic and poignant.

This trope relies on feelings and emotions in lieu of love scenes and physical expressions of attraction, affection, or love. At its core, this is a trope of minds and souls—of two people connecting intellectually and emotionally to fall in love or remain in love.

ADJACENT TROPES
--Coming Home
--Reunion
--Sacrifice
--Separated/Marriage in Trouble

WHY READERS/VIEWERS LOVE THIS TROPE

--how romantic it is for someone to love you deeply enough that their love can span vast distances or separations

--experiencing a spiritual love that relies on words and letters and transcends physical love

--a steadfast lover/partner/spouse who is willing to stand by you, stay loyal to you, love and support you through a long and difficult separation

--he or she loves you enough wait at home, hold down the fort, raise the kids, and manage alone until you return

OBLIGATORY SCENES
THE BEGINNING:

Two things have to be established in the beginning of this story—a relationship between two people and a separation between these people. The hero and heroine may begin the story already in a relationship. They may know each other but not have developed a romantic relationship yet. Or, this couple may meet, physically, or even virtually, at the beginning of your story.

They could meet by becoming random pen pals when a volunteer writes letters to soldiers he or she has never met. One partner in a married couple may take a job in a remote location or may begin a job in a new place while the other partner sells a house, children finish out a school year, or some other necessity keeps this other partner in the old home for a period of time.

The couple may have control of choosing the separation or it may be completely out of their control. The possibilities for introducing this couple, establishing a relationship, and then separating them or keeping them separate are endless. Have fun and feel free to come up with something novel, creative, and clever.

THE MIDDLE:

The hero and heroine are almost without exception apart by the middle of the story. The long distance has been introduced between them, and now they must commence building, growing, maintaining, or saving their relationship.

The method(s) of communication available to this couple commence being used.

It's entirely possible for your couple to have virtual dates, get to know each other if they already don't know each other well, communicate honestly and openly, learn about each other, hang out, have fun, discuss anything under the sun...and yes, commence having conflicts. In fact, they may run into things they disagree about sharply or at a fundamental level of core values.

This type of relationship is unique, however, in that your characters have time to consider their reactions and responses to each other between communications. This delay allows them plenty of opportunity to consider their words, to calm down, to see the other person's side of the argument, and to moderate their own behavior in a way that an in-person relationship often lacks.

If the hero and heroine weren't in love before, they fall in love now. If they've fallen entirely out of love, they start falling back in love. A couple that was in love may stay in love.

It's also in the middle of the story that the lovers start turning their attention to being together. They typically make plans for one of both of them to travel to join the other one. A contract or deployment may be ticking down toward its end.

And of course, obstacles to physically getting together may crop up at this point in the story.

Into every romance, however, a fly must enter the ointment. Something must enter into the relationship that is a source of stress, disagreement, and potential crisis.

Often this thing is a development, event, or change in status that threatens to create an even longer, or heaven forbid, permanent separation between the lovers.

Perhaps one character is being presented with another relationship where he or she is now. Perhaps one of them faces a threat of death. Or perhaps the situation changes at one end of the relationship or the other to prevent the lovers from getting together as planned.

Whatever you choose, this is a real crisis that threatens to end this relationship.

BLACK MOMENT:

Whatever crisis threatening the relationship happens or appears to happen. Both partners quit the relationship, walk away from it, or declare an end to it.

You might not want to kill off one of the lovers if you want to pull off a happy ending to your story. Even in the case of a tragic ending, you might choose to delay the actual death of one (or both) of the lovers until the end for the sake of getting your audience to actually read or watch your story through to the end.

THE END:

By the end of the story, the crisis is resolved. You may need to get creative to solve this problem if the lovers are still far apart when your story ends...or making that separation permanent may be the resolution to the crisis.

At any rate, the couple may stop communicating for a period of time, or their means of communication may be slow enough that they can't communicate anyway. There's a blackout, as it were, between the lovers, giving them each plenty of time to think about what has happened. This pause to reflect may help them realize they don't want to live forever without the other person in their life.

Typically, the lovers do finally get together, with one or both of them traveling to a place where they can physically be in the same place at the same time. The long-awaited meeting or reunion occurs.

Resolution of the crisis that tore them apart may or may not be resolved before they unite. Resolution may have to wait until they can finally be face-to-face.

If they've broken up fairly permanently or angrily in the black moment, they may not initially "reunite" as lovers, but rather to resolve the crisis and finish separating their lives. But it may be this reunion that finally opens their eyes to how much they love each other and want to be together forever.

This story ends with the lovers in love, and the relationship stronger than ever after being tested by a long-distance separation. Usually, it ends with the lovers finally together and living out their happily ever after.

KEY SCENES

--the farewell in the beginning if they already know each other

--the first correspondence, call, or communication from long distance

--the virtual love scene, which may be a deeply romantic letter, call, or declaration that stands in for a physical love scene

--The Dear John letter or call

--the first physical meeting or reunion

THINGS TO THINK ABOUT WHEN WRITING THIS TROPE

How do the hero and heroine know each other already when your story begins or do they meet when the story begins?

Does your story begin with the couple in close physical proximity or not?

Do they start out the story as strangers, just friends, or more?

What forces them to be apart or stay apart? That is, what injects the long distance into their relationship?

How do they each feel initially about being so far apart? Is it a big deal or not?

What does each of them fear will happen in their relationship when they are apart for a long distance and/or a long time? Are those fears founded?

What kinds of communication will they use throughout your story? What limitations are there to this communication? What frustrations? Is it private or not?

Will you use two points of view to tell this story from each end of the long-distance relationship, or will you stick to one person's point of view? If one, whose?

Each character will, in effect, live their own story in this trope. How will you convey what's happening in each, separate story? Will this be through point of view shifts, running two parallel plot lines, a third-party narrator, or some other device? Or will you rely on the communications between the characters to relay one of the storylines to the main character whose point of view you stay in?

How will you inject fun into this relationship?

How will you inject tragedy into this relationship? Do they miss important moments in each other's or other people's lives by being absent?

What's the overall tone of their communication? Does it remain constant or change over the course of the story?

If they don't start the story fully in love, how will they fall in love with each other? What do they learn about each other that makes them fall in love?

What do they disagree about? Is this a source of serious conflict between them?

What threatens to keep them apart forever? Is it the failure of their relationship or some external force or event that could end their relationship?

How do their separately lived timelines mirror each other or contrast with each other?

Do they keep secrets from each other? Why or why not?

What, besides the mere fact of being long-distance, threatens to end their relationship?

What does the end of the relationship look like when it happens? What triggers it to appear to end?

Is there one external plot crisis at one end of the relationship that breaks it up, or are there crises at each end of the relationship that destroy it? If there are plot crises at each end of the separation, how do they mirror each other or contrast each other? Are they related crises or two completely unrelated ones?

How will the couple overcome these crises?

Will the couple ultimately overcome the separation and get together physically? If this happens, how does it happen?

What does a reunion or first physical meeting between these two look like? Is it big enough? Romantic enough? Satisfying to your audience, which has waited through the entire story for this climactic moment?

Is this couple together forever, never to be pried apart again, or are they likely to face more separations going forward? If so, are they equipped to deal with those, now?

What does happily ever after look like for this pair?

TROPE TRAPS

Creating a story set-up that, if implausible, isn't adequately sold to the audience in a way that readers or viewers are willing to suspend their disbelief to go along with the story.

Creating characters not sympathetic and likable enough for readers to buy into their story.

Failing to create a necessary backstory if these two characters already have a history together.

Dumping the entire backstory of these people's lives up front in your story and killing the pacing.

Using a clumsy method of telling the parallel plot lines of what each of these characters is experiencing that doesn't make sense in the story you've developed.

Not actually growing or mending the relationship over the course of your story and just keeping these two people in touch but not truly communicating.

Having one or both characters fail to communicate honestly or freely, fail to reveal their feelings honestly, or fail to put real effort into the long-distance relationship.

Failing to introduce a real problem into this relationship. Without problems, this story just becomes a series of love letters that, while romantic, don't really go anywhere beyond extended I miss you's and I love you's.

If you're relying solely on the long distance to be the big threat to the relationship, I'm going to go ahead and say you can do better. Reach for more than that. The long-distance is the starting point for this couple's problems, not the be all and end all of them.

Failing to introduce a real threat to the expectation of them ever getting together or back together.

Delivering a weak or inadequately satisfying reunion or first meeting when the lovers finally do get together at the end of your story.

Failing to write an emotionally satisfying romantic arc in the absence of physical contact between these two people. This is a challenging trope to pull off for this reason, but ever so satisfying to audiences when you can really engage their emotions in such a poignant tale of longing.

LONG DISTANCE ROMANCE TROPE IN ACTION
Movies:

- Going the Distance
- Sleepless in Seattle
- Kissing Booth 2
- The Time Traveler's Wife
- You've Got Mail
- The Lake House

- An Affair to Remember

Books:

- Dear John by Nicholas Sparks
- The Wedding Date by Jasmine Guillory
- The Forever of Ella and Micha by Jessica Sorenson
- Mine by Katy Evans
- The Time Traveler's Wife by Audrey Niffenegger
- Landing by Emma Donoghue
- The Middle Ages: A Novel by Jennie Fields
- Beijing: A Novel by Phillip Gambone
- Dear Aaron by Mariana Zapata
- In Your Room by Jordanna Fraiberg

24

LOVE TRIANGLE

DEFINITION

Historically, a love triangle involves one woman who loves and is loved by two different men, or one man who loves and is loved by two different women. The resolution of this traditional structure is that the hero or heroine must choose between the two other people competing for his or her love.

In the modern world, many, *many* more variations upon this theme are possible. There's no requirement to limit the love interests to two—feel free to write a love dodecahedron if you feel like it and can pull it off. There's no requirement to stick to a male-female model. The main character could be male or female and choosing between competing male and female love interests. The multiple characters entwined romantically can be bisexual, pansexual, gender fluid, transgender, or some other identity that you invent wholesale.

Another modern variation on the old story is that the main character isn't necessarily required to choose just one long-term love interest. Polyamory and ménage arrangements are full possible as outcomes for the lovers.

For the sake of discussing this trope as clearly as possible, however, I'm going to stick to a simple triangle with one main character and two potential love interests.

In general, this trope is defined by two potential love interests competing for the love of the main character, who ultimately must choose between them. Typically, the two love interests bring very different strengths and weaknesses to the table. Both love interests are deeply appealing and make the hero/heroine's choice very difficult.

Traditionally, the hero or heroine does choose one person to love in the end. But it's entirely possible that your main character may choose more than one potential love interest to be happily with ever after.

ADJACENT TROPES
--Engaged to/Marrying Someone Else
--Best Friend's Sibling
--Best Friend's Boyfriend/Girlfriend
--Best Friend's Ex

WHY READERS/VIEWERS LOVE THIS TROPE
--how flattering is it having not one, but two, attractive, sexy, ultra-appealing people fighting over you
--being the one with all the power to choose who you want--being the heartbreaker and not the heartbroken
--being so attractive and appealing that multiple people want to be with you
--being WANTED

OBLIGATORY SCENES
THE BEGINNING:

The main character may begin the story in one relationship, to which he or she adds another relationship in the beginning of the story.

OR

The main character meets two potential love interests in quick succession, or at the same time, at the beginning of the story.

In either case, the main character finds both people attractive and is drawn equally to both of them. It's too early for this person to choose the one person he or she wants to be with, and the main character chooses to develop both relationships a bit more before deciding which one to stick with...assuming he or she has a compelling reason to choose just one lover.

The potential love interests may commence competing for the attention and affection of the main character right away, or this may unfold more slowly in the middle of the story. But either way, the two potential love interests find out about each other.

Before long, a love triangle begins to brew.

THE MIDDLE:

The different qualities the potential love interests bring to the table are demonstrated, and the main character's dilemma deepens as he or she begins to fall for both potential love interests.

The competition between the potential love interests heats up. The main character may choose one love interest, but as soon as that happens, the other love interest ups the stakes and does something to throw the decision back into doubt. It's a seesaw of attention, affection, and feelings that the main character and audience are both riding.

The main character bounces back and forth between the two love interests as they each romance her separately. It's fair to say that shenanigans usually ensue. The love interests probably try to sabotage each other, to steal time with the main character from each other, and to outdo each other in the romance department.

While this competition may start out all in good fun, at some point it takes on a more serious quality, and the urgency for the main character to make a final choice begins to ratchet up.

As the story unfolds, the main character may learn that the kind of person who really makes him or her happy isn't what he or she initially thought. The main character may waffle back and forth between which competing love interest he or she prefers.

Friends, family, and co-workers may weigh in—a lot—on who they think the main character should choose. They may try to influence the choice and may interfere or even sabotage one or the other love interest.

The need to choose one or the other builds into a full-blown crisis. The tension between the competing love interests can become so extreme that the main character must choose for everyone's safety and sanity. Or there may be some external reason that the main character must make a choice *now*.

BLACK MOMENT:

The main character chooses one lover and the other reacts badly. Very badly.

OR

The main character is unable to choose and loses both love interests.

There are, of course, many variations on what the main character's choice can be. No matter what genders, numbers, or combinations of lovers there are, your mission is to make a complete mess of it in the black moment. It all has to go terribly. All the relationships blow up, and in the midst of the chaos, the main character is left with no one at all whom he or she loves and who is willing to be in a relationship with him or her.

If there's an external plot crisis that has forced the choice or lack of a choice, that crisis also has to go to hell in a hand basket.

THE END:

You may have multiple crises to resolve in the ending of this trope. There may be an external plot crisis to resolve and multiple individual relationships to resolve. The convention is to solve the most important plot line last, so, you would typically solve the external plot problem, then let down the love interest who was not ultimately chosen, and then the main character would, last of all, reconcile with and resolve the relationship with the love interest he or she has finally chosen to be with for the long term.

In variations where more than one love interest is chosen, you may want to resolve these relationships at the same time or in very quick succession.

The main character has discovered his or her perfect mate and, in spite of the drama getting to a decision, has ended up with the person he or she truly belongs with. The love interest who was not chosen typically understands by the end of the story that he or she was not the perfect person for the main character and can go on with his or her life sadder but wiser, and armed with what he or she has learned in this story, hopefully finding his or her perfect mate soon.

KEY SCENES

--meeting each or both potential love interests

--the love interests finding out about each other and/or realizing they're in a competition

--the main character's refusal to choose

--the competing love scenes (which may or may not include sex, but probably do include a certain amount of steam)

--the main character's moment of realization that one of the love interests is not the One and the other love interest is

THINGS TO THINK ABOUT WHEN WRITING THIS TROPE

How do the main character and the love interests meet? Do they already know each other when this triangle forms, or does it form soon after they all meet?

Who are the competing love interests? How do they differ? How are they the same? What distinguishes them as two polar opposite choices for the main character to choose between?

How does each love interest appeal to some different side of the main character's personality? What is that aspect of the main character's personality?

What do friends and family think of the love triangle? Do they judge the main character for its existence or do they judge the love interests? Is it scandalous? Gossiped about? Followed with interest? Bet upon?

Do friends and family interfere in the love triangle? If so, how? Can you make their interference bigger and worse? Can it really mess with the main character or get the love interests in trouble?

What about the main character do each of the love interests find irresistible?

What is the relationship between the competing love interests? Are they friends, frenemies, or enemies? How does this relationship change over the course of the story?

Is the competition for the main character friendly or not? Does it get ugly? Violent? Why? How?

How does the main character feel about the relationship between the love interests? Does it bother him or her? Make him or her acutely uncomfortable? Secretly amuse or please him or her?

How does the way each of the love interests romances the main character differ? How is each way the same? How is each way irresistibly appealing to the main character?

What external reason could force the main character into having to choose one love interest over the other? Can you make that reason bigger, more compelling, or more urgent?

Why does the main character refuse to choose one or the other? When does this refusal happen? What happens in the story because the main character can't or won't choose? Does this make the external crisis worse? Can you make this effect on the external crisis much worse?

What does the main character learn about himself or herself over the course of the story that the two love interests teach him or her? How does discovering this shape his or her choice of partner?

Why does the main character finally choose when he or she does? Who does he or she choose? Why?

How does the love interest not chosen react? How does the main character react to that? Is the love interest not chosen going to become an enemy to the lovers? How will they deal with that?

How will the external crisis resolve once the main character finally makes a choice?

How does the main character tell the one not chosen that he or she lost out on love?

Will the main character and the chosen love interest stay in contact with the love interest not chosen? Does he or she leave town? Vow revenge? Gracefully accept the loss? Become an enemy of the lovers?

TROPE TRAPS

Creating a flat, unlikable second potential love interest whose sole purpose in the story is to cause conflict between the hero/heroine and the "real" love interest.

Creating a one-dimensional main character who really only has one "type" of partner and who wouldn't plausibly love two very different people.

Signaling to the audience too soon who the main character is going to choose.

Not justifying to the audience why the main character ultimately chooses the love interest that he or she does.

Creating two love interests who get so caught up in competing with each other that they lose sight of the main character and are more focused on winning than on actually finding the love of their life.

Readers and viewers get super aggravated when the hero/heroine chooses the love interest they believe is not the best choice. This may be inevitable with some readers who happen to fall for the love interest that the main character doesn't ultimately choose (for example Team Jacob fans of the Twilight franchise who have yet to forgive Stephanie Meyer for Bella choosing Edward). But, if the majority of readers or viewers hate the choice the main character made, you have a problem.

A main character who comes across as wishy washy or unlikeably indecisive for not choosing one lover or the other.

A main character who's unlikable for causing or exacerbating a crisis because of his or her inability to choose one love interest over the other.

LOVE TRIANGLE TROPE IN ACTION
Movies:

- Eclipse
- Something Borrowed
- My Best Friend's Wedding
- Bridget Jones's Diary
- The Notebook
- Titanic

- Gone With the Wind
- Casablanca

Books:

- Fourth Wing by Rebecca Yarros
- New Moon and Eclipse by Stephanie Meyer
- Clockwork Prince by Cassandra Clare
- The Great Gatsby by Sinclair Lewis
- The Hunger Games by Suzanne Collins
- The Summer I Turned Pretty by Jenny Han
- Collide by Gail McHugh
- The Selection by Kiera Cass

25

MARRIAGE PACT/MARRIAGE BARGAIN COMES DUE

DEFINITION

This trope involves a bargain or pact of some kind that, if a certain set of conditions are met, requires the hero and heroine to get married.

The hero and heroine themselves might have made a pact—the most common one being, "If we're not both married by age __, we'll marry each other." Or, a family member, typically a parent, makes a marriage bargain on behalf of a child.

This isn't an arranged marriage per se because a set of conditions have to be met before the marriage can or must happen. This trope could be based on a bet, a contract, or any other types of promises.

The hero and heroine may or may not know each other before the bargain is made. They may be friends who have agreed to marry someday if a set of conditions are or are not met.

In most cases, the hero and heroine are not romantically involved or in love before the bargain is triggered.

You could technically write about a long-term couple that has never married but has created a set of conditions under which they would agree to marry. In this case, your story risks lacking a proper conflict.

You'll need to create some strong objection to marriage by one partner or strong negative consequence of the marriage that the pair has been avoiding to give yourself a real conflict between two people who already love each other.

Once the marriage bargain is invoked, the couple must decide whether or not to honor their promise. If they both do, then these friends or strangers must fall in love and forge a romantic relationship that is a real and lasting marriage, which is no small task even between two people who love each other deeply.

At its core, this is a trope of change of relationship status. Strangers must become friends, friends must become lovers, and lovers must become committed spouses...and all of these may need to happen within the same relationship.

ADJACENT TROPES
--Friends to Lovers
--Arranged Marriage
--Only One Not Married
--Right Under Your Nose
--Commitment Phobia
--Everyone Else Can See It

WHY READERS/VIEWERS LOVE THIS TROPE
--being rescued from loneliness

--the fantasy of your best friend becoming your true love

--somebody else takes care of the hassle of finding a perfect mate for you

--being saved by a mysterious stranger who swoops in and transforms your life

--secretly, you and your future lover have been waiting for each other all this time

. . .

OBLIGATORY SCENES
THE BEGINNING:

This story usually begins with the bargain or pact coming due. Your audience can catch up on the backstory later—throw them into the heart of the story right away.

This trope often has a complicated backstory that would slow down your opening greatly to slog through—friendship, failed relationships with others, desperation, the formation of the pact or bargain, the intervening years, and finally, the triggering of the conditions of the bargain or pact. You'll have plenty of time to drop in the highlights of this long and sordid past over the course of the story, so I strongly against doing it in chapter one or even a prologue.

At any rate, the bargain comes due and the hero and heroine may or may not be horrified that a promise they made, or someone made for them, a very long time ago is actually being called in.

The first major plot point in this story is the decision by both parties of whether or not to honor the bargain.

THE MIDDLE:

If the hero and heroine do honor the bargain, then, the middle of the book will center around the two of them working toward building a relationship and falling in love.

If the hero and heroine don't honor the bargain immediately, then the middle of the book will center around the consequences of not honoring the bargain and pressure on the person(s) refusing to honor the pact to do so. In this case, the middle will typically lead up to a marriage.

In either case, the hero and heroine are thrown into a relationship, like it or not. Your plot will need to throw them together over and over—even if they hate each other's guts initially—so the relationship can grow.

In this story type, the plot will be a subordinate tool for letting the relationship unfold (as opposed to the main thrust of your story being the action and external problems of the plot).

If there is some external plot consequence of the marriage bargain not happening or the marriage failing, that will develop and become a burgeoning crisis through the middle of the story.

The hero and heroine get to know each other through the middle of the story. This getting-to-know-you phase may take up much of your book as shenanigans, arguments, moments of romantic awareness, attraction, and seduction ensue.

If they're not already friends, the hero and heroine become friends. If they're already friends, they fall in love. If they're already in love...they get to jump ahead to the discovery of a problem, difference, or crisis that threatens to ruin the relationship.

In every case, the middle of the story concludes with this couple together, in love, but facing some possibly insurmountable problem that could end the relationship altogether.

BLACK MOMENT:

There are a bunch of variations upon a black moment depending on the other conditions I've already discussed of how this couple came to be together.

If the hero and heroine didn't agree to honoring the marriage bargain, the black moment may be the moment when they're forced to marry. In this scenario, your black moment may happen very early relative to most stories and may involve an extended unwinding of the black moment as the relationship ultimately winds its way to a happy ending for the hero and heroine together or apart.

OR

If the hero and heroine were friends who made their own marriage bargain, the black moment is when the marriage relationship fails and they not only lose the marriage but the underlying friendship. All is lost.

OR

If the hero and heroine were strangers, forced to marry, and fell in love over the course of the story, some intractable disagreement or crisis—external or relationship-based—tears them apart.

Maybe their spouse is a stranger after all. Maybe they're stuck in a marriage neither of them wants. Maybe the marriage has stopped being a game and become all too real, and one or both of them doesn't want to be shackled forever. The options are limitless in this scenario.

OR

If the contract was arranged by the families for political or business reasons, the consequences that the contract was meant to avoid may happen anyway, or the problem it was meant to solve is, in fact, fully solved and no longer an issue. The whole marriage may have been in vain or is fully mission accomplished.

In either case, now the couple needs to decide whether or not to carry on with the marriage anyway, even if the reason for it existing has disappeared.

THE END:

Any crises surrounding the marriage pact are solved and the couple has the freedom to choose to stay together or to part ways. However, the hero and heroine realize they are in love and decide to stay together and make a go of the marriage, for real.

As simple as this ending sounds, it may involve multiple steps for your couple to arrive at this moment.

If an external crisis is resolving at the same time the couple decides to stay together, it's conventional to solve the less-important plot crisis first and the more important relationship crisis second.

That said, this trope often lends itself well to an even more elegant ending where both the plot crisis and the romantic crisis are solved simultaneously in the same climactic confrontation or moment.

KEY SCENES

--the hero and heroine are presented with the pact and react to it being invoked

--the first scene with the hero and heroine alone together, often where they try out relating to each other romantically for the first time. This isn't necessarily a kiss or seduction, but rather the first time they look at each other through the lens of being potential life mates

--one or both lovers reneges on the contract

--the first love scene. This doesn't have to be fully realized sex. It can be the first physical expression of romantic love—a kiss, a dance, or even a touch depending on the story and setting

--the moment when the marriage becomes real...meaning they each volunteer to be in the marriage, bargain or no bargain

THINGS TO THINK ABOUT WHEN WRITING THIS TROPE

Do the hero and heroine know each other or not before this story begins?

What is the bargain? What are its conditions of activation? Do the hero and heroine know the bargain exists or not?

Who made the bargain? The couple themselves or someone else?

Why did the bargain get made?

How do the hero and heroine feel about the bargain before it's invoked and immediately afterward?

Who invokes the bargain? Is it the hero or heroine? Someone else?

Do they each choose to honor the bargain or not?

What will acting on the bargain do to the hero and heroine's current lives? What problems will it cause? Will one or more of these problems become a crisis later in the story? If so, what?

How do friends and family around the hero and heroine feel about and react to the marriage pact? Do they support it or try to talk the hero and heroine out of it?

Is there some external consequence that happens if the marriage pact isn't honored? If so, what? How can you make that consequence worse? Much worse?

How willingly do the hero and heroine commence getting to know each other, either before they marry or afterward?

What attracts them to each other? What do they dislike about each other? What makes them unable to resist falling in love with each other?

How will you throw the hero and heroine together often and alone so their relationship can grow?

When in the story will the marriage actually happen?

Who or what is trying to pull the hero and heroine apart? Why? What does this person or force have to gain by keeping this couple apart?

What crisis will unfold that threatens the marriage? How will this crisis ultimately be solved?

At what point are the hero and heroine released from the marriage pact? Under what conditions are they both free to walk away? Does some outside force make that possible, or do they make the decision for themselves to release each other from the bargain?

When, why, and how do the hero and heroine each choose to stay in the relationship and be married for real?

TROPE TRAPS

The marriage bargain is a stupid or unrealistic one that two reasonable adults wouldn't expect someone else to honor.

The hero or heroine who balks at honoring a promise they made seems dishonorable, unheroic, and unlikable.

If someone else forces them into the marriage, the hero and heroine should have refused to go along with it and look weak for allowing themselves to be bullied into a marriage they don't want.

Having married, one or both partners fail to give the marriage their best shot and come across as petty and selfish for not doing their best to make the thing work.

Failing to portray both ups and down in the relationship—two people who argue and snarl at each other all the time are not only unrealistic but can't possibly fall in love for real. Vice versa, two people who get along perfectly at all times aren't the least bit realistic and won't look as if they have any real passion in their relationship.

Failing to have the friends blossom into passionate lovers. Being just friends in bed might be okay, but it's not great. Your audience wants a grand love story, not just an okay love story.

Creating no negative consequences if the relationship fails. If these two people can give marriage a try, it doesn't work, and they can both walk away no harm no foul, then what's the point of your story? Who cares? Where's the drama? Where's the risk?

Never releasing the hero and heroine from the pact. They both need and deserve agency before the end of the story. Nobody wants to be forced into marriage or feel trapped in it—it's a deeply unromantic way to leave this couple at the end of your story.

MARRIAGE PACT/MARRIAGE BARGAIN COMES DUE
TROPE IN ACTION
Movies:

- The Wedding Pact
- The Wedding Bargain
- In Name Only
- The Young Victoria
- The White Princess (although this remains a loveless marriage)

Books:

- The Contract by Melanie Moreland
- The Pact by Karina Halle
- The Marriage Bargain by Jennifer Probst
- If We're Not Married by Thirty by Anna Bell
- Terms and Conditions by Lauren Asher
- The Wall of Winnipeg and Me by Mariana Zapata
- Radiance by Grace Draven

26

MARRIAGE OF CONVENIENCE/FAKE MARRIAGE

DEFINITION

Two people, for some purely unromantic reason, decide to get married and be married in name only. Or, two people, for some purely unromantic reason, decide to fake or pretend being married. Obviously, the movement of this trope comes from the fake or convenient marriage becoming real over the course of the story.

Typically, the hero or heroine has a need to be married or appear to be married, and the love interest has some compelling need that the hero or heroine can fulfill, and hence agrees to the marriage or convenience or fake marriage to get what he or she needs. It's common for the love interest to need money, a job, or something equally urgent to agree to this fake marriage.

Fake marriages in particular tend to have a time limit upon them. The ruse of being married will last a fixed period of time, say a year, or until a will is executed, until a jealous ex leaves town, or until a sports season ends.

A marriage of convenience is generally meant to be a permanent arrangement. Both partners know it will be a marriage in name only and they both agree to that up front...until, of course, they start living together and experience irresistible attraction or fall in love.

. . .

ADJACENT TROPES
--Arranged Marriage
--Fake Fiancé/Fiancée/Boyfriend/Girlfriend
--Boss/Employee
--Friends to Lovers

WHY READERS/VIEWERS LOVE THIS TROPE
--being saved from disaster financially or otherwise
--being thrown together with a mysterious and attractive stranger
--catching the uncatchable fish
--breaking through the walls of your lover's emotional defenses and they let only you in
--someone trusts you and no one else
--a secret or forbidden romance
--he or she can't keep their hands off you, and you alone

OBLIGATORY SCENES
THE BEGINNING:
The hero and heroine may or may not know each other when the story begins. The love interest is usually established as having a crisis of some kind. He or she desperately needs a job, needs money, or something else vital to his or her survival or the survival of a loved one.

The hero or heroine is established as someone who can take care of the love interest's problem and make it go away; however, the hero or heroine has a problem of his or her own. He or she doesn't want to get married, but being married would solve some irritating or intractable problem that he or she faces, too.

The bargain is struck. The hero/heroine and love interest will enter into a marriage of convenience or a fake marriage. If it's to end at some point, that condition is set.

The couple may marry in the beginning, or that may be delayed until the middle of the story.

THE MIDDLE:

If preparations for the wedding must happen, those take place and the marriage happens if it hasn't already. The newlyweds settle down to the business of living together, and shenanigans ensue. The couple goes out in public, posing as a happy couple if necessary.

In a marriage of convenience, it's possible that the hero/heroine withdraws to his or her own life immediately after the wedding and emotionally or physically disappears. If this happens, somewhere in the middle of this story, the abandoned spouse has had enough of being left alone and goes after the hero/heroine to force him or her to engage in the relationship at least a little.

If the love interest married to solve a crisis, that crisis is taken care of by the hero/heroine. But now the love interest must pay for the aid and stay in the marriage as long as was agreed to.

This couple usually has serious disagreements and does not find simpatico right away. Friction and tension rule the day. Some of that friction and tension probably is sexual tension or attraction growing between these two.

Because they're already married, they may skip friendship and go straight to being lovers and then have to develop friendship later. Or they may choose to become friends first and then progress to being lovers.

The act of becoming lovers may introduce a new complication to the relationship that causes an external plot problem. It certainly causes loads of questions in the couple themselves. Are they making a mistake? This was not supposed to become real. What if the other person doesn't love them back? Have they shown their cards too soon? What will happen when the term of the deal is expired and one of them leaves as promised?

Someone who knows the marriage is fake or one of convenience may challenge the couple as they display affection in public, insisting that it's not real and is all an act. This may happen before the hero and heroine become a couple, in which case they'll have to deny the accusation and pretend even harder to be happily married. Or this accusation may happen after they've developed real feelings for each other, in which case the couple will probably respond heatedly and with a dramatic display of affection.

If there's an external plot crisis to go along with the conflicts and difficulties of forming a romantic relationship with a stranger to whom you're already married, both of these obstacles reach a crisis at the end of the middle.

BLACK MOMENT:

This can take many forms in this trope. One of the partners may leave or completely withdraw emotionally. The terms of the arrangement can expire, causing both partners to end the relationship. One partner has demanded a declaration of love or commitment from the other and doesn't get it.

Regardless of how it happens, the marriage that was well on its way to being real, falls apart entirely. Even if they don't separate or divorce, the relationship is over. It may not only go back to where it began, but it may become much more distant even than it was originally. If there was friendship before, there's none now. If there was politeness, that's gone. If there was mutual respect, that, too, is blown.

An interesting variation on this black moment is when the external reason why they married or pretended to marry in the first place clears up, which is to say its black moment is resolved, and there's no reason for the couple to continue on with the sham. Passing through the plot's black moment and resolving the external crisis—an event that would normally be withheld to the end of the story—actually precipitates the black moment in this case. This leads to a second black moment—a double-bounce if you will—where the relationship collapses.

THE END:

The hero and heroine, now parted, realize they love each other and aren't happy apart. They individually decide they want to make the marriage real. Any external crises are resolved, and both partners clear the way for a return to the relationship for real this time.

They meet with each other, resolve any remaining differences, reconcile, and reunite. One of the partners may need to make a grand gesture of apology to bring the couple back together, but who doesn't love a good romantic grand gesture?

Last but not least, they announce to the world that they are back together. What they pretended to before is real now.

KEY SCENES

--the love interest's desperation or desperate need for something the hero/heroine has

--the striking of the bargain

--the first real romantic encounter

--a declaration of love by one and a rejection of that declaration by the other

--the abandoned partner confronts the partner who has walked out or walked away

THINGS TO THINK ABOUT WHEN WRITING THIS TROPE

How do the hero and heroine know each other? What does each one need that makes a marriage of convenience or a fake marriage helpful enough to actually consider doing it?

What are the terms of the marriage? Is it permanent or temporary? If temporary, for how long? Who is most insistent that there be no sex?

How do people around them react to this sudden marriage? Do they buy it as real or not?

How does moving in together go? What goes wrong? What's awkward? What drives them nuts—in a good or bad way? What, if anything, do they each like about living with another person?

Who woos whom first? What does that look like? How does it go?

What do they like about each other as they get to know each other? What do they find attractive about each other besides the other partner looking hot?

Does one of them fall for the other one first? Who? Why?

What public appearances do they make as a "couple"? How do those go? How do they react when they get home or get in private afterward?

Is there an external crisis brewing that threatens to tear them apart or expose their deception? What is it?

Who knows this isn't a real marriage besides the couple? Is he or she a threat to expose it? Could this person accidentally let something slip? What would happen then?

When do they finally give in and consummate the marriage? Does one or both of them feel obligated to stay in the marriage now? Does one or both of them think that having had sex changes nothing about the arrangement? How does either reaction cause conflict between them?

What finally blows the relationship apart? Who walks out first?

Who confronts whom when it's time to reunite this couple?

Does one of them make a grand apology? If so, what does it look like? How is it received?

TROPE TRAPS

The wealthier/more successful character comes across as patronizing or having a savior complex.

The character offering the marriage of convenience or fake marriage is such a jerk that your audience cheers for the marriage to fail.

The couple does nothing but argue constantly. While this is fun for a while, at some point, this pair has to actually learn to like each other and learn to live together in relative peace.

The love interest comes across as clingy and needy. Just because he or she needs something they get from agreeing to the marriage that doesn't mean the love interest will roll over and become a wet sponge or pushover.

The sex between the couple is hot but you never develop real and deep emotions in your hero and heroine. Marriage is about much, *much* more than sleeping together.

The shift from arranged or fake marriage to real one is too abrupt or not believable.

Their first sex together is a "mistake", and the one who initiated it thinks they can go back to the pre-sex arrangement just because he or she says so. Having sex and then failing to follow and step up and be a responsible part of the relationship is sleazy at best and sexual assault at worst.

The person who walks out at the black moment not being appropriately devastated, too. Both people need to be wrecked when the marriage falls apart.

Failing to be sure that even though the marriage started unequally—one had something the other needed—the real marriage that develops needs to be one of equal partners with no one maintaining all the power or control in the relationship.

. . .

MARRIAGE OF CONVENIENCE TROPE IN ACTION
Movies:

- The Proposal
- What Happens in Vegas
- Green Card
- Loco Love
- Purple Hearts

Books:

- To Love Jason Thorn by Ella Maise
- The Favor by Suzanne Wright
- Devil in Winter by Lisa Kleypas
- King of Wrath by Ana Huang
- The Unhoneymooners by Christina Lauren
- Jasper Vale by Devney Perry
- The Penalty Box by Odette Stone
- A Not So Meet Cute by Meghan Quinn

27

NO ONE THINKS IT WILL WORK

DEFINITION

In this trope, two people launch into a romantic relationship. While they may think it's a grand idea, everyone around them who knows one or both of them believes they aren't suited for each other and that this relationship will never last for the long term or be a healthy, functional relationship.

The lovers, of course, ignore everyone's advice and forge ahead with their relationship.

In spite of nobody else having faith in the couple, the hero and heroine have faith in themselves and see their way through their conflicts to a happily ever after.

At its core, the relationship between this hero and heroine may not have much—or anything—wrong with it based on this trope. All the pressure on this relationship that comes from this trope is truly external and comes from other people.

Because of this, it's not uncommon for this trope to be combined with other tropes that do give the couple a serious conflict to overcome between themselves. In a heavily plot-driven story or a story that's not primarily a love story, this trope is a good choice because it relies mostly on external events, actions, and people for its core conflict.

This trope can be as simple as people around the couple being an ongoing annoyance, or it can be a trope of outsiders ripping this couple apart with judgment, threats, and ultimatums. The degree of misery this trope inflicts on your hero and heroine depends largely on the secondary characters who are skeptical of this couple's chances.

ADJACENT TROPES
--Bad Boy/Girl Reformed
--Across the Tracks/Wrong Side of the Tracks
--Cross Cultural/Interethnic/Interracial
--Feuding Families
--Scandalous Hero/Heroine
--Opposites Attract

WHY READERS/VIEWERS LOVE THIS TROPE
--proving everyone else wrong and showing up your doubters
--achieving the impossible
--finding love in the least expected place
--being loved enough and loyal enough that he or she will stick with you through thick or thin

OBLIGATORY SCENES
THE BEGINNING:
The hero and heroine meet and hit it off. In its initial phases, this relationship may unfold like most normal relationships—after meeting, there's mutual attraction and enjoyment of each other's company. There's a getting-to-know-you period followed by progression of the relationship to more than friendship.

At some point, however, the people around the hero and heroine jump in to cause problems. It's up to you who will be the naysayers around the hero and heroine. They may each have their own naysayers, or they may share skeptics who know them both. These outsiders can be friends, family, co-workers, or anyone else who knows the couple or knows of the couple and who has a strong opinion on the subject of their relationship.

These skeptics are likely to show themselves fairly quickly after the relationship goes public since they're absolutely convinced this relationship is a mistake and is never going to work. They will probably try to intervene before the relationship becomes too serious and before it's too late to get the hero and/or heroine to "see reason."

THE MIDDLE:

The hero and heroine's relationship continues to develop. You may choose only to show your audience why this pair is actually well-suited to each other, or you may choose only to show the audience the problems that are inevitable between this pair and why the skeptics around them are right. But most likely, you'll do both.

You have a range of choices in points-of-view you'll use to show these opposing perceptions of the couple and their relationship. You can stick to the point of view of either the hero or heroine, you can shift between the two, or you can include points of view of your main skeptic(s).

At any rate, in the middle of this story, problems and conflicts must arise that threaten to break up this couple. Whether it's the problems everyone around them forecasted that causes them conflict or some other problem(s) nobody anticipated is up to you. The problems can be related to the plot of the story or can stem from internal conflict between the lovers. Regardless of what causes this couple to struggle, it's likely the people around the lovers will engage in I told you so's and continuing predictions of doom.

The couple may become defiant in the face of all this criticism and choose to hide their relationship or conversely, to flaunt it even more publicly.

Their problem(s) and conflict(s) continue to mount, and the situation begins to spin out of their control. This supposedly easy relationship isn't so easy anymore, and maybe they won't be able to pull it off. A sense of impending doom closes in around them as the big crisis and black moment approach.

BLACK MOMENT:

The problems and conflicts pulling the hero and heroine apart succeed and the couple's chance at love appears destroyed. Worse, everyone around them is probably delighted. The lovers are devastated but may or may not get any sympathy from their family and friends. The suckage is complete.

THE END:

The hero and heroine have to pull themselves together, take a deep breath, and in spite of everyone else appearing to be right, try one last time to salvage their unlikely relationship. They find a way to solve their problems and conflicts and to be together. This final test proves not only to them but to everyone around them that they really do belong together. These star-crossed lovers finally earn their happily ever after together.

KEY SCENES

--the hero and heroine reveal who they've met and like to friends, family, or co-workers for the first time and experience their first push-back against the relationship

--the decision to proceed with the relationship in spite of all the naysayers

--the hero and heroine part ways forever

--the hero and heroine reveal their repaired relationship to the naysayers at the end of the story

THINGS TO THINK ABOUT WHEN WRITING THIS TROPE

How do the hero and heroine meet? Will the friends, family, or co-workers who will be skeptical of the relationship later be present or not? Is the way they meet or where they meet part of the reason the naysayers are skeptical later?

What attracts this hero and heroine to each other?

When do the people around the couple find out about this nascent romantic relationship?

Who are the people around the hero and around the heroine who object to this relationship? Do the hero and heroine have separate acquaintances who hate the relationship, or do they share the same critics?

How widespread is the naysaying? Is it only a few close friends or is the skepticism widespread? Is it very widespread...as in one or both of the lovers is famous and the whole world is against them?

Do these people dislike the hero or heroine? Or is this a case of them liking the hero and heroine individually but just not seeing the two of them working together?

What do the naysayers see in the new romantic partner of their friend, family member, or co-worker that makes them so sure this relationship is doomed?

What, in fact are the problems or conflicts that arise to cause trouble between the hero and heroine? Is it externally plot based or is it internal and personal conflict between the hero and heroine?

Will the naysayers actively try to sabotage the relationship, or will they stand back and let it take its inevitable course to failure?

Is there a way to give the hero and heroine both external and internal conflicts...and can the two mirror each other in some way?

How will the conflict(s) grow in seriousness over the course of your story? What factors will cause the conflict to continue to escalate from bad to worse to terrible?

Do any of the couple's friends, family, or co-workers actually support the relationship? If so, why?

What, besides sheer, cussed stubbornness (or determination to prove someone wrong) will keep the hero and heroine genuinely engaged in and trying to make the relationship work as their troubles mount? What, besides physical attraction, pulls them together enough to survive as a couple?

What ultimately breaks them apart? Why?

How do the naysayers react to the disintegration of the relationship? Are they thrilled? Smug? Sympathetic? Supportive?

If the naysayers actively helped wreck the relationship, how will the hero and heroine react to them?

How will the hero and heroine solve the external and internal problems that broke them up? Will any of the former naysayers help them?

What about their unlikely relationship makes both of them willing to dust themselves off and give the relationship one last try in the end? What do the naysayers think about that?

Once they've gotten back together, how will the couple let the naysayers know they're back together and have found their happily ever after? How will the naysayers react?

If the naysayers ultimately approve of or support the final relationship, what has changed their minds about the relationship by the end? Is this a slow process that unfolds throughout the story? Is it a sudden epiphany? If so, what event precipitates the epiphany?

How do the lovers feel about the naysayer(s) at the end of the story? Is all forgiven? Is the relationship over? Something in the middle?

TROPE TRAPS

The hero and heroine really aren't suited to be together and the naysayers aren't wrong.

Forcing two characters together into a relationship that feels fake or unnatural.

Creating a relationship with a toxic core that will someday wreck this relationship no matter how you end your story now.

Giving this beleaguered couple no support at all.

Creating characters that give in to peer pressure too easily and appear weak and manipulated.

Creating lame or superficial reasons for the naysayers to dislike the hero and heroine.

Painting a hero or heroine who isn't ready for a healthy long-term relationship regardless of who he or she falls in love with.

Failing to give the lovers a compelling attraction and chemistry to justify their stubborn persistence through all the peer pressure trying to force them apart. And the corollary to that...keeping the hero and heroine together primarily or solely because they're determined to prove someone wrong, not because they truly love each other.

Breaking this couple up using purely an external plot device. If two people truly love each other, they'll move mountains to be together. And, if the external plot device is enough to actually break them up, it's probably enough to keep them apart forever. This means they're unlikely to overcome it at all.

Failing to create a serious internal, personal conflict between the lovers. They're very stubbornly determined to have this relationship. It's going to take something real and serious to actually destroy the relationship.

Using a lie to break them up. (Obviously, some lies would absolutely ruin a relationship, even a strong one. But if a naysayer friend simply makes up something to sabotage the relationship, such things are easily proven to be false.)

The naysayer(s) being exceptionally vicious in breaking up the couple for no good reason. That is, failing to give the naysayer(s) a valid reason and motivation to dislike this relationship and to interfere in it.

Keeping the naysayers and lovers close and cordial at the end of the story if the naysayers have, in fact, made a good faith effort to destroy the most important relationship of their friend/relative/co-worker's life and deny that person true love.

The naysayers change their minds and become supportive the minute they see the couple "happily ever after" at the end of the story. This comes across as fake and shallow and isn't believable. People don't change their opinions on a dime.

The happy couple at the end isn't believable to your audience. They haven't grown and changed enough for their ability to sustain a long-term relationship to be believable.

NO ONE THINKS IT WILL WORK TROPE IN ACTION
Movies:

- Pretty Woman
- Romeo and Juliet
- Say Anything
- The Age of Innocence
- Portrait of a Lady on Fire
- New Moon
- Titanic
- Avatar

Books:

- Make Me Sin by J. T. Geissenger

- Fourth Wing by Rebecca Yarros
- The Age of Innocence by Edith Wharton
- New Moon by Stephanie Meyer
- The Mortal Instruments by Cassandra Claire

28

NURSING BACK TO HEALTH

DEFINITION

Either the hero or heroine in this story suffers or has suffered some sort of injury or illness that involves a lengthy recovery. The love interest is typically the person in charge of nursing the hero or heroine back to health, or the love interest is, at a minimum, a key person supporting the patient and his or her medical team.

The hero or heroine may eventually make a full recovery and the couple then gets their happily ever after.

OR

The recovery may never be complete, and the lovers will have to take that into account as they craft their long-term relationship.

No surprise, the central conflicts of this story revolve around the challenges of the patient recovering and/or the challenges of being a caregiver and supporter to the patient during this time.

If there's a primary character whose point of view you mainly or solely tell the story from, that character will determine whether the emphasis is on the patient's journey or the caregiver's.

You can raise the stakes on whether or not the patient recovers by making recovery the condition for something to happen or not happen in your story's plot. A character might refuse to marry unless he or she can walk down the aisle on their own. A character might not inherit an estate unless he or she can prove mental competence. A criminal will not get prosecuted unless the patient wakes from a coma and can learn to communicate again to testify against the bad guy.

It's not uncommon to layer this trope with another trope to increase the stakes even more. For example:

- there's an arranged marriage on the line
- a secret identity that must be preserved
- the patient is a bully turned nice guy

By adding a secondary trope, ou can turn what might seem to be a fairly bland and straightforward story into one that intrigues and engages your audience deeply.

In reality, recoveries from serious injuries or illnesses can be slow, difficult, tedious slogs. They can be emotionally wrenching and psychologically exhausting for both patients, caregivers, and their loved ones.

The challenge with this trope, then, is to make your story interesting and exciting—or at least emotional—enough to pull readers forward through the story and hold their interest all the way to the end.

ADJACENT TROPES
--Amnesia
--Disabled Hero/Heroine
--Damaged Hero/Heroine
--Recovery/Rehabilitation
--Back from the Dead

. . .

WHY READERS/VIEWERS LOVE THIS TROPE

--being safe when you're helpless

--getting to let go of all responsibility for a little while, as if we're a child again

--someone loving us generously and loyally, even in a bad time

--my love is strong enough to pull someone back from the brink of death or through an unrecoverable illness/injury

--he/she fought to live for me

--the person who loves me *never* abandoned me (even when it might have made sense to do so)

OBLIGATORY SCENES
THE BEGINNING:

The hero or heroine becomes injured/ill/incapacitated or it's established that this character is already in that state. The love interest gets his or her entrance onto the stage. This person might be an old acquaintance, a new friend, or perhaps an employee. It's not uncommon for the love interest to be a professional caregiver who is part of the team assembled to help the hero or heroine recover.

There's a spark of attraction between the patient and love interest, or perhaps a spark rekindled. Regardless of their past, a new hope for a possible romantic relationship going forward is planted as a seed in the beginning of your story.

The patient and love interest sometimes do have a backstory together. They may even be married already. It's not uncommon that they're engaged, betrothed, dating, or otherwise romantically involved before the injury/illness occurs. This backstory may or may not be introduced in the beginning of your story, the caveat being that backstory almost inevitably slows down the pacing of your story and should be kept to an absolute minimum in any story.

The inciting incident is often the moment of incapacitation and anything that came before is left for short flashbacks and snippets of information dumping later in the story. The other usual inciting incident is the first meeting between the patient and love interest post injury or illness. Neither of these are mandatory, however, if your story should logically start somewhere else.

If you plan to introduce an external plot reason why the hero/heroine must or must not recover over the course of the story, that plot element is usually introduced near the beginning of the story.

THE MIDDLE:

The romantic relationship between the patient and love interest grows as they work together climbing this mountain of recovery before the hero/heroine. They get to know each other or get to know each other in a new way. If they knew each other before, they see sides of each other they've never seen before—both good and bad. If they have some intractable personal difference in values or beliefs, a crisis of this magnitude is likely to reveal it, and it will become a source of conflict between them.

If the external plot deadline or condition for the patient recovering has not been established in the beginning, this is often the big plot reversal that starts the middle of the story.

The patient begins working on his or her recovery with the help of the love interest. This recovery will have successes and failures, fits and starts, ups and downs. Depending on the type of injury or illness your hero/heroine is suffering, there may be large physical challenges to overcome. In almost all cases, there will be large mental, emotional, and psychological challenges to overcome, as well.

If the caregiver is part of the medical team healing the patient, conflict may arise over the ethics of this person becoming romantically involved with the patient.

Friends and family may support the patient's recovery. They may enter into conflict with the love interest over the methods being used to pursue recovery for the patient. Or these well-meaning but misguided people may interfere outright with the patient's recovery.

It's also possible that friends, family, detractors, or enemies may sabotage the patient's recovery in some way. Feel free to have fun with how the characters around the patient and love interest interact with the couple. These secondary characters can be an excellent source of interest, excitement, suspense, or emotional twists to help this trope engage your audience.

As the middle concludes something typically goes off the rails in the patient's recovery. The rehabilitation work may become so difficult that he or she wants to give up. A medication may not do what it's supposed to. The patient may be running out of time to recover (either medically or because some external deadline is approaching). A personal conflict between the patient and love interest may be approaching the breaking point.

BLACK MOMENT:

The patient hero or heroine's recovery fails. As hard as he/she and the love interest have worked and tried, the treatment hasn't worked and the hoped-for recovery isn't going to happen. If there was an external plot device riding upon this recovery, it won't be achieved now. Worse, the relationship between the patient and love interest completely falls apart. Either the patient or the love interest or both walk away from the relationship in despair, exhaustion, frustration, or something else.

If there have been an ongoing series of crises with the patient's health, this is when the "big one" hits. The big crisis that's going to kill the patient or completely destroy any chance of recovery happens.

Whatever bad thing is triggered in the external plot by failure of the patient to recover happens. The bad guys in your story triumph and get what they want (and possibly the thing they've been maneuvering, manipulating, and machinating to achieve).

. . .

THE END:

Something happens that allows the patient to recover. Perhaps some medical intervention finally works, although do beware of the implausibly miraculous and unexplained recovery. Perhaps the patient digs deep one last time and overcomes the final obstacle in his or her path to recovery. This can be a physical, emotional, or psychological obstacle.

The love interest decides to give the relationship and the patient one last shot. This may be the catalyst for the patient's final recovery, or it may be an entirely separate event in your story.

The bad external plot outcome is typically reversed, but this may not always be the case. The patient may still lose his or her position as CEO or a noble title, but the patient may be okay with that if he or she has achieved health, happiness, and family.

The patient and love interest find their happily ever after. This may or may not include a full recovery to health. Either is totally fine. All that matters is the lovers are at peace with the outcome of the recovery journey and happy with each other.

KEY SCENES

--the big reveal of the full extent of the patient's injury/illness/incapacitation to the love interest

--the patient doesn't want to or is afraid to embark on the journey required to recover and the love interest talks him or her into it. Or vice versa...the patient talks the love interest into it

--the patient tries to quit and the love interest doesn't let him or her do it

--the (first) big romantic scene between the patient and love interest

--the patient's final refusal to continue the recovery process

--the big breakthrough for the patient medically, emotionally, or psychologically

. . .

THINGS TO THINK ABOUT WHEN WRITING THIS TROPE

What's the hero or heroine's injury, illness, or incapacitation? Is it visible to the naked eye? Is it an invisible injury?

Do the patient and love interest know each other before the injury/illness occurs? If so, what's their past relationship? What's the status of their relationship at the time the injury/illness occurs? What's their relationship at the beginning of the story if that's not the moment the injury/illness occurs?

If the patient and love interest meet after the injury/illness occurs, what are their initial impressions of each other? Are they romantically attracted from the start, or does that grow later? Does the love interest pity the patient? Admire him or her? Fear him or her or the injury/illness itself?

Will you start the story before or after the injury or illness occurs? Why?

How did the injury or illness occur? How will you show this to the audience—

directly in current action, in flashback, in narrative, obliquely, never?

How long will a plausible recovery take? This doesn't have to be entirely medically accurate...just plausible.

Is the love interest a medical caregiver? If so, what kind? Is it ethical for him or her to be involved with the patient?

If the love interest is not a medical caregiver, how does he or she have frequent access to the patient?

What does the love interest do to help along the patient's recovery?

How self-sacrificing is the love interest? Does he or she have a vested interest in the patient's recovery? Is he or she helping out of the goodness of his or her heart at first?

At what point does the love interest begin to fall in love with the patient? How does this change the nature of what he or she is doing to help the patient? Does it change the love interest's motivation to help with the recovery? How does he or she feel about that?

What steps in the recovery will you show in your story? Which steps will go well, which will go badly?

Where will you find humor, joy, and romance in this story? Where will you find tragedy, loss, grief, trauma?

What do the patient and love interest learn about each other that they didn't know before or that are new sides revealed of each person's personality as they deal with this crisis?

Is there an external plot reason the patient must recover? Is there a deadline for that recovery? Who wants him or her to succeed? Who wants him or her to fail?

How do friends and family treat the patient and love interest? Are they helpers in the healing process? Well-meaning interferers? Outright saboteurs?

What do friends and family of the lovers think of the growing romance between the patient and love interest? Will they try to help, hinder, or destroy the growing romance?

What prevents or stops the patient's recovery?

What personal crisis comes to a head between the patient and love interest?

What external plot event goes all wrong for the patient and love interest that costs them everything that they thought mattered?

What restarts the patient's recovery in the end or causes a treatment to finally succeed? Is it medically plausible? Again, it doesn't have to be real...just plausible.

How will the patient and love interest solve their intractable personal crisis? Does one or both apologize? Compromise? Change their mind? Have an epiphany?

Does the "lost" external prize come to the patient after all when he or she recovers? Or does that plot McGuffin stay lost to him or her? How do the patient and love interest feel about that?

What lessons do the patient and love interest learn over the course of this story?

How completely or incompletely will the patient's recovery be by the end of the story?

What does this couple's happily ever after look like?

TROPE TRAPS

The patient has an injury/illness/incapacitation that they can't plausibly recover from, ever.

Using implausible and flatly unbelievable medical information to describe the illness/injury. Or worse, getting the science of it wrong.

Painting an injury or illness that real people have and deal with and not portraying it accurately enough to avoid hate mail and/or howls of outrage (that you richly deserve for not doing your home-work and treating this condition with respect)

The love interest, with little or no medical training, comes up with a brilliant solution for the patient's injury or illness and imple-ments it successfully but wildly implausibly.

Creating a passionate romance in the middle of a painful, trau-matic, or debilitating injury/illness that would distract any patient to the extent that they wouldn't possibly be interested in romance.

Failing to include any moments of happiness, joy, or lightness in the heaviness of fighting the recovery that would make any romance plausible.

Being so steeped in the suffering, misery, pain, hard work, and negatives of the recovery process that your audience walks away rather than puts itself through any more depressing reading/viewing. While stories of this type may have reputations for being Oscar or Pulitzer bait, you still have a responsibility to entertain your audience at least a little. And no, this story doesn't have to be a laugh-fest by any means. But give your audience at least a fighting chance of getting through your story without having to resort to anti-depressants.

Creating a love interest who doesn't engage in any self-care and sacrifices everything all the time for the patient. This character can come across as having no self-esteem and being unlikable, or at least unrespectable. Or this character can come across as holier than thou and sanctimonious.

It's fine for the love interest to love the patient fiercely and fight with everything he or she has for their recovery but try to keep them human. They, too, will have moments of doubt, rebellion, exhaustion, frustration, and desire to give up or walk away.

Creating cardboard characters who are too consistently noble and self-sacrificing to be believable.

Creating a selfish patient who's unlikable and unredeemable. It's fine for a patient to start out in a bad head space or descend into one. But the audience needs to see some glimmer of something lovable (that the love interest sees as well), to make them keep rooting for him or her to recover.

Creating a wildly implausible miracle cure at the end.

Magically and without any pushback having the bad thing that happened because the patient didn't heal (or heal on time) reverse itself when he or she does heal.

Failing to acknowledge the importance of health, love, family, and friends over any material reward.

Failing to resolve the relationships between the couple and any family, friends, or other characters who weren't fully supportive in a positive way of the patient's recovery.

Failing to address any likely long-term side effects or aftereffects of the injury/illness/incapacitation that the couple may have to deal with in the future and what they plan to do about it.

Creating a full, everything's wonderful, recovery when only a partial recovery is plausible to your audience.

Failing to integrate the lingering effects of the injury or illness or some aspect of it that remains into the couple's long-term relationship.

NURSING BACK TO HEALTH TROPE IN ACTION
Movies:

- The English Patient
- Land
- The Outsider
- The Secret Life of Words
- Coming Home

Books:

- Forbidden by Elizabeth Lowell
- Flowers From the Storm by Laura Kinsale
- Yours Until Dawn by Teresa Medeiros
- When Beauty Tamed the Beast by Eloisa James
- A Virgin River Christmas by Robyn Carr
- Lover Unbound by J.R. Ward

29

ON THE RUN/CHASE

DEFINITION

In this trope, the hero and heroine are chased or are on the run. They may start the story on the run or, shortly after the story begins, they may commence being chased. It may be only the hero or heroine who is actually the target of the chase, or it may be both of them.

Typically, once a love interest joins the hero/heroine who is being pursued, the love interest, too, becomes a target of the chase if for no other reason than proximity to the hero/heroine or because the love interest is providing aid to the hero/heroine.

The person or persons chasing the hero/heroine are vital to this trope and will provide much of the mood and movement of this story.

It's entirely possible this pursuer stays completely off the page or screen, but even then, the pursuit is the action the hero and heroine will spend much of the story reacting to.

The hero or heroine may or may not be caught by their pursuer(s) over the course of the story, but the reason they're on the run/being chased typically is resolved by the end of the story, so the couple can finally stop running.

Of course, there are exceptions to every rule, and some stories may best end with the hero and heroine merely able to take a break from running and catch their breath, as it were. This may particularly be the case if this story is part of a series or you're planning a sequel to this story that resumes the chase before ultimately resolving the reason for the pursuit.

At its core, this trope is about solving an external problem that will tear the lovers apart if they don't find a way to end the chase. While this external problem can cause plenty of stressors to the romantic relationship, writers often layer this trope with other tropes that create more internal, personal conflict between these two characters, who might otherwise be in perfect sync throughout this story.

ADJACENT TROPES
--Road Trip/Adventure
--Hero/Heroine in Hiding
--Running Away From Home
--Dangerous Secret
--Redemption

WHY READERS/VIEWERS LOVE THIS TROPE
--who doesn't love a good desperado
--being sucked into a secret world or secret life that makes you feel special and different
--being loved so much that your lover is willing to leave behind their normal life to run with you
--walking (or running) away from everything and everyone you've known and starting a new life
--not being tethered to any responsibilities anymore
--traveling and seeing new places

OBLIGATORY SCENES
THE BEGINNING:

The hero and heroine meet. While this might seem obvious, for the person on the run or about to be on the run, the act of meeting anyone and engaging socially with him or her may be a huge risk.

The initial attraction between the hero and heroine is strong enough that the character in jeopardy is willing to pause an existing flight or risk not running yet.

If the hero or heroine is already on the run when the story begins, you may not want to reveal immediately why that character is a fugitive and who he or she is running from.

If the reason for the hero and heroine running hasn't occurred when the story begins, it is probably the inciting incident to start the story. The hero, the heroine, or both of them get caught up in whatever event that forces one or both of them to go on the run.

THE MIDDLE:

In the case where the love interest is not part of the inciting chase in this story, the relationship will have to develop enough—probably quickly—that the love interest is willing to join the hero/heroine in their flight from pursuit.

While the love interest may not technically be in jeopardy if he or she is caught, he or she will be emotionally invested in not getting caught because he or she cares deeply about the hero/heroine and his or her cause.

OR

The uninvolved love interest will need to become involved with the chase and be forced on the run, as well. The love interest can be mistaken for an accomplice of the hero/heroine, or the love interest can intentionally or unintentionally help the hero/heroine run and end up being pursued as well.

If the couple has any friends, families, or allies willing to help them, they will call in favors as needed to avoid being caught. Even though their first priority is not getting caught, the couple's second priority is to find a way to end the chase. Whatever event, misunderstanding, crime, or other cause of the pursuit you construct, the lovers will become increasingly focused on finding a way to resolve it and get themselves off the hook. The more they fall in love, the more urgent it becomes to end the chase so they can have some sort of normal life together.

As the chase progresses, the lovers come closer and closer to getting caught and the misses with getting caught get nearer and nearer...until they are finally cornered or trapped with no escape left.

BLACK MOMENT:

The worst happens and the hero and heroine are caught. They are torn apart as they feared they would be. The love interest may or may not be in trouble, depending on how the pursuer(s) perceive their involvement in the hero/heroine's flight.

The hero/heroine has failed to resolve the reason for the chase or to exonerate himself or herself. Rightly, or wrongly, the hero/heroine must now face the consequences he or she was trying desperately to avoid.

All is truly lost.

THE END:

The hero/heroine may rely on the love interest, who's not in custody, to complete the work of exonerating him or her. Or, if both of the lovers are in custody, they may need outside help from someone to resolve the problem that has forced them on the run. Or the couple may need to find a way to escape so they can finish the work of clearing their names.

The emotional conflicts that have arisen as they've been on the run and become more and more stressed are fully resolved. They have external peace and internal peace, now, and can finally stop running. The hero and heroine start to establish a normal life for themselves.

KEY SCENES

--the love interest is dragged into his or her first chase by the hero/heroine, or the pair runs for the first time

--the big reveal to the love interest of why the hero/heroine is on the run

--the pursuer and his or her reasons for chasing the lovers is revealed

--the lovers pause to rest...and finally can have a romantic interlude

--the lovers *barely* avoid being caught

THINGS TO THINK ABOUT WHEN WRITING THIS TROPE

Why is the hero/heroine on the run? From what event? For how long?

Who's chasing the hero/heroine? Why? What's the pursuer's emotional motivation—is he or she determined? Angry? Relentless? Driven by justice or vengeance?

What will happen to the hero/heroine if he or she is caught?

Does the hero/heroine start your story already on the run or does the chase start during your story?

How do the hero and heroine meet?

Is the love interest a totally uninvolved outsider to the chase initially? Is the love interest involved in the reason the hero/heroine is on the run?

How does the love interest get sucked into the chase and end up on the run as well? Is he or she in trouble for joining the hero/heroine? Why or why not?

How does the hero/heroine feel about dragging the love interest into the chase? How does the love interest feel about it?

Why is the love interest willing to give up his or her current life to go on the run as well?

What do the run and the pursuit look like? How much distance will be covered? Where will it take place? What conveyances will everyone use? How much technology is brought to bear in pursuing the lovers?

Does anyone help the lovers along the way? Who? Why? How?

Does anyone double cross the lovers along the way? Who? Why? How?

What conflicts will develop between the lovers as they continue to run and are having progressively more difficulty avoiding being caught?

What are the hero and heroine trying to do to resolve the reason for the chase? Do they have to find something? Prove something? Disprove something? Get evidence? Get a confession from someone? Are one or both of them avoiding some event?

How is the search for a resolution complicating the chase? Are the hero and heroine being forced to go to or return to a place that increases the odds of their being caught? How risky is this search? How can you make it even more risky?

How and when will the pursuer(s) close in on and finally trap the hero and heroine?

What event is triggered by the lovers getting caught?

How and why are the lovers separated when they're caught?

How will you get the lovers back together in the end?

How does the big problem causing the chase get resolved in the end?

Is the chase over forever? If not, why not, why is it pausing now and for how long?

What does normal look like for the lovers after they stop running?

. . .

TROPE TRAPS

The fleeing hero/heroine is being irresponsible and skipping out on a duty as opposed to fleeing for an important reason. Which is to say, not making the reason for being on the run life-threatening literally or metaphorically.

The reason the hero or heroine is on the run could be solved readily enough if they just faced it or the person pursuing them.

The hero/heroine looks like an idiot for pausing his or her flight or not starting it because he or she has met somebody attractive.

The love interest agrees way too readily to drop his or her entire life and take off with this person they barely know.

Revealing all the details about who and why is pursuing the hero/heroine way too early and not building any mystery or suspense around it.

The hero and heroine fall in love way too hard, way too fast, to be plausible.

The hero/heroine is a jerk for ripping the innocent love interest out of his or her safe life and into danger.

The love interest seems gullible, completely lacking common sense, or self-destructive to fling himself or herself into unnecessary danger.

Failing to put the love interest in enough danger once he or she joins the flight.

Not having any near misses as the pursuer(s) close in.

In the middle of this dangerous chase, having the lovers stop, drop, and take a (completely foolish and implausible) roll in the hay that allows the pursuers to get perilously closer. As a rule, nobody feels romantic when bullets are literally or metaphorically flying overhead, and characters who ignore this look unrealistic or TSTL—too stupid to live.

The excitement and attraction between the lovers has more to do with the thrill of the chase and the shared danger than actual compatibility between the hero/heroine and love interest.

The way the hero and heroine get free after being caught is completely implausible or lame.

Failing to resolve the reason the lovers were being chased satisfactorily.

ON THE RUN/CHASE TROPE IN ACTION
Movies:

- Bonnie and Clyde
- The Getaway
- Wild at Heart
- Thelma and Louise (although not a romance, it's a classic on the run movie)
- True Lies

Books:

- Devil of Dublin by B.B. Easton
- Blood Guard by Megan Erickson
- The Bourne Identity by Robert Ludlum
- Crown Duel by Sherwood Smith
- Children of Blood and Bone by Tomi Adeyemi
- A Thousand Pieces of You by Claudia Gray

30
QUEST/SEARCH FOR THE MACGUFFIN

DEFINITION

In this story, the hero or heroine—or both of them—are on the hunt for something. They're determined to do or find something, to complete a quest, or find something of great value for some reason.

One or both of the characters may not be involved with this quest to begin the story. However, soon enough, they're completely consumed by this search. The relationship may develop over the course of this hunt, or it may develop as one character supports the other in his or her quest, or the relationship may be threatened by the singlemindedness with which the hero/heroine pursues the MacGuffin.

Whether or not the search for the thing is successful, the hero/heroine does find true love along the way. It's up to you to decide if this is enough to satisfy this questing character or not.

At its core, this trope is about obsession over a quest or a search and whether or not love can thrive and survive in the face of this obsession. Because the focus of this trope is purely on finding something, it's often layered with another trope that will give the hero and heroine some additional personal conflict and potential for personal growth over the course of the story.

. . .

ADJACENT TROPES
--Treasure Hunt
--Road Trip/Adventure
--Oblivious to Love
--Dangerous Secret

WHY READERS/VIEWERS LOVE THIS TROPE
--who doesn't want to find treasure and get rich
--leaving behind your boring, mundane life to go on an exciting, life-changing journey
--being rescued from your terrible life by a romantic stranger
--finding the thing no one else has been able to find

OBLIGATORY SCENES
THE BEGINNING:
The hero or heroine may already be on the quest when the story begins, and in the course of that search meets the love interest. Or the quest may actually be given to the hero/heroine as the story begins. The love interest may be "assigned" to help the hero/heroine, may be a friend of the hero/heroine, or may start on the same quest, causing the hero/heroine and love interest to join forces.

OR

The hero/heroine is on the quest or starts the quest, and while it's in progress, meets the love interest, who has nothing whatsoever to do with the quest. In this scenario, the love interest is sucked into the quest voluntarily or involuntarily. The love interest may not be prepared for the rigors or dangers of the search and may find himself or herself in way over their head initially.

. . .

THE MIDDLE:

The hero and heroine get serious about the search. They may collect allies and friends along the way...or they may collect enemies and competitors in the search. The more time they spend together and the more challenges they face together, the closer they become. If they started the story as strangers, they become friends and eventually become romantically involved.

If there's a time limit on the search, the clock ticks down and the urgency of the search grows. If there's a looming consequence of failing to find the MacGuffin, that consequence draws closer and more threatening with every passing day, hour, and minute.

If conflicts arise between the lovers as to how to conduct the search, how to proceed, and what risks are too much to dare, these conflicts grow until they take on the stature of a crisis that threatens to derail both the quest and the relationship.

The couple may get close to finding the thing they seek, but each time it slips out of their grasp at the last moment. If there are competitors racing the lovers to find the MacGuffin, those competitors threaten to take away the prize.

BLACK MOMENT:

The hero and heroine fail to find the MacGuffin and fail at their quest. The negative consequences of that happen, and the thing that was *so* important to the hero/heroine is lost. The hero/heroine is devastated (and possibly the love interest is devastated for the same reason). The couple may be torn apart unwillingly as part of the consequences of failing in their quest.

OR

The conflicts that have been simmering within the relationship that have been threatening to tear it apart from the inside out finally succeed and the couple breaks up. They cannot resolve their differences, which may or may not be tied to the hero/heroine's obsession with the quest.

THE END:

The hero and heroine make one last ditch effort to complete their quest, and this time it works. They find what they're searching for or find the MacGuffin. Disaster is averted, or conversely, the great reward is received. Now that this crisis that has obsessed one or both of them is complete, they have time to complete the promise of their relationship and be together, happily ever after.

KEY SCENES

--the hero/heroine tells the love interest what it is he or she is searching for

--the love interest joins the search

--the couple takes time out from the search for romance

--they nearly lose the MacGuffin because of personal distraction or conflict

--the hero/heroine chooses the quest over the love interest and causes conflict and/or a full-blown crisis

THINGS TO THINK ABOUT WHEN WRITING THIS TROPE

What is the search, quest, or MacGuffin the hero/heroine is going after?

How obsessed is the hero/heroine with his or her search?

How do the hero and heroine meet or already know each other? What do they think of each other as the story begins? What are the friction points (both positive and negative friction) between them?

How does the love interest get involved in the search, too? Is he or she as obsessed about it as the hero/heroine? Are they competing against each other to complete the quest or find the MacGuffin?

Who else is trying to do or find the same thing they are? What will this competitor do to win and to sabotage the hero and heroine?

What are the stakes, consequences, or reward of completing the quest or finding the MacGuffin? What are the consequences of failing? Is there a way to make those consequences even more devastating or dangerous?

Do the hero and heroine immediately become romantically interested in each other, or is that a slow burn development over the course of the quest?

What steadily more difficult challenges do the lovers have to overcome as they get closer to completing their search? Can you make those challenges harder? Closer to impossible? Test the hero and heroine more?

What conflict(s) develop between the hero and heroine as the story progresses? How do these conflicts threaten to tear them apart? How do these conflicts threaten the search itself?

When does the hero/heroine choose the quest over the love interest? How does the love interest react to that?

How and why does the hero/heroine fail in their quest? Does he or she blame the love interest?

How will the lovers collect themselves and give the quest one last try at the end? What changes that makes them willing to try it one last time? Do the stakes go up so much it's worth dying in the attempt?

Do they get any help from allies in their final push to finish the quest?

What happens when they finally succeed?

How will the lovers forgive each other or reconcile in the end?

What does happily ever after look like for this couple?

• • •

TROPE TRAPS

The hero or heroine is so obsessed with his or her quest that he or she wouldn't plausibly even notice the love interest, let alone get romantically involved.

The love interest dives into a dangerous quest without any sense of self-preservation or without any real understanding of the risks involved and comes across as wildly naïve or stupid.

The love interest is too willing to just drop his or her life and take off on this quest with no thought to the responsibilities he or she is leaving behind...making him or her look feckless and unreliable.

The hero/heroine and love interest fall in love for no apparent reason, meaning they have to actually develop a full-blown relationship, even in the midst of their concentrated search.

The quest is so important and so much is riding on it that the hero/heroine comes across as irresponsible for allowing himself or herself to be distracted by romance in the middle of the quest.

The quest isn't important enough to merit the hero/heroine's obsession with completing it.

Failing to give the couple any friends or allies.

Creating a competitor *so* much smarter or with *so* many more resources than the hero and heroine that they have no plausible chance at all to win. It's fine to outmatch them by a lot, but your audience has to believe the good guys have at least a fighting chance. Luke had no chance of destroying a Death Star all by himself, but with the aid of stolen plans, he at least had a fighting chance.

Not creating serious enough consequences for failure.

Failing to provide a reward of any kind to the hero/heroine for successfully completing the quest.

The lovers bicker—or argue outright—so much over the course of the quest that they wouldn't ever plausibly fall in love.

The lovers stop at some critical moment in the quest to have a romantic interlude that distracts them from the quest, gives the competitors time to catch up or get ahead, and may cost the lovers their shot at success.

The hero/heroine ultimately values finding the MacGuffin over his or her relationship with the love interest, proving himself or herself unworthy of having true love or a happily ever after. (The hero/heroine can choose wrong as part of the black moment, but in the end, this character needs to get his or her priorities straight.)

Failing to create a powerful enough dilemma for the lovers where they have to choose between their love for each other and completing the quest.

QUEST/SEARCH FOR THE MACGUFFIN TROPE IN ACTION

Movies:

- The Little Mermaid
- Mr. and Mrs. Smith
- Casino Royale
- Avatar
- Romancing the Stone
- The Thomas Crown Affair
- Crouching Tiger, Hidden Dragon

Books:

- The Hunger Games by Suzanne Collins
- Graceling by Kristin Cashore
- Throne of Glass by Sarah J. Maas
- The Iron King by Julie Kagawa
- Shadow and Bone by Leigh Bardugo
- Divergent by Veronica Roth
- The Gentleman's Guide to Vice and Virtue by Mackenzi Lee

31

RAGS TO RICHES/CINDERELLA

DEFINITION

Historically, this trope was called the Cinderella trope. However, in modern times more characters than dispossessed princesses turned scullery maids are allowed to experience being swept out of poverty into great wealth and privilege. Hence, the name of this trope has evolved to the more generic Rags to Riches story.

You will still hear stories called retellings of Cinderella or modern Cinderella tales from time to time. This term is usually applied when a female character is the one transformed from a life in rags to a life of riches.

In this trope an impoverished character and a very wealthy character fall in love. The poor character (the one in rags) is swept away by a wealthy love interest into a world of luxury and ease (riches).

The wealthy love interest sees through the rags and poverty to find a person worthy of his or her love. Typically, the character in rags is kind, loving, attractive, intelligent, long suffering, and any other positive qualities you'd care to attribute to him or her.

A strong theme underlying this trope is that if you are good enough for long enough, someone will eventually recognize your goodness and you will be rewarded for it. This can be a problematic theme to some readers or viewers as the realities of life do not, in fact, promise reward of any kind for anyone who works hard, is patient, kind, and a good person.

Nonetheless, this dream of being seen and rescued from a difficult life remains one of the most popular and aspirational tropes of all.

ADJACENT TROPES
--Hidden Wealth
--Across the Tracks/Wrong Side of the Tracks
--Forbidden Love
--Makeover
--Billionaire

WHY READERS/VIEWERS LOVE THIS TROPE
--being plucked out of poverty into wealth
--being seen for who you really are in spite of the circumstances you come from or live in
--someone who could have anyone chooses you and only you
--he/she loves you enough to go against everyone to fight for you and have you
--living a life of ease, beautiful things, being waited on hand and foot, never having to think about money, being able to relax and not work or not work so hard
--being taken care of by someone else

OBLIGATORY SCENES
THE BEGINNING:
The hero and heroine meet. While this might seem an obvious place for a story to begin, for this couple, the fact of their meeting is unusual for one or both of them. These are two people whose worlds

would never normally collide. The opportunities for a meet-cute are very high in this trope, since the couple's meeting is probably an accident or had to be engineered by one of them (usually the impoverished hero/heroine).

The wealthy love interest may or may not realize the hero/heroine is impoverished when they meet, depending on how they meet. The rags hero/heroine probably recognizes that the love interest is rich but may not depending upon how they meet.

The pair are obviously attracted to each other immediately and see something special in each other right away. They may or may not find out who the other one is in the beginning of the story, and they may or may not find out the financial circumstances they each come from right away.

THE MIDDLE:

The hero and heroine begin spending time together. One of them may pursue the other one. Traditionally, the wealthy character pursues the poor one, otherwise the impoverished character may be perceived as a gold digger without sincere romantic feelings for the wealthy character.

The external plot of the story usually must do the heavy lifting of throwing these two characters together because the worlds they come from are so separate and different. At some point, their growing attraction and budding romance can take over the work of explaining how and why these two characters continue to spend time together.

If the two characters don't know where the other one comes from and their financial situation, it surely becomes known in the middle of the story. The two worlds then collide. The impoverished character is introduced to an unfamiliar world of wealth and must learn to navigate it. The wealthy character may or may not be introduced to the impoverished character's world and learn to navigate it as well.

The couple may keep their relationship completely secret, or friends and family may begin to find out about it...and have very strong opinions about it. Traditionally, the wealthy character's friends and family are violently opposed to the interloper who's obviously chasing after his or her money. Of course, you're not bound by this traditional and stereotypical reaction and should feel free to paint a much more complicated picture of the wealthy friends and family's reactions.

The friends and family of the impoverished character often have a much more nuanced reaction to the budding romance. They may think it's a fantastic idea to get involved with someone rich. They may hope to benefit financially from the hero/heroine's good financial luck themselves. They may distrust the motives of the wealthy character. They may be flatly opposed to the relationship because obviously the wealthy character is simply planning to use and discard the poor character and break his or her heart.

The friends and family of this couple may, in fact, go out of their way to sabotage the relationship. The rags character may be accused of thinking he or she is too good for old friends and family anymore. The rich character may be accused of turning his or her back on everything he or she stands for or has been blessed with in his or her life. And the friends and family of both lovers may simply dislike the other partner and go out of their way to break up the couple—out of jealousy, distrust, societal frictions, or any number of other reasons you can cook up.

Conflict(s) between the rags hero/heroine and rich love interest grow as the story progresses. They may run into issues of culture, values, beliefs, or trust. The wealthy love interest may not be entirely convinced the hero/heroine loves him or her and not his or her bank account. Likewise, the impoverished character may be concerned that the wealthy love interest is operating out of some displaced savior complex and not true love for him or her.

The pressures, both internal and external, that are pulling these two people apart grow toward a full-blown crisis.

. . .

BLACK MOMENT:

The internal conflicts and social status differences pulling the hero and heroine apart succeed. The chasm between their worlds is just too big to bridge. Everyone who said it would never work was right. Any sabotage by friends and family has worked. The external plot forces blocking these two getting together have worked.

The couple breaks up, and both characters are devastated.

THE END:

The hero and heroine can't live without each other and make one last big effort to overcome the obstacles keeping them apart. If it's internal conflict that has parted them, one or both will compromise or apologize. If family and friends have broken them up, the family and friends may relent after seeing how miserable these two are apart. The lovers' misery may be the thing that finally convinces the skeptical family and friends that this is true love, after all.

The external plot problem may be resolved in a way that allows the lovers to be together. Or the lovers may choose to let the horrible consequences of choosing to be together to stand and to be together anyway. This act of defiance may cause the perpetrator of the horrible consequences to relent, and the lovers may avoid the bad thing in the end. Or, indeed, they may simply move on with their lives in spite of the bad thing their relationship has triggered.

It's worth noting, however, that this is a rags to RICHES story. Regardless of the consequences the lovers may suffer or accept to end up together, the impoverished character always ends up in a better financial circumstance. The one ironclad promise of this trope is that the impoverished character is lifted out of poverty, difficulty, stress, and misery into a much better life of ease, safety, comfort, and less grindingly hard work.

KEY SCENES

--the main characters discover the difference in their financial circumstances

--the impoverished character's first introduction to the wealthy world and vice versa

--the pair's values have a serious clash

--the wealthy character is threatened with losing everything if he or she proceeds with this relationship

--each character makes a great sacrifice for the other

THINGS TO THINK ABOUT WHEN WRITING THIS TROPE

How do the hero and heroine meet? It is an accident or not? Is the meeting machinated by one or the other? Is it a collision of their differing worlds or not? What's the tone of this meeting and how does it set the tone for the rest of the story?

Does each character realize who the other one is or not? Does each character realize the relative poverty or wealth of the other character immediately or not?

When do these two figure out who the other one is and how little or how much wealth the other one has?

How will these two people be thrown together plausibly often enough and for long enough to form a real and romantic relationship?

What bad thing will happen to each of them if they pursue this relationship? Will something bad besides losing all of his or her money happen to the wealthy character?

What do friends and family think of this budding romance? Will any of them help it along? If so, who—from each character's worlds?

Will friends and family from each world try to sabotage the relationship? If so, who? How? Why?

What conflicts of values, beliefs, culture, and customs do the lovers run into between the two of them? Will any of these threaten to break up the couple? If so, which one(s)? How? Why?

What doubts and fears will each of the lovers have about this new relationship? Are the fears valid? Can you make these fears bigger? Scarier? More personal? Deeper-seated?

What external plot problem will threaten to break up the couple? Does someone level a threat of some kind at them? Is there a contractual problem like a will, trust, inheritance, or pre-nup? Is there some condition on who the wealthy lover must marry, or is a job, education funds, or other financial support tied to the wealthy character breaking up with the impoverished character?

How will the lovers overcome this external plot problem, or will they choose to live with it?

What will each of them sacrifice to have the other one?

If family and friends relent and accept the relationship, what makes them relent and how do they do it?

What does happily ever after look like when these two finally create a life together? Is the wealthy character less wealthy than before? How much better is the new life for the impoverished character? Did all of his or her dreams of being swept away into great wealth come true, or did he or she compromise to some degree?

TROPE TRAPS

The wealthier/more successful character comes across as patronizing or having a savior complex. Conversely, the impoverished character comes across as a gold digger.

The chemistry between these two very different characters is forced or feels fake.

The lovers have nothing in common.

The impoverished character is so completely unprepared to deal with the degree of wealth and privilege the wealthy character lives in that he or she can't possibly fit into this world in the timeframe of your story. It's worth pointing out that Princess Kate dated Prince William for eight years before he proposed and they didn't marry for another year. She needed *all* of that time to be trained and prepared to step into her royal role. While this is an extreme case, the demands of being a spouse in an extremely wealthy household nonetheless can be very high and very different from what most 'normal' people have any experience with.

Suggesting that money somehow makes a person better than other people.

The impoverished person isn't acceptable just the way he or she is and needs to change some fundamental aspect of himself or herself to be acceptable to the wealthy person and his or her family and friends.

Suggesting that just because a person has wealth, he or she is necessarily shallow, superficial, or obsessed with the trappings of wealth.

Only one of the lovers has to change, sacrifice, or compromise to be with the other one—traditionally the impoverished character is expected to do all the changing to fit into the fancier, "nicer" world. Love is a two-way street, and just because you have money doesn't mean your partner has to do all the work to make love work.

Relying solely on everyone else seeing in the end that the lovers really do love each other for all their problems to magically melt away. While this romantic fantasy ending may be exactly what your particular story calls for, if you did set up real problems, external or internal, your lovers do need to find real solutions to those.

RAGS TO RICHES TROPE IN ACTION
  Movies:

- Pretty Woman
- Crazy Rich Asians
- Maid in Manhattan
- Trading Places
- My Fair Lady
- The Sound of Music

- Ella Enchanted

Books:

- The Perfect Play by Jaci Burton
- Cinder by Marissa Meyer
- A Kiss at Midnight by Eloisa James
- An Offer from a Gentleman by Julia Quinn
- Throne of Glass by Sarah J. Maas
- Lord of the Fading Lands by C. L. Wilson
- Maid for Love by Marie Force
- The Beast in Him by Shelly Laurenston

32

RESCUE ROMANCE/DAMSEL OR DUDE IN DISTRESS

DEFINITION

This trope has its roots in a very old story—the rescue of the damsel in distress by the knight in shining armor. In its modern incarnation, however, either the hero or heroine may be rescued, and the thing this person is being rescued from need not be a dragon or physical assault.

Any time a hero or heroine is in need of a rescue of some kind and the love interest swoops in to accomplish said rescue, this trope is at work.

A rescue can happen as the way the hero/heroine and love interest meet. In this case, the story and the romance proceed from there with the damsel/dude already fully rescued. In this case, the rescue isn't actually the trope of the story but merely an element of describing how the main characters meet.

If you *do* want to rescue the hero/heroine up front and *do* want this to work as a trope, the aftermath of the rescue, reaction to the rescue (perhaps an attempt to re-jeopardize the damsel/dude), or the consequences of the rescue would have to flow through the rest of the narrative causing obstacles to the lovers finding their happily ever after.

That said, for a rescue to become the driving force that moves the action of the story forward, and hence a full-blown trope, the rescue must typically stretch across a good chunk of the story, if not all of it, culminating in the big rescue at the end of the book.

One reason you as a writer may choose to delay the rescue until late in the story is to avoid a perception of the person who was rescued falling in love with his or her rescuer more out of gratitude than of real attraction and romantic interest.

The threat to the damsel/dude—be it a person, an event, or something else—will set the entire tone of your story.

Remember, the badness of the bad guy will define the goodness of the good guy. The threat needs to be big enough and hard enough to defeat that the good guys will be pushed to their limit (or beyond) if they're going to prevail.

ADJACENT TROPES
--Hero/Heroine in Hiding
--On the Run/Chase
--Lone Wolf Tamed
--Stranded/Marooned/Forced Proximity

WHY READERS/VIEWERS LOVE THIS TROPE
--being rescued from all your problems by an outsider who makes them all go away
--being safe, taken care of, and cherished
--who doesn't love a good knight in shining armor? He or she is the perfect romantic hero
--being loved so much that your lover is willing to risk his or her life for you

OBLIGATORY SCENES
THE BEGINNING:

The hero/heroine begins the story in jeopardy or enters into grave danger very shortly after the story begins. The knight-in-shining-armor love interest swoops in to rescue the beleaguered hero/heroine from their crisis.

If the damsel/dude is fully rescued at this point, then the remainder of your story will probably focus on the aftereffects of this rescue and the couple's struggles to manage the fallout and consequences.

If the damsel/dude is only partially rescued, perhaps is saved from immediate danger but a larger threat still looms, then the love interest commits to protecting the hero/heroine until he or she is fully safe. The love interest may feel obligated to do this since by affecting a partial rescue, the love interest has unleashed the wrath of the bad guy on the hero/heroine who is now in even greater danger than before.

If the damsel/dude in distress's predicament is complex and is going to take a while to extricate him or her from it, the love interest commits to helping him or her stay safe and find a way clear of the danger for good.

The love interest probably doesn't commit to this protective duty out of attraction to the damsel/dude. Rather, he or she probably does it out of a sense of duty, right and wrong, honor, or some other noble motivation (whether or not the love interest is willing to admit to it or not). Whatever this motivation is—both stated and actual—these are made clear to the audience if not to the damsel/dude.

THE MIDDLE:

The threat to the damsel/dude becomes clear. The identity, goal, motivation, and degree of danger of the bad guy is revealed. The love interest now knows what he or she is up against and begins to make plans and to confront the threat to the damsel/dude.

The hero and heroine must work together to face the looming threat to the damsel/dude. They may take a physical journey. They may investigate a problem. They may search for a MacGuffin. The number of ways they can seek safety for the damsel/dude are endless. Over the course of this externally plot driven action, the main characters fall in love.

As these two fall in love, their fates become inextricably entwined. If one of them dies, they both die—literally and metaphorically.

As each confrontation between the bad guy and the love interest occurs, the danger increases, the stakes get higher, and the knight-in-shining-armor has a harder time holding off the bad guy.

In the case where the couple is dealing with consequences of the initial rescue, these also need to get worse and worse as the story progresses and ultimately to be worse and more dangerous than the thing the damsel/dude was initially rescued from.

The middle of this story is all about continually raising the stakes and raising the danger to the damsel/dude and, by extension, to the knight-in-shining-armor love interest.

BLACK MOMENT:

The knight-in-shining-armor is defeated. The damsel/dude is not saved from the big threat, and the bad thing the lovers have been trying to avoid all this time happens.

If something bad happens to one of the lovers, they're so emotionally tied to each other that the fate might as well have happened to both of them. That said, the bad fate *may* happen to both of them.

Typically, the lovers are torn apart and something terrible is going to happen to the damsel/dude that the love interest is powerless to prevent. The love interest is devastated by his or her failure to protect the person he or she loves. The damsel/dude is devastated because the one person they entrusted their safety to has failed him or her.

The drama and tragedy are usually outsized in the black moment of this trope—desperate lovers torn apart. The knight stripped of his shining armor. The damsel or dude on the verge of a fate worse than death. The lovers grieving. The guilt. The loss of will to live...you get the idea. All the big emotions are in play.

THE END:

Through one final heroic effort, and likely a grand sacrifice, the love interest—possibly with help from the damsel/dude herself or himself—rescues his or her true love. The bad guy (or whatever threat these lovers face) is vanquished. The ecstatic and relieved lovers throw themselves at each other in a swoon-worthy reunion. Again, big emotions tend to dominate in the ending of this trope.

With the threat eliminated, the damsel/dude is safe at last, the love interest rescuer victorious, and the lovers can return home or ride off into the sunset to their happily ever after.

KEY SCENES

--the threat to the damsel/dude is revealed to the audience and probably to the love interest

--the first confrontation between the bad guy/threat and the knight-in-shining-armor

--the damsel/dude is rescued (for the first time)

--the love interest/rescuer nearly fails and has a crisis of confidence

--the grand sacrifice by one or both characters

THINGS TO THINK ABOUT WHEN WRITING THIS TROPE

What threat does the hero or heroine face? Why can't he or she marshal the resources to deal with it himself or herself? Which is to say, why does he or she need to be rescued?

Why does the love interest rescuer jump in to help rescue this damsel or dude? What draws him or her to this particular problem and this particular person?

What does the damsel/dude think when the rescuer first shows up to attempt a rescue? Is he or she grateful? Suspicious? Disbelieving?

Does the damsel/dude tell the rescuer not to get involved? If so, why? If not, why not?

What attracts these people so strongly to each other that fairly quickly they're willing to die for each other? While the knight-in-shining-armor may be willing to lay down his or her life for duty, honor, or doing the right thing immediately, how and when does that transition to being willing to die for his or her true love occur?

Who is the big bad guy associated with the big threat? It's okay to have the main threat not be a physical person, but with no personification of the threat for the rescuer to fight, your audience will have to be willing to go along with a story where the threat is intangible and can't be fought or defeated directly. This can work, but it's harder to pull off than a direct, human threat.

How will the threat get bigger, closer, scarier, and more dangerous as your story progresses?

How will the rescuer have a harder and harder time staying one step ahead of the threat to keep the damsel/dude safe?

What conflicts arise between the main characters? Does the damsel/dude have trouble letting the rescuer control the situation? Do they have trust issues with each other? Communication problems? Are they working at cross purposes? Do they have motives that come into conflict?

What does complete failure look like for the knight-in-shining-armor? Can you make that failure even worse? Can you make *that* happen?

How will the lovers come back from this utter failure?

How will they muster one last effort to overcome the threat? What does that effort look like? Will the rescuer do most or all of the heavy lifting in this final rescue, or will the damsel/dude take an active and important role in his or her own rescue?

What happens to the threat once it or he/she is defeated? Is it possible that this threat will come back someday, or is it permanently eliminated?

What does happily ever after look like for this couple?

TROPE TRAPS

The damsel/dude falls in love with his or her rescuer more out of gratitude than actual attraction.

If he or she had been given a chance, the damsel/dude could have rescued herself or himself.

The audience resents the fact that the damsel/dude wasn't given a chance to rescue herself or himself.

The love interest rescuer is holier than thou or barges in to help where he or she hasn't been asked to assist.

The love interest comes across as chauvinist or sexist for not trusting the damsel/dude to take care of herself or himself and instead busting in to take care of the little lady or little man.

The threat or bad guy is not scary enough or dangerous enough to truly threaten the damsel/dude or the love interest. The audience doesn't believe that the bad guy or threat has a good chance of succeeding.

The knight-in-shining-armor never makes a grand sacrifice or never at least offers to make a grand sacrifice.

The lovers get a wimpy reunion. (They've been through a lot and deserve a big reward commensurate with the emotional upheaval and danger they've endured.)

The writer fails to show even a glimpse of the well-deserved happily ever after for this couple, who has been to hell and back along with the audience.

. . .

RESCUE ROMANCE TROPE IN ACTION
Movies:

- The Little Mermaid
- Titanic
- The Lost City
- Shrek
- The Shape of Water
- Romancing the Stone
- Last of the Mohicans

Books:

- Protecting Caroline by Susan Stoker
- Don't Kiss the Bride by Carian Cole
- Goodbye Paradise by Nealy Wagner
- Without Words by Ellen O'Connell
- River Wild by Samantha Towle
- Safe Haven by Nicholas Sparks
- Broken Vow by Sophie Lark
- Axel by Harper Sloan
- Fighting Temptation by K.C. Lynn

33

RICHES TO RAGS

DEFINITION

This trope is characterized by one or both of the lovers in the story giving up something of great value to be with their true love. While this thing of great value is traditionally monetary wealth, it can also be power, influence, position, title, rank, a magical ability, or anything else of great value to your riches to rags character(s).

While a character making this sacrifice may go from riches to rags literally or metaphorically, in return he or she receives the greatest wealth of all, true love that's steadfast, loyal, and will provide happiness ever after.

This trope is an ancient one with roots stretching back into Greek mythology, such as the tale of Jason and the Argonauts, where he attained great wealth through his exploits, then treated his wife, Medea, badly, left her, was punished by the Gods for his lack of gratitude, and died poor and alone in the rubble of his ship. It's also a common trope in religious writings—the story of a wealthy person realizing how truly impoverished he or she is until giving up all worldly possessions in favor of love or faith.

In its modern incarnation, this trope typically features someone born into great wealth, keeping in mind that "wealth" doesn't always mean money. This character lives in idle excess until finding love, which opens his or her eyes and teaches him or her the value of hard work, perseverance, and other virtues embraced by the non-wealthy.

A variation is when a wealthy person has his or her wealth taken away in punishment for arrogance, ingratitude, laziness, spending too much, or some other negative behavior.

Another variation on this trope is when a person born wealthy discovers the "evil" source of his or her wealth. Perhaps it comes from criminal activity or exploiting others in some way. Alternatively, this person might discover that aristocrats are evil and cut ties with his or her family, wealth, and/or ill-gotten income.

Yet another variation on this Riches to Rags character is the impoverished patrician, who might have experienced wealth at some point or was only raised as if he or she were wealthy. This character may greatly desire real wealth to begin with. His or her character arc typically includes coveting and pursuing wealth but eventually learning that actually having wealth isn't all it's cracked up to be.

In all these cases, the wealthy, formerly wealthy, or wannabe wealthy character meets a "poor" love interest, and ultimately embraces a new and simpler life without the luxuries and wealth of his or her previous life.

While this trope is often perceived at its core as a trope of sacrifice, the riches to rags character would probably strongly disagree with that assessment. This is a trope of defining one's values, of moral choices, and finding what's truly important to this particular character. Thus, I would posit that this is a trope of self-discovery and a search for moral clarity.

ADJACENT TROPES
--Bad Boy/Girl Reformed
--Across the Tracks/Wrong Side of the Tracks
--Sacrifice

. . .

WHY READERS/VIEWERS LOVE THIS TROPE

--it's gratifying to know that being rich isn't all it's cracked up to be

--someone loves you enough to sacrifice SO MUCH to be with you

--the virtues the riches to rag character ultimately embraces align with what most

readers believe to be good, right, and honorable, and readers love having their own morals reinforced as correct

--happiness and true love are possible in any financial situation

--happiness happens where you make it

OBLIGATORY SCENES
THE BEGINNING:

The hero/heroine usually begins the story living in great wealth, be it financial riches, great power, great title, privilege, or rank, or great abilities.

For the impoverished patrician version of this main character, his or her actual poverty is probably contrasted against his or her perception of self as "ought to be rich" or "will be rich again one day".

The riches to rags character may lose his or her wealth to begin the story, or this character may choose to abandon their wealth as late as the very end of the story. If the character loses his or her wealth up front, this often happens when the riches to rags character is first introduced in beginning of the story, well before he or she meets the love interest.

In this case, the wealthy character typically meets the impoverished love interest in the aftermath of losing everything. The impoverished future love interest typically rescues the formerly wealthy main character, who is helpless when trying to function in the "real" world.

If the wealthy main character meets the impoverished future love interest BEFORE his or her loss of wealth, the love interest's initial tone after the loss of wealth may be amused, arch, or "I told you so" toward the formerly wealthy character who has suddenly fallen low and joined the love interest in poverty. Often this version of the trope includes these characters disliking or hating each other when they first meet, before the wealth has been lost.

THE MIDDLE:

If the wealthy character hasn't already lost his or her wealth in the beginning, this character is still probably experimenting with living in the impoverished character's world. In this case, the friends, family, and colleagues of the wealthy character are probably pushing back against this wealthy person falling in love with a poor or lower status person. Likewise, friends and family of the impoverished character may dislike the idea of their loved one falling for a wealthy person who might be using the love interest, be leading on the love interest, or have no intention of making a serious commitment to the poor love interest. This couple may sneak around as a result of others disapproving of their relationship. By the end of the middle of this story this wealthy character is either close to losing his or her wealth or is seriously contemplating walking away from it.

If you're working with the trope variation where the wealthy character discovers an evil source of his or her wealth or discovers that his family, friends, or peers are evil, this investigation takes place in the middle of the story. It's up to you to choose when the wealthy character finds proof positive of the criminal or evil activity—it's often a midpoint reversal in a story of this type, or it can be delayed until the black moment. This discovery typically precipitates a crisis whenever it happens. Now the wealthy character has a critical choice to make—stand on his or her morals and lose everything, or sell his or her soul for wealth, in whatever form that wealth takes. If the wealthy character hesitates at all in his choice, the love interest may take offense at not being worth giving up everything for immediately.

The love interest may spend the middle of this story teaching the newly impoverished character how to survive in this new world in which he or she finds himself. Power shifts to the love interest and the riches to rags character is often at the mercy of the love interest—a state to which the newly impoverished character is not accustomed and may struggle to adapt to. Conflict between the lovers often revolves around these power dynamics in the middle of the story. The middle of this story can be humorous as the formerly wealthy character tries to adapt to being poor, or it can be fraught with tension and even danger, now that the formerly wealthy character no longer has the protection of his or her "wealth."

The external conflict between the lover's different worlds and backgrounds, and any external conflict revolving around the source of the original wealth reaches a crisis point by the end of the middle. Any internal conflicts between these two characters—which may revolve around conflicting moral values, different goals for their lives and for the relationship, insecurities, whatever—also build toward a crisis.

BLACK MOMENT:

If the riches to rags character hasn't lost his or wealth by now, it definitely happens now. If this character hasn't already walked away from wealth gained by evil means or evil people, he or she walks away now.

If the riches to rags character lost his or her wealth to begin the story, this is the moment where he or she must choose to return to that life of wealth or to devote himself or herself to pursuing regaining wealth to the exclusion of all else, including love.

If external forces or people have been trying to break up this unlikely and socially unacceptable couple, this is the moment that plan works.

It's possible that what finally breaks up this couple is their intractable moral differences. Often, it's the morally steadfast love interest who breaks up with and walks away from the formerly wealthy character who has been living on a slippery moral slope for the entire story.

In the black moment, the riches to rags character must either give up the last vestige of his or her wealth or power or must accept that he or she is never going to get that "wealth' back. When faced with this ultimate sacrifice, this character chooses wrong. He or she fails to make the great sacrifice, and in so doing loses the love interest or drives away the love interest.

THE END:

The gigantic conflicts of the black moment must be resolved. The riches to rags character finalizes walking away from his or her previous wealth. He or she rejects the idea of trying to get back that former wealth.

If external forces or people have torn the couple apart, the lovers must overcome that separation. Doing so often requires the riches to rags character to permanently give up his or her wealth, power, status, title, magical ability. In return, the love interest is allowed to live, go free, or live in peace, or the riches to rags character is allowed to live, go free, or live in peace. In both of these cases, the couple is allowed to reunite.

In this story, a happy ending does NOT include getting back the wealth the riches to rags character ultimately must let go of. Instead, the riches to rags character accepts that wealth is not measured in money, power, or status. He or she accepts that love and happiness are more valuable than anything else in life and embraces a simpler life with his or her true love.

Because it can be a bit difficult for an audience to believe that this formerly wealthy character will really be happy for the long term in his or her "reduced" circumstances, the ending of this story often includes a denouement or epilogue that shows the couple living a happy life together at some point in the future.

· · ·

KEY SCENES

--the moment the wealthy character is stripped of wealth or walks away from it

--the moment the love interest finds out about the main character's current or former wealth

--the first time the wealthy character encounters the impoverished world the love interest lives in

--the love interest glimpses the world the riches to rags character came from

--an argument about money, or whatever form the wealth took, between the lovers

--the moment the formerly wealthy character encounters a crisis that his or her wealth would have solved...and he or she doesn't have access to it anymore

--a scene that starkly illustrates the moral differences between the lovers that they will have to overcome

THINGS TO THINK ABOUT WHEN WRITING THIS TROPE

What form does the riches to rags character's wealth take? Is it straight financial wealth? Is that wealth tied to something else, like a title, an inheritance, family obligations, a job, or some special skill—like being a professional athlete or having a magical ability?

Will the main character only lose/reject their money, or will he or she also lose/reject anything else that is tied to that wealth?

What is the source of this character's wealth?

Why and how will the wealthy character lose his or her wealth?

When in your story will the wealthy character lose his or her wealth? Does it happen before or after he or she has met the love interest?

If the lovers meet BEFORE the wealthy character loses everything, what do these two characters think of each other when they meet? What conflicts are established that will carry forward through the rest of the story?

If the lovers meet AFTER the wealthy character loses everything, what do these characters think of each other in this situation? How helpless or out of his/her element is the formerly wealthy character?

What "impoverished" situation does the formerly wealthy character find himself or herself in? What does this setting look like? How does it differ most sharply from the wealthy world he or she has just exited?

What is better in the impoverished world than it was in the wealthy world? Are friendships stronger? Families closer? Is there more laughter? Is there more sense of community and people helping and looking out for each other?

What about the impoverished world most strongly draws the riches to rags character to it? What does this world teach the riches to rags character about his or her former life?

What aspects of the wealthy world does the riches to rags character bring to the love interest's impoverished world that makes it better?

How do their wildly different backgrounds and worlds collide?

What tone does the relationship between the lovers take when the formerly wealthy character enters the impoverished world? Is the love interest amused at the riches to rags character's lack of survival skills? Exasperated? Protective? Confused?

What do the friends, family, coworkers, and peers of these two characters think of their budding romance? Will these people try to break up the lovers? Machinate to throw them together? Approve or disapprove of the relationship? Think the worst of the other partner from the one they know well?

What internal, personal conflicts develop between the lovers as their relationship grows? Does one or both of them have personal insecurities to overcome? Do they have ethical or moral differences? How do their values differ? How do their expectations of the future differ?

Will some external plot element force the lovers apart?

What are the stakes if the riches to rags character either walks away from his or her wealth for good or never recovers it? Are the stakes high enough to cause a profound personal crisis for the riches to rags character? How can you make those stakes even higher and the choice even more tortuously difficult to make?

How does the love interest feel about this moral crisis his or her partner faces? What choice does the love interest think the riches to rags character should make?

How does this choice become a crisis between the lovers?

When and in what way does the riches to rags character fail to choose to make the great sacrifice for love? How does the love interest feel about this? How does the love interest react to this failure?

How will the lovers overcome any external plot elements that have succeeded in breaking them up?

How will the lovers resolve their personal conflicts? Will only one of them have to change his or her morals, values, or beliefs, or will both of them have to make a major personal change?

How will you convince your audience that the riches to rags character is genuinely okay with—and in fact, happy with—giving up their wealth for good?

Why doesn't the riches to rags character try to regain his or her lost wealth? What makes that permanently impossible or permanently undesirable to him or her?

What does happily ever after look like for this couple? How will you show a slice of this life to your audience?

TROPE TRAPS

Creating a wealthy starting character who is so unlikable initially that the audience never warms up to him or her, even after this character loses everything.

Setting up an implausibly stupid reason for the wealthy character losing everything. NOTE: you surely have more leeway in a romantic comedy to play with an absurd or unlikely way this person loses his or her wealth.

The wealthy character is too stupid to deserve any wealth at all based on how easily he or she loses it in your story. In reality, most wealthy people have many safeguards in place to prevent going instantly from great wealth to total destitution.

Some or all of the wealthy characters in your story come across as caricatures of spoiled elites and not real people with both good and bad qualities.

The love interest is too suspicious or not suspicious enough of the riches to rags character when he or she first shows up in the impoverished world.

The love interest is painted as too saintly and long suffering for your audience to identify with or connect with.

The morals, ethics, and values between the lovers are so wildly different that these two people would never plausibly fall in love, let alone like each other.

Suggesting that a few weeks or months of "living poor" is enough to cause major changes in the riches to rags character's core values. Once formed (typically by about age seven), human beings' core values almost never change. At all.

Depicting the riches to rags character as having "changed", when the audience knows that he or she can probably sustain these changes for a little while but won't be able to sustain them for the long term. Which is to say, creating a relationship that looks good on paper or the screen, but that has no chance or lasting forever.

Failing to show both characters putting in the hard work (or at least starting the process) to make real and lasting changes in themselves before your story ends.

Failing to resist the impulse to give back some or all of the wealth to the riches to rags character in the end—which completely negates the size and value of the great sacrifice this character makes to attain true love.

Bonus trap: by giving back some or all of the riches to rags character's wealth in the end, you also tell your audience that the entire theme of this story arc—that love is more important than wealth—isn't true at all.

RICHES TO RAGS TROPE IN ACTION
Movies:

- Kate & Leopold (and before you argue, he has to go back to his time and invent a bunch of things before he can possibly, eventually, save his impoverished family)
- Titanic
- Schitt's Creek (TV series)
- Broke Girls (TV series)
- Overboard

Books:

- It Happened One Summer by Tessa Bailey
- Drive Me Wild by Melanie Harlow
- Daughter of the Forest by Juliet Marillier
- Call It What You Want by Brigid Kemmerer
- The Dutch House by Ann Patchett
- King of Hearts by L.H. Cosway

34

RIVALS/WORK ENEMIES

DEFINITION

The short version: a hero and heroine who clash on a professional, public, or interpersonal level nonetheless are irresistibly drawn to each other romantically.

The long version: This trope is often confused with the enemies to lovers trope, but the two are, in fact, different. In the enemies to lovers trope, the hero and heroine have goals, beliefs, or desires in direct opposition to each other's. They're on opposite sides of a conflict that is angry, possibly violent.

In the rivals to lovers trope, the hero and heroine are both working toward the same goal, but typically in competition with each other. They probably share the same or similar goals, beliefs, or desires. They each just want to achieve it before the other character does.

Likewise, when we talk about work enemies, they probably work for the same organization or work in cooperating organizations. They both (should) have the same goal of promoting the good of the organization, advancing their own career, and achieving success as measured by the organization.

But, for some reason, the hero and heroine have been thrust into competition with each other in pursuit of their goal. Classically, the hero and heroine are competing to earn the same promotion, land the same client, or finish the same deal.

Because the hero and heroine have their core beliefs and goals in common, odds are good that at some point they'll end up cooperating with each other as opposed to destroying each other, which is a real possibility in the enemies to lovers trope.

This is also why this trope appears in a volume of external tropes as opposed to a volume of backstory tropes. In the rivals/work enemies trope, a boss, a company, an opportunity, or some external force throws two basically compatible people into competition with each other. The source of their conflict is external in source.

In the enemies to lovers trope, the characters have core beliefs, goals, or desires already baked into who they each are when they meet that throw them into conflict with each other. These values and goals were developed in the past, long before the hero and heroine meet. Hence, enemies to lovers is categorized as a backstory trope.

So, why doesn't Enemies to Lovers fall into the internal tropes category? After all, internal values, beliefs, and goals form an obstacle to love between the hero and heroine.

In this trope, the hero's beliefs pose no problem to him, and the heroine's beliefs pose no problem to her. Neither character has any need to change, overcome, or fix his or her beliefs to achieve love in general.

It's only when this pair meets that a problem in their beliefs arises. Hence, it is a set of ideas formed in their pasts—in their backstory—that's the source of conflict in their romance going forward.

So, the core of this trope is resolving competition between lovers. This trope revolves around rivals or work enemies who have common beliefs, common values, and common goals but who are competing to achieve something better or sooner than the person with whom they're falling in love.

. . .

ADJACENT TROPES

--Enemies to Lovers

--Friends to Lovers

--Boss/Employee

--Right Under Your Nose

WHY READERS/VIEWERS LOVE THIS TROPE

--friction causes sparks...and heat. Which is even sexier at work or in a public situation, where it's a little taboo

--he or she loves me enough to let me win in the end

--who doesn't love being noticed...even if it takes the form of teasing, humor, snark, and some good-natured needling

--he or she loved me enough to push me to be my best...and ultimately helped me be more than I knew I could be

--the fantasy of an attractive or otherwise unattainable co-worker falling for you

OBLIGATORY SCENES
THE BEGINNING:

The hero and heroine enter into some sort of competition with each other. This opening has all kinds of opportunity for a meet-cute. Two realtors want to sell the same house. Two ad execs are assigned to create campaigns—the client will choose one. Two athletes can prepare to compete against each other. A bet gets made. Sky's the limit on how you throw this pair together.

What matters in this opening is that some sort of rivalry or work competition is introduced. The hero and heroine may or may not know each other well or at all to start the story, or they may be long time colleagues and have a lot of history.

Often, the reward for winning and the stakes for losing are established as part of setting up the rivalry or competition.

You may or may not set up romantic sparks between this pair right up front, or you may choose to develop those over the course of the story.

THE MIDDLE:

A work romance or a romance between supposed rivals often needs to remain secret. Many organizations have strict policies against dating co-workers. In the case of a rivalry, friends, family, and colleagues of each character may doubt their commitment to the team or the big goal if the character is distracted by love or appears disloyal to the "home team".

The hero and heroine compete against each other. The rivalry deepens, the competition grows fiercer. At the same time attraction forms if it hasn't already. This attraction grows apace with the heat of the competition between them. The hotter the work/rivalry sparks, the hotter the romantic sparks.

This may be a pair who fights by day and makes up by night. They may bring their friction and external conflict into their romantic encounters, or they may make some sort of pact to set aside outside friction whenever they're together romantically.

Conflict from their external rivalry bleeds over into the romantic relationship, causing personal conflict between them. For example, one or the other may cheat or pull a dirty trick to win and not understand when their partner is angry with them personally.

Vice versa, personal, romantic conflicts may bleed over into the work environment. If they're arguing over whose house they want to move into or how many kids they want to have, that may carry over into the work/public environment. They're supposed to be professionals (or at least polite), but as that private conflict becomes way too public, it interferes with both of their abilities to achieve their goals.

If their relationship is supposed to be secret, that secrecy may be seriously threatened as the competition and friction between them build to unbearable levels.

This combination of external and personal conflict builds toward a crisis that threatens both the success of whatever they're trying to achieve at work and the survival of their romantic relationship.

BLACK MOMENT:

One of the lovers wins, and the other fails. The stresses of this on the relationship break them up. The winner regrets winning, because in the end, he or she has lost everything.

OR

The hero and heroine both fail to achieve their external objective. Their internal conflict has ruined everything for both of them. The weight of their dual failure not only blows their external goal but tears them apart as well.

OR

The internal conflicts between the hero and heroine break them up. In turn, this causes one of both of them to fail in the external objective they've both been chasing. This is a chicken-and-egg situation. You can choose to implode the rivalry or work competition and then the relationship, or you can reverse that order with equally successful effect as a black moment.

The key is to both destroy the relationship and have one or both of them fail to achieve the big goal.

THE END:

The hero and heroine, typically joining forces at last and working together, reverse the failure to achieve the big goal they've both been working toward. They resolve their internal conflicts—either as a result of working together or because one or both of them has learned a lesson and is choosing to change his or her behavior, beliefs, or goals. The couple works together harmoniously going forward. The moral of this version of the story is, of course, that working together as a team is more effective than competing against each other.

OR

One of the lovers moves out of the rivalry or workspace so they will never come into direct competition against each other again. This is, in fact, the more realistic ending of the two. Competitive people tend to stay competitive. Nobody changes a core personality easily, and this doesn't usually happen quickly, either.

However, competitive people can pick and choose whom they compete against and in what environments. This hero and heroine can choose to leave competition out of their personal relationship going forward. They form a supportive, cohesive unit and are together against the world going forward.

KEY SCENES

--a stolen romantic scene at work or in the environment in which the rivalry occurs (usually, they almost get caught)

--the first big argument about work or their rivalry in a private, romantic setting

--the moment of disillusionment that the other person is choosing competition over loving him or her

--a moment or scene that foreshadows one or both characters choosing the rivalry or the win at work over the other character. This is the warning shot across the bow of the crisis to come

--if one character wins and the other loses, the moments of reward for one and negative stakes for the other happening

--the consequences of failing to separate their personal and work lives land upon the hero and heroine

· · ·

THINGS TO THINK ABOUT WHEN WRITING THIS TROPE

What is the thing that the hero and heroine will compete over in your story? Is this thing merely a MacGuffin—a relatively unimportant thing that's more of an excuse for competition than an important goal in and of itself?

Is there a way to make the thing they're competing over VERY important to each of them? To outsiders? To the world?

What are the potential rewards for achieving the goal? What are the consequences of failing to achieve it? Can you make these rewards and consequences a lot bigger? Can you make them a LOT more important personally to the hero and to the heroine?

Have you created a hero and heroine who are both likable enough that the audience will root for each of them to win and will be torn over who they want to win the most?

Do the hero and heroine already know each other when your story starts or not?

How did the hero and heroine meet or how do they meet in your story? What's the tone of that meeting? Do they snipe at each other instantly? Irritate each other instantly? Do sparks of attraction fly right away?

How will this first meeting set the tone for their relationship and for the rest of your story?

Does somebody outside the hero and heroine set them against each other, or do they each choose a goal that set them in competition with each other? If it's an outsider, who? How does this person put them into competition?

Does the budding romance between the hero and heroine have to remain secret or not? Why or why not?

Who else knows, suspects, or finds out about their budding romance? What do these people think about it? Do they help or hinder the romance? Help hide it? Threaten to expose it? Blackmail one or both main characters?

How does the hero and heroine's pursuit of their goal parallel the growth in their romantic relationship? If you lay out a list of steps necessary to achieve the big goal, is there a parallel step to be taken in the romance?

How do each of them mess up at some point along the way as they pursue the big goal?

Does the hero help the heroine or does the heroine help the hero at any point in the competition? Do they ever set aside their rivalry to help each other?

Does the hero or heroine ever sabotage the other one in pursuit of the big goal? If so, does the other lover find out about it? If so, when? How? How does he or she react to learning about the sabotage?

How unpleasant does their competition get, particularly as it approaches a crisis point?

What personal conflicts between the lovers stem from the professional conflicts between them...and vice versa, what professional conflicts stem from their personal conflicts?

Do their personal and professional conflicts parallel or complement each other in some way? Is there a similar lesson to be learned from both? Is there a similar flaw at work in both conflicts? Do the hero, heroine, or both of them need to address a single flaw to rectify both sets of conflict(s)?

Who will win their competition if one of them wins at all? Will somebody else swoop in and steal the win from both of them? Will they sink their own chances individually or together by failing to resolve their various conflicts?

What do the consequences of failing look like when they land on your loser or losers?

What breaks up this couple?

Does the personal conflict wreck the professional competition, or does it happen the other way around?

How will they deal with the professional failure? Will they fix it, turning failure into a success? Leave it behind and move on to a new job or new goal? Will they both have to accept failure and move on?

Does one of the lovers sacrifice winning in the rivalry or work competition for the sake of love? If so, how? How does the other partner feel about that sacrifice?

How will they resolve their personal conflict? If doing so requires an honest, mature conversation, why haven't they had that talk long before now?

Does one or both of them learn a lesson that allows them to repair their broken relationship? If so, what lesson?

Do they set aside their rivalry/competition for good and work together going forward? Do they eliminate the rivalry by one of them moving to another job or goal?

What does happily ever after look like for this couple? How will you give your audience a glimpse of it at the end?

TROPE TRAPS

The hero and heroine are actually enemies and not merely rivals or work enemies.

The hero and heroine's goals are in fundamental opposition such that only one of them can win and the other must lose...which is to say, they're really enemies.

The hero or heroine is so competitive that he or she is completely unlikable to your audience.

The rivalry/work competition and the couple's personal conflicts bear no resemblance to each other. There's no thematic parallel structure.

Resolving each conflict requires a totally separate lesson learned that has nothing to do with the other required lesson, thereby splitting your audience's attention between two entirely separate story lines.

Failing to create meaningful personal conflicts that threaten the romantic relationship and relying solely on the friction from work to separate this couple.

Relying solely on the friction and sparks from work to draw this couple together romantically.

Neither character shows any grace or mercy toward the other professionally. Neither of them ever relent to help each other a little or warn each other of a problem or threat.

If one or both sabotages the other in the midst of the competition, it comes across as mean or mean-spirited, and hence, deeply unheroic.

The competitiveness between the hero and heroine is weighted too heavily to animosity and dislike for them to plausibly fall in love.

When the rivalry or competition ends, there's no vibrant relationship left between this pair. All the sparks, banter, and heat were ultimately work related and not personal.

One or both main characters is too competitive to be lovable by the other, to let go of winning at all costs, or to sacrifice winning for the sake of love.

One or both characters let go of being competitive for the sake of love WAY too quickly or easily at the end of the story to be plausible.

RIVALS/WORK ENEMIES TROPE IN ACTION
Movies:

- The Proposal
- You've Got Mail
- How To Lose A Guy in Ten Days
- The Hating Game
- The Ugly Truth

Books:

- Rival Radio by Kathryn Nolan
- We Shouldn't by Vi Keeland

- The Worst Guy by Kate Canterbary
- Shipped by Angie Hockman
- See Me After Class by Meghan Quinn
- Kiss My Cupcake by Helena Hunting

35

SECRET BABY

DEFINITION

Rather obviously, this trope revolves around a baby whose existence is being kept secret for some reason. Because of biology, it's almost always the baby's mother who is keeping the child secret from someone else. Typically, it's the father of the child from whom the baby's existence is hidden, but that's not always the case.

This trope works perfectly well without an external villain. In this case, the story revolves around an enormous secret being kept for personal reasons and its revelation to the person(s) it's initially being kept from.

If you choose to have a villain, in the form of some person besides the mother and the love interest from whom the baby's existence is being kept secret, the story will revolve around dealing with the compelling reason why the villain mustn't find out about the baby's existence.

It's entirely possible, of course, to craft a version of this story where the father or a guardian is raising a baby whom he or she is keeping secret from someone. But, for the sake of simplicity in this trope write-up, I'll refer to the custodial adult hiding the baby as the mother.

A baby may need to be kept secret from someone who poses a threat to the child, for example an enemy of one or both of the parents, or someone who covets a title, inheritance, or position the baby stands to inherit. The mother may hide her pregnancy and subsequent baby from someone who would inflict repercussions on her if the baby's existence were discovered—a boss who forbids pregnancy, the spouse of the baby's father, or an enemy of the mother's, to name a few.

It goes without saying that if a secret is being kept at the beginning of a story, it's bound to be revealed before the story ends. Whatever consequences the person keeping the secret of the baby's existence is trying to avoid probably happens—or else measures must be taken to avoid the consequences before or after the baby's existence is revealed.

As a rule—one of the few I would encourage you to think very carefully about before breaking—babies do not get harmed or killed in fiction stories. Audiences universally take deep umbrage at the idea of an innocent baby being hurt in any way. If it's taboo to kill cats and dogs in fiction, it's doubly taboo to harm helpless infants.

In classic secret baby stories, the mother of a baby usually keeps the child's existence secret from the birth father, who also ends up being the love interest. In this scenario, this trope, at its core, is a story of transgression by the mother for keeping the secret and by the father for acting or being a person from whom the mother feels compelled to keep the secret. It's also, at its core, a trope of forgiveness—forgiveness by the father for the mother keeping the baby secret, and forgiveness by the mother for the father acting or being someone from whom she had to hide the truth.

In most versions of this trope, not only does the love interest have to deal with how he or she is going to react to finding out there's a baby in the main character's life, but he or she also must reckon with the fact that the main character has been keeping a gigantic secret.

Although it's possible that the baby is being kept secret from a secondary character, usually the villain, it's more frequent that the main character is keeping the baby secret from the love interest himself or herself. The love interest may not be the biological parent of the baby but usually steps into a parental role before the end of the story.

ADJACENT TROPES
--Baby on the Doorstep

--Insta-Family

--Accidental Pregnancy

--Dangerous Secret

WHY READERS/VIEWERS LOVE THIS TROPE
--mother as protective hero—we all love to be loved by a mama bear

--struggling single mother is rescued by the father of her child

--what's more lovable than a man who steps up to be a good father and good partner to his family?

--being rescued by a knight in shining armor who'll keep you and your child safe

OBLIGATORY SCENES
THE BEGINNING:
We may start at the conception of the baby, or the story may start as late as well after the child is born. Your choice of when in the life of the secret baby to start your story will depend on how important it is to your audience to see who the baby's parents are and to know the circumstances of the child's conception or upon your choice to keep secrets from your audience as well. If you start your story after the child is born, the audience will likely need to see the circumstances of the child's conception at some point to help members understand why mom is keeping this child such a deep, dark secret.

You may or may not choose to fill in your audience up front on the identity of the father or details of his life and how these impact the mother's decision to keep the baby's existence secret, particularly if it's the father she's hiding the child from. But at some point, this secret must also be revealed to the audience.

If the person the mother is keeping the baby secret from is not the birth father, we're typically introduced to this person in the beginning of the story, along with the reason why the mother cannot reveal the baby's existence to this person.

At a minimum, this trope requires you to establish the existence of a baby or baby-to-be and the need for his or her existence to be kept from someone for some reason.

Very early in the story, the mother usually gets in contact with the love interest, be this person the baby's father or someone else with whom she's going to end up romantically involved. Mom usually reveals the baby's existence to the love interest before long. After all, it's awfully hard to hide a baby, who can be both loud and needs constant care and attention.

THE MIDDLE:

The reason why the baby's existence is being kept secret is made abundantly clear in the middle of the story. The full complications of the secret and the multiple reasons for the secret unfold. The audience learns what would happen if the secret were revealed, and tension builds as both mother and audience worry about the secret being revealed.

It's typical that the love interest finds out about the baby somewhere in the middle of the story if he or she hasn't found out about the baby as part of the book's beginning or inciting incident.

Revealing the baby (or his or her previously secret parentage) sends the story careening off in another direction entirely—dealing with the baby and the revealed secret in the middle of mom and the love interest trying to form a long-term relationship or sort out a previous one.

The love interest may enter into a conspiracy of silence with the baby's mother and help keep the secret from a third-party villain who threatens the child. The love interest may also step up to act as a protector of both mother and child from the villain.

Internal conflict builds within and between the mother and love interest as they deal with the revelation of the enormous secret she's been keeping.

In the external plot, the threat to the baby or mother or both builds toward a crisis. This may be an actual threat to the baby's safety, or it may be a looming custody battle, looming loss of the mother's job, or some other crisis that threatens mom's ability to keep and care for her child.

BLACK MOMENT:

The secret of the baby's existence is revealed to everybody in the story. The terrible consequences the mother has been trying to avoid by hiding her baby's existence happen.

The mother and the love interest's relationship implodes, and they break up. The love interest may not be able to forgive the mother for the deception, or the reason the mother kept the baby secret in the first place causes her to exit the relationship with the love interest.

Mom is back to being a single parent, but now she's suffering the consequences she was trying to avoid. If you really want to torture your characters and audience, the mother may even lose custody of her child.

THE END:

Mother and child are reunited if they were separated. The mother and the love interest resolve their personal differences. If mom and/or the baby are in need of rescuing, the rescue happens, almost always accomplished by the love interest or at least assisted by the love interest.

Whatever consequences from the baby's existence being discovered have threatened mom or the baby, these are reversed, negated, fixed, stopped, or otherwise dealt with. I apologize for the vagueness of that sentence but this trope has many possible specific outcomes that will depend on a variety of story choices you make.

The bottom line is the baby is safe, the threat posed by a person(s) finding out about the baby's existence is gone, mom and baby are together, mom and the love interest are together, and the love interest has probably stepped into a parental role beside mom.

KEY SCENES

--the love interest discovers or is introduced to the baby

-- a near miss with disaster as the secret of the baby's existence is almost revealed to the person from whom mom is trying to keep it

--the love interest is left alone with the baby for the first time

--the confrontation between mom and the love interest over her having lied by keeping this important secret

--a romantic or almost love scene interrupted by the baby

THINGS TO THINK ABOUT WHEN WRITING THIS TROPE

Who are the parents of the baby in your story? Under what circumstances was this child conceived? How and why did the mother end up on her own, with a baby, protecting it from some threat?

What threat to the baby is making mom keep its existence secret? (Keeping in mind that "mother" refers to whatever adult is caring for the child and protecting it.)

Who threatens the child in some way and why is this person threatening a child?

If the father poses a threat to the child, what compelling reason does he have for threatening his own child? Does the mother perceive something the father is doing as a threat that the father doesn't consider a threat?

Who is the love interest in your story?

If the father from whom the baby's existence is being hidden is to become the love interest in your story, what makes his reason for posing a threat to the child forgivable to your audience and redeemable in the eyes of your audience? How will you transform this man into someone acceptably heroic to your audience that they'll cheer for him and mom to end up together?

What lesson does the father learn and how does he learn it that makes him ready to step into the baby's life now? This may also apply to the love interest if he or she is not the birth father.

If someone other than the birth father will be the love interest, does this person know the birth father? If so, how, and what do these two think of each other? If not, what will these two think of each other if and when they meet?

Is there an external villain who threatens the baby's safety? If so, who? Why is this person a threat to the kiddo? What's your villain's motivation?

When will you start your story? Before, at, or after the baby's conception and/or birth?

How old is the child when your story starts?

How will the love interest come into the mother's life or come back into the mother's life? Does she reach out to him? Does he reach out to her? Does some external circumstance throw them together?

What are more reasons that just the one primary one that the villain or threatening adult have for threatening this child. Even if the main problem is huge, you may want to consider making the issue more complex than a single problem.

What actions and events in your story will throw the mother and love interest together in a way that allow romance to blossom between them? Where will the baby be during these encounters?

Bless them, but infants can be quite the buzz kill to a romantic interlude.

How will the baby interfere with the developing romance between mom and the love interest?

What personal conflicts arise between the mother and the love interest that are purely about the two of them and their relationship and have nothing to do with the baby?

How will the threat to the baby rise to the level of a crisis? Is there a way you can make it an even bigger crisis? (Look at additional threats to the baby beyond the big, main one for help with this question.)

How will mom (and probably the love interest) overcome or negate the threat to the baby?

How will mom and the love interest solve their personal problems so they can be together as a family?

How does the villain—if your story has one—cease to be a threat to the baby and to mom?

What does safety and security look like at the end for mom and baby? Did the love interest provide some or all of this safety, or was it a team effort between mom and her partner?

TROPE TRAPS

Creating a father for the child who's so terrible initially that the audience desperately doesn't want him to end up anywhere near the child...even if he says he has changed.

Failing to create a compelling threat to the child that would cause mom to keep the baby's existence secret.

Mom just assumes the birth father will try to take away the child, and she assumes he would win custody because he's rich and powerful. The courts try hard to think of the child's best interests, not just which parent has the most money.

Creating a one-dimensional threat to the baby. One dimensional problems tend to have simple, one-dimensional solutions that won't sustain a strong plot.

Relying on the baby to be the only conflict keeping the mother and love interest apart. While becoming a parent unexpectedly is a big obstacle to love, a heroic character would probably step up to the responsibility if he or she truly loves the mother and wants to be with her forever.

Creating a villain who's dastardly without having a compelling reason for being that way. Villains should have motivations for doing what they do and sincerely believe they're doing the right thing to achieve an end they believe to be right or deserved by them.

Harming or killing the baby. You can technically do it. But particularly in a romantic story, brace yourself for hate mail and slash-and-burn reviews.

Relying on an honest, adult conversation to solve all the issues between the adults fighting over this baby. If that was all it took, why didn't that conversation happen right up front?

Failing to show the love interest gradually growing into a parent. It's a really big life shift and shouldn't be entirely easy or automatic. There should be some bumps along the way.

Failing to show how the baby is cared for and who's doing it throughout your story. Don't just dump the baby in a crib in another room for hours on end or have the parents runoff and leave it alone. It's a child, not a football. The baby needs responsible care and attention throughout your story. Yes, it's a pain to write. But it'll save you hate mail.

SECRET BABY TROPE IN ACTION
Movies:

- Knocked Up
- Revenge of the Sith
- Tulip Fever

- The Object of My Affection
- Three Men and a Baby
- A Jazzman's Blues

Books:

- Sweet Regret by K. Bromberg
- Forever My Girl by Heidi McLaughlin
- The Resurrection of Wildflowers by Micalea Smeltzer
- The Baby Bargain by Jennifer Apodaca
- Tattered by Devney Perry
- Reckless by Elsie Silver
- From Here to You by Jamie McGuire

36

SECRET IDENTITY

DEFINITION

In this trope, either the hero, heroine, or both have...you guessed it...a secret identity. This alternate persona can be a public one, meaning they appear as a superhero, highwayman, or other public figure. Or the secret identity can be a private one, meaning he or she has taken on an assumed name, is part of a witness protection program, is undercover and using a fake identity, or is hiding his or her real identity for some reason.

The love interest may actually meet, interact with the main character as their real persona, falling in love with the real person and having no idea that the alternate persona exists. Conversely, the love interest may meet and fall in love with the alternate persona and have no idea the real persona exists. The last possible scenario is that the love interest meets and interacts with the main character in *both* his or her real persona and in his or her alternate persona.

The main character has a compelling reason for having and maintaining a secret identity that probably includes a compelling need for his or her real identity to remain secret and separate from the secret identity.

Over the course of the story, the main character either feels a need to be honest with the love interest and reveal the secret identity or the love interest may stumble across the secret identity accidentally (or through nosy prying). In either case, the love interest ultimately finds out about the secret identity and complications ensue as the love interest is sucked into the secret.

At its core, this is a story of a (typically necessary) deception made by an exceptionally heroic and self-sacrificing character or pair of characters. The main difference between this trope and the hero/heroine in disguise trope is that the hero/heroine in disguise is choosing to hide his or her real identity for personal reasons whereas the character maintaining a secret identity is typically doing it for altruistic reasons. The secret identity is usually a long-term creation meant to keep the hero/heroine's real identity unrevealed indefinitely. The hero or heroine in disguise typically maintains the disguise for a short period of time with no intent to maintain the disguise for the long term.

The difference between this trope and false identity is that in the secret identity, a character becomes someone entirely different and steps into an entirely different life while living the secret identity. In the false identity trope, a person chooses to portray some aspect(s) of himself or herself differently from his or her real self. This person maintains his or her real life but lives a lie within it.

ADJACENT TROPES
  --Hero/Heroine in Disguise
  --Secret World
  --Dangerous Secret
  --False Identity

WHY READERS/VIEWERS LOVE THIS TROPE

--who doesn't covet escaping their mundane life to live an exotic or heroic second, secret life full of adventure, romance, and excitement

--getting to be a superhero, complete with rescuing people who need help and being admired greatly

--being in on a big secret

--the person with the secret identity loves you enough to risk everything by letting you into his or her secret world

OBLIGATORY SCENES
THE BEGINNING:

The main character and love interest meet with the main character either acting in his or her real persona or in his/her alternate persona. They may have immediate sparks...or you may choose to have there be no sparks at all with the understanding that when they meet with the main character in his/her other persona, sparks will fly like crazy.

The two completely separate worlds of the character with the secret identity are established. He or she may or may not interact with the love interest in both worlds, which will be a primary source of conflict in the story as the main character navigates the lie and not being found out by the love interest.

If the couple interacts in only one of the main character's identities, then keeping knowledge of the other identity away from the love interest will become a primary source of conflict in the story. The main character will struggle to keep such a huge secret as he/she falls in love, and there will be near misses with the love interest figuring out who the main character also is.

THE MIDDLE:

The main character's two worlds collide, with the couple's budding romance caught squarely in the middle. If aspects of one of the main character's personas would cause a huge obstacle to a romance in the world of the other persona, that becomes an increasing problem as the story progresses. If there's a threat in one persona, it bleeds over into the other persona's life, endangering the love interest at the same time.

The love interest figures out the main character is keeping something from him/her and commences digging for the truth. This may take the form of difficult questions, spying on the main character, snooping, whatever.

Characters with secret identities are almost always honorable characters with heroic qualities. Hence, lying to the person they're falling in love with will get harder and harder as the romance progresses.

If both characters are maintaining a secret identity, the stress of managing their respective lives and trying to grow a long-term relationship gradually becomes too much for both of them to control.

The main character may or may not reveal the secret identity somewhere in the middle of the story. If he or she does so, the remainder of the middle of the story is taken up with the love interest being sucked into the dangers of the alternate life (or the dangers of the real life that has been left behind). Both of the lovers struggle to keep the secret identity secret as the dangers around them mount exponentially.

The main character is increasingly torn between maintaining and living the secret identity and a need to be with the love interest. The love interest may actually demand that the main character choose between him or her and the secret identity.

BLACK MOMENT:

Not only does the love interest find out about the secret identity if he or she didn't know it before now, but something catastrophic happens within the main character's secret identity. He or she is captured, attacked, exposed, or defeated by the bad guy threatening one or both identities (the real one and the secret/alternate one).

The couple is torn apart by events imploding in one or both identities. Or the couple breaks up as the main character chooses the secret identity over the love interest.

All is lost. The relationship has failed, and the main character has let down the people he/she cares about or is responsible for in one or both of his/her identities.

THE END:

How this story ends will depend greatly upon how badly you've chosen to implode the main character's identities. Regardless, the lovers resolve their differences and reconcile as a couple. One or both of them may learn a lesson that allows them to be together, or one forgives the other, or one apologizes to the other. They may both have to make personal concessions to allow for a long-term relationship. The love interest may have to accept playing second fiddle to the demands of the secret identity, the main character may have to trust the love interest with his or her safety, and they both may have to learn how to live in both identities in harmony.

If the main character was fully exposed in the black moment/big crisis and the secret identity is ruined, the lovers will probably reconcile and build a life in the real world (as opposed to the alternate world of the secret identity).

If the main character's secret identity or real identity was threatened by a bad guy, that bad guy is defeated in the end and the main character resumes his or her dual life, but living with the love interest in both worlds after they reconcile.

· · ·

KEY SCENES

--the love interest encounters the main character for the first time in the other identity from the main one in which he or she will mostly interact with the main character

--a romantic moment between the main character in his/her secret identity and the love interest

--the moment when the love interest first suspects not all is as it seems with the main character and he or she is hiding something

--an argument or disagreement between the lovers that would be solved if the main character revealed his/her secret identity

--a near miss with the love interest discovering the secret identity

--the love interest is endangered and the main character may have to revert to or reveal his or her secret identity to save or protect the love interest

THINGS TO THINK ABOUT WHEN WRITING THIS TROPE

What is the main character's secret identity? What does he or she do in the secret identity? Why is it important? Why is it heroic? Why is it appealing to your audience?

What is the main character's real identity? Why can't he or she do the same thing he/she does in the secret identity in this real identity?

In which identity does the main character spend most of his or her time? Why?

How often does the main character switch identities? What causes a switch from one to the other? What does it take to switch identities? How fast can it happen? How abruptly does he/she have to disengage from one identity to assume the other one?

How do the main character and love interest meet? In which identity does the love interest first meet the main character?

What character traits draw the two of them together? What does the main character find irresistible in the love interest?

How are these two people extremely different? What about them is different enough to cause real friction or disagreement?

Will the main character and love interest meet in the main character's other identity? If so, when? Where? How? How does the main character feel about having to interact with the love interest in two different personas?

If they meet in both of the main character's personas, is the love interest attracted to both identities or to just one of them? What conflict does this cause in the couple's relationship?

Does the love interest feel as if he/she is cheating on one of the personas if he/she is attracted to both of them? Does this cause conflict between the lovers?

Does anyone besides the main character know about both identities? Who? Why?

What terrible thing could happen if the main character's secret identity is revealed?

What terrible thing could happen to the love interest if he/she is associated with one of the main character's identities?

Who is the bad guy in your story? Is there a separate bad guy for each identity, or is there one that threatens both identities, or is the main character safe in one identity but in danger in the other?

Why can't the main character trust the love interest with his/her secret identity quickly? What keeps the main character from sharing the big secret?

What causes conflict between the lovers? Is it the secret itself? Is it a lack of trust between them? Is it secrecy and lack of open sharing between them?

Will the big threat endanger both of the main character's personas? Will it endanger the love interest? How can you make this threat bigger, scarier, more necessary to stop at all costs?

How will the main character be forced to choose between upholding his/her secret identity (to stop the big threat) and the love interest?

Does the love interest get in the way of the main character

defeating the bad guy? Does the main character have to choose between defeating the big bad guy and saving the love interest?

How will the big bad guy ultimately be defeated? Does the love interest help in some way? Does someone or some outside force help the main character or does he/she win the day solo?

Does one or both of the lovers make some sort of grand sacrifice to save the other and/or prove their love to the other?

Is the main character's secret identity revealed to the world or kept secret?

How will the lovers ultimately resolve their personal conflicts?

Which world will the lovers live most of their time in after they've resolved their differences? What will their lives look like going forward?

TROPE TRAPS

Creating a lame or ridiculous secret identity that there's not a necessary or compelling reason to maintain or hide.

The love interest is too stupid to live for not realizing the main character is the same person in both the real-world identity and the secret identity. I'm sorry, but Superman™ is hot whether he's wearing glasses or not. Just how dimwitted was Lois Lane for not figuring out Clark was the same guy?

There's no good reason for the main character not to let the love interest in on the secret much sooner than he or she actually does.

The bad guy or dangers are not big enough or bad enough to justify all the trouble of building and maintaining a secret identity. Remember, the goodness of your good guy is determined by the badness of your bad guy.

There's no conflict between the main character's two identities that causes him or her any internal dilemmas or angst.

The love interest isn't worthy or doesn't become worthy of this heroic main character.

There's no real threat of the main character losing to the bad guy.

The love interest is never in any real danger.

The main character never has a terrible choice to make between his or her secret identity and the love interest. What's the point of this story if this doesn't happen?

Neither character is required to make a grand sacrifice to have the other one. Again, what's the point if these two aren't willing to sacrifice to have the other? This is supposed to be a heroic arc.

The love interest is too helpless and weak to be likable to your audience.

The main character isn't vulnerable enough emotionally to be likable to your audience.

The main character has to completely give up his or her heroic activities, for good, to have love with the love interest. While it's romantic to make that big a sacrifice, it's also a waste to society to have it lose a hero who did good deeds.

The love interest comes across as supremely selfish to ask the main character to (or let him/her) give up his/her heroic activities.

Failing to justify why and how the main character will be happy being completely normal. It's unrealistic to expect a character accustomed to living a double life to be comfortable and satisfied living a completely mundane single life forever.

SECRET IDENTITY TROPE IN ACTION
Movies:

- Superman
- True Lies
- Buffy the Vampire Slayer (movie and TV show)
- The Flash
- Green Arrow (TV show)
- The Departed
- The Americans (TV show)

. . .

Books:

- The Scarlet Pimpernel by Emmuska Orczy
- Code Name Verity by Elizabeth Wein
- The Prince and the Dressmaker by Jen Wang
- Beneath a Scarlet Sky by Mark Sullivan
- The Personal Librarian by Marie Benedict and Victoria Christopher Murray
- Ninth House by Leigh Bardugo
- Firekeeper's Daughter by Angeline Boulley
- Aphrodite's Kiss by Julie Kenner
- A Rose in Winter by Kathleen Woodiwiss

37

SECRET ORGANIZATION/SECRET WORLD

DEFINITION

Either the hero or heroine in this trope belongs to some sort of secret organization or is part of some secret world.

It's rare that both characters start out aware of and part of a secret world together because this eliminates the entire tension of one of them keeping a huge secret from the other. A possible exception might be if they each belong to different secret organizations or worlds and each need to keep that secret from the other.

Whereas in a secret identity story the main character assumes a secret identity for some of the time, in this trope, the main character retains his or her identity, but is part of a secret world.

Also, in the secret identity story, the main character is typically working alone and there may only be a few others who know who he or she really is. In the Secret organization/secret world story, a large group of people are in on the secret together, and they typically work together toward some large, long-term objective like making the world safe from evil.

I would be remiss if I didn't point out that villains also may be part of a secret organization or secret world, and this can also be the source of a full-fledged story as the hero and heroine attempt to uncover that secret group and stop it from doing the evil or dangerous thing.

It's also possible that the main character starts the story as part of an evil secret organization or world. He or she may spend the story trying to extricate himself or herself from that group, or the love interest may set out to remove the main character from this secret group.

So, the variations in this trope revolve around who exactly is part of the secret organization/world, what this group's orientation is on the scale of good and evil, and if the end goal is to draw the love interest into the secret world, remove the main character from the secret world, or defeat the villain's secret world.

At its core, this is almost always a story of a character in jeopardy and a knight in shining armor coming to the rescue.

This is also, at its core, a story of secrets withheld until ultimately revealed and forgiveness granted by the love interest to the main character.

ADJACENT TROPES
--Secret Identity
--Divided Loyalties
--Mafia Romance
--Redemption

WHY READERS/VIEWERS LOVE THIS TROPE
--getting to be part of the cool secret
--protected by a powerful, secret organization and will never be in danger again
--he or she trusts me enough to let me into his or her secret world
--he or she loves me and wants to be with me enough to risk not only his or her own safety but that of an entire organization and a lot of teammates

. . .

OBLIGATORY SCENES
THE BEGINNING:

The hero and heroine meet, often when the love interest accidentally stumbles into the path of the secret organization or secret world of the main character.

This story often opens with a rescue of an unaware and unsuspecting love interest who is in the wrong place at the wrong time, but please don't feel at all limited by these comments in how you open this story.

Frequently, the love interest starts the story in some kind of jeopardy or becomes jeopardized as part of the inciting incident in the story. He or she is abruptly in need of help or protection.

The main character is frequently called in to protect or defend the love interest. They may or may not already know each other. The love interest may reach out to the main character for help, they may have a friend in common who introduces them, or the secret organization may assign the main character to look after the love interest.

The love interest may not be introduced to the secret organization or world right away, but the audience probably will be shown at least a glimpse of it as we meet the main character.

THE MIDDLE:

Shenanigans aplenty ensue in this story.

If, in fact, the love interest is in jeopardy in this story, the danger to him or her builds toward a crisis throughout the middle of the story.

If the lovers are tasked with stopping a bad guy over the course of the story, it becomes more and more difficult until it becomes entirely impossible to achieve.

The external plot elements of this type of story will fly thick and fast, with danger, near misses with disaster, and ever-increasing peril as the race against a ticking clock or imminent danger races onward.

The internal tensions of this story often start with the main character's need to keep his or her organization or world secret from the love interest and spiral from there.

Often people who work for secret groups tend to compartmentalize their lives and emotions heavily. They tend to be secretive and very guarded about what they say and how they express their emotions. All of these are fertile ground for relationship conflict.

The main character starts the story already intensely loyal to his or her secret organization or world. The love interest is an interloper who threatens that world. As the main character falls in love with the love interest, his or her loyalties are going to be deeply divided.

As soon as what the main character needs to do to grow the relationship comes into conflict with his or her responsibility to the secret group, there's going to be conflict galore.

BLACK MOMENT:

The secret organization or world may be revealed publicly, and potentially catastrophically.

The bad guy appears to have won. All the efforts of the lovers and the secret group have failed to stop the villain's dastardly plan. The terrible thing the bad guy aims to do appears unstoppable. The last gambit by the lovers to stop him or her has failed. It's clear sailing for the bad guy to his or her awful goal.

Even worse, the hero and heroine have failed to resolve their personal conflicts and their relationship blows up, often spectacularly.

If the main character is forced to choose between the secret organization/world and the love interest, he or she chooses the organization/world over love. The love interest can't or won't forgive this and breaks off the romantic relationship.

.   .   .

THE END:

Even though the hero and heroine's relationship has imploded, they may still be in forced proximity and/or forced to work together to make one last ditch effort to stop the bad guy or bad thing from happening.

Conversely, the act of the two of them breaking up and separating from each other may be just the opening the bad guy needs to fulfill his or her dastardly goal.

Either way, the lovers—and possibly other members of the secret organization/world—work together in one last, Herculean effort to stop the bad guy or bad thing from happening. This time, they succeed.

One or both of the lovers makes a grand sacrifice, meaningful gesture, or heartfelt apology that breaks the ice between the estranged couple and puts them on the road to resolve their personal conflicts.

Thelovers find their way back to each other with a renewed appreciation of their relationship and stronger than ever commitment to it.

The love interest is fully aware of the secret organization/world by the end and may even become part of it.

The main character fully trusts the love interest and no longer holds back any secrets. His or her heart is an open book.

The lovers establish a new life together that incorporates the secret organization or world (and/or members of this secret group) into their life.

KEY SCENES

--the love interest almost, but not quite, discovers the secret organization or world

--the love interest confronts the main character about his or her secret (the main character may or may not admit to its existence in this scene)

--the main character gives the love interest a tour of the secret sanctum. After all, what's the point of being part of a secret organization or world if there's not a good secret clubhouse or warehouse of insanely cool gadgets to go with it

--the main character and love interest confront the lie(s) the main character has been telling the person he or she professes to love or at least to care about deeply

--the main character almost fails to keep the love interest safe and freaks out...which may be his or her first hint of how deep his or her feelings are becoming

--the lovers get a moment's respite from the constant danger. You'll actually need several of these scenes so the couple's relationship has time to breathe and grow

THINGS TO THINK ABOUT WHEN WRITING THIS TROPE

What secret organization or world is the main character part of? Is it military? Paramilitary? A spy organization? Government-based or private?

What about your secret organization or world will make audience members wish they were part of it?

Who runs the secret organization or world? Where does the main character rank in this group? What's his or her job within this group? What's the goal of this group?

How morally white, black, or shade of gray is this secret group? Does the main character's moral compass align with the group's or his or her personal moral compass pointed in some other direction?

How do the hero and heroine meet? Does it have anything to do with the secret organization/world or not?

Is the love interest put into jeopardy in your story? If so, by whom, how, and why? If not, what is his or her main goal in the story? How is the love interest's goal thrust into direct conflict with the main character's goals?

Who is the villain in your story? What's his or her main goal? Is there a way you can make this goal bigger, badder, more dangerous to more people? Why does he or she think the ends justify the means in pursuing and obtaining this goal? Which is to say, why does the villain perceive himself or herself as the hero in his or her story?

Why does the villain's goal cause the secret organization to go after him or her?

Do the lovers try to keep their relationship secret from the other members of the group or not? Why or why not?

How do other people from inside the secret organization/world feel about the budding romance between the main character and the love interest? When do they find out about this relationship? How do they find out about it?

What does the boss or leader of the secret group think of the lovers' relationship? Does he or she forbid it? Support it? Warn the main character to be careful?

When in your story will the hero and heroine get down time in safe spaces to get to know each other and spend romantic time together? How few and far between will these interludes be?

How will the tension and danger keep rising through your story? How can the disaster the hero and heroine are trying to prevent go from bad to worse? How can it get even worse than that? How can it become truly terrible to them? How can it grow to catastrophic proportions that are much larger than just the two of them?

What personal problems will threaten the hero and heroine's relationship? What baggage does each of them bring to the relationship? Is there a way to make each of them particularly upset by, sensitive to, or triggered by the problems or behaviors the other one brings to the relationship?

What breaks up the main character and love interest? Are they forced to continue working together while estranged or do they separate?

Does anyone outside the lovers intervene to try to fix their relationship?

How does the climactic crisis bring the hero and heroine back together at least partially...or do they have to reconcile before they can confront the big bad guy? (If you can't resolve both the plot and romance in a single climactic finish, you solve the most important story last. In a primarily romantic story, you would usually resolve the relationship last. In a primarily suspense-based story where the romance is a sub-plot, you'd resolve the suspense plot last.)

What big gesture or sacrifice does each of the lovers make in an effort to save their relationship?

Does the main character leave his or her secret world, or offer to leave it?

Does the love interest join the secret organization or world at least in part?

Do the co-workers of the main character embrace and feel at ease around the love interest by the end of the story?

What does happily ever after look like for this couple, particularly in relation to the secret world?

TROPE TRAPS

The secret organization isn't that big a deal for the love interest to not know about.

The main character is way too chatty, outgoing, or forthcoming for a person who has such a big secret to keep.

There aren't any cool gadgets, skills or perks built into the secret world to make it super interesting and appealing to your audience.

The love interest is so unsuspecting of or oblivious to a secret organization or world existing that he or she comes across as TSTL—too stupid to live.

The bad guy isn't bad enough to justify all the angst this couple goes through to stop him or her.

Revealing the secret organization or world wouldn't actually damage it in any way.

Right in the midst of tense chase scenes, huge danger, or risky situations, having your lovers stop, drop, and boink. Don't. Do. This!

Failing to develop a believable relationship in the middle of all the suspense, action, and danger.

The members of the organization are TSTL for not realizing the lovers are in love.

Not justifying the main character's loyalty to the secret group sufficiently to make his or her choice of the group over the person he/she loves plausible.

Creating a crisis at the climax of your story that's too easy to solve. Failing to have the good guys fail a time or two as they try to solve this crisis.

Creating a love interest who couldn't keep a secret if his/her life depended on it. He or she needs to have some secretive tendencies of his or her own to be a plausible love interest for this main character.

Creating personal conflicts between this couple that could be solved if they just had an honest adult conversation...even if having such a conversation is not in their natures.

SECRET ORGANIZATION/SECRET WORLD TROPE IN ACTION
Movies:

- Kingsman: The Secret Service
- Fight Club
- Spectre (James Bond)
- Buffy the Vampire Slayer (TV show)
- The Black Book

Books:

- A Hunger Like No Other by Kresley Cole
- The Ritual by Shantal Tessier

- Hell on Wheels by Julie Ann Walker
- Until the Sun Falls From the Sky by Kristen Ashley
- The Unsung Hero by Suzanne Brockmann
- Night Pleasures by Sherilyn Kenyon
- I'd Tell You I Love You, But Then I'd Have To Kill You by Ally Carter
- Dark Lover by J.R. Ward

38

TWINS SWITCH PLACES/LOOKALIKES

DEFINITION

While twins are genetically related and lookalikes are not, the only major difference between the two in this trope is that the twins probably know each other very well, and lookalikes, doppelgangers, or clones may or may not have ever met or know anything about each other.

In this write-up, Twin #1 is the twin who's replaced by the main character, Twin #2, who replaces his or her sibling is the star of this story.

If you're writing a story about lookalikes, doppelgangers, or clones, for ease of reading this write-up without repeating those three words constantly, I'm still going to refer to your pair of identical-looking characters as Twin #1 and Twin #2, with Twin #2 being the main character who replaces his or her lookalike, doppelganger, or clone.

In this trope, a pair of twins or lookalikes switch places for some reason or one twin/lookalike is mistaken for the other one, typically by someone that the replaced twin is romantically involved with, works with, or interacts with regularly.

The reason the twins/lookalikes switch place will determine the tone of this story. Is it a joke? A mistake with repercussions? A response to a serious threat?

Often the twins are polar opposites and hilarity or misunderstandings ensue as the opposite twin #2 replaces twin #1. The twins may have different talents and switch places so twin #2's special skill set or knowledge of something or someone can be taken advantage of.

Another variation of this is the good twin/evil twin pairing. Sometimes, it's the evil twin who replaces the good twin and chaos ensues. The evil twin may be reformed or redeemed in this story, or the good twin may eventually "defeat" the bad twin and resume his or her life. Conversely, the good twin may learn how to loosen up and relax as his or her twin implodes Twin #1's formerly uptight and unhappy life.

NOTE: If Twin #2 is going to be your romantic lead, he or she is probably the good twin—audiences want the heroic character to end up rewarded with true love in the end.

Sometimes, this story follows only twin #2 who's replacing twin #1, and twin #1 is more of a device for getting the story moving than an important character in the story and only shows up at the end to force the big reveal of the switch.

Sometimes, this story is set up as a dual timeline, following both twins individually. Their experiences with switched lives come together at the end of the story when they solve a problem they've been coming at from opposite directions, switch back, or decide to remain in the other's life permanently.

Sometimes, BOTH twins are a heavy focus in the story and their lives remain tightly intertwined as one twin impersonates the other. Throughout, they work together to solve some problem. In this scenario, they may switch back and forth multiple times as the situation requires, or they may work together to be in two places at once.

Twin stories often revolve around one twin thinking his or her twin's life is better than his or her own and wanting to experience the greener grass on the other side of the fence. In these stories, the twins who've switched lives generally learn that everyone's life has challenges of its own and nobody's life is perfect, no matter how it looks from the outside.

At its core, this story revolves around deception. The motive(s) of the twin(s) in switching places are going to be very important in determining if your audience likes and cheers for the twin(s) or not.

At the end of the day, the deception is going to have to unwind and the consequences of it will have to be dealt with.

ADJACENT TROPES
--Mistaken Identity
--Hero/Heroine in Disguise
--False Identity

WHY READERS/VIEWERS LOVE THIS TROPE
--someone takes over your life and deals with all the crises overwhelming you while you escape it all

--getting to step into a much better life than your own and live the fantasy

--you're not alone in dealing with your problems and someone who loves you has your back

--in effect, you get to be in two places at once

--someone acts as a placeholder in your "real" life so you can go do something else much more exciting, interesting, fulfilling, or safe without having to exit or throw away your real life

OBLIGATORY SCENES
THE BEGINNING:
The life of Twin #1 is introduced. If they exist, whatever problems or crises in this life that cause Twin #1 to want to leave it or escape are introduced. If Twin #1 has a fantastic and enviable life, then that is introduced instead.

Twin #2 replaces twin #1. The mechanics of how this happens and why are laid out for your audience.

If you're writing a lookalike story, the lookalike, doppelganger, or clone (Twin #2) is mistaken for Twin #1. The compelling reason why this Twin #2 goes along with the misidentification is introduced to your audience.

The beginning typically ends with a complication or development that makes Twin #2 stopping the impersonation of Twin #1 exponentially more difficult to stop.

It's worth noting that I'm just getting around to mentioning the love interest in this story several pages into this trope write-up. In this story, the love interest is often deeply secondary to the interaction and interplay between the twins. He or she sometimes is little more than a device to cause conflict between the twins or an object for the twins to fight over—a tug toy caught between two dogs who both want it.

Your mission is to create a love interest who can hold his or her own in this story where the conflict between the twins threatens to overwhelm everyone else.

The love interest usually is expected to fall in love with Twin #2 in this trope. Indeed, Twin #2 is the main character, and that would usually be who the love interest ends up with. This is the rare trope, however, where Twin #1 can get the happily ever after in the end with the love interest.

If Twin #1 and the love interest were romantically involved before your story begins, when Twin #2 steps into Twin #1's life, he or she also steps into the middle of this ongoing relationship. Inevitably, Twin #2 quickly takes the relationship in a different direction or does something to shock and fascinate the love interest. This moment of shock can be positive or negative. Twin #2 can start the relationship down the road to a break-up, or he or she can start the relationship down the road to a passionate love affair between Twin #2 and the love interest.

. . .

THE MIDDLE:

The complications continue to pile up as Twin #2 continues to live the life of Twin #1. Twin #2 makes decisions that Twin #1 would not that will significantly complicate Twin #1's life if and when Twin #1 returns to his or her regularly scheduled life. Twin #2 may try to fix these problems, but fails, and these efforts inevitably lead to even worse complications. While that may sound comic on its surface, it can also be a series of increasingly problematic, suspenseful, or even dangerous developments.

If the relationship with the love interest was the main problem in Twin #1's life, that will be the focus of the middle of the story. Twin #2 has an interesting job in this case. He or she needs to get the love interest to fall in love with him or her specifically and to fall out of love with Twin #1...all while making the love interest think he or she IS Twin #1. To be clear, Twin #2 needs the love interest to love this new and improved version of Twin #1 more than the love interest loved the original.

If Twin #2 has taken over Twin #1's life to solve some other problem—work related, safety-related, whatever, the middle of the story will be taken up with Twin #2 trying to manage the increasingly challenging issues of that problem. There will be successes and setbacks, and the problem will barrel forward toward the crisis that Twin #2 promised to fix for Twin #1. In this scenario, Twin #1 and the love interest may or may not have been romantically involved before Twin #2 shows up on the scene. In this case, Twin #2 and the love interest fall in love through the middle of the story. This may be a forbidden love for some reason. Or, Twin #1 may have no romantic interest in the love interest at all and be horrified at the prospect of stepping back into his or her own life, complete with this romance he or she doesn't want. This relationship will greatly complicate how and when the twins reveal their switch and step back into their own lives...and the more in love Twin #2 and the love interest become, the harder that switch is going to be.

Twin #1 may try to return to his or her life in the middle of the story. Odds are good that Twin #2 resists this. Twin #2 is in the middle of falling in love with the love interest and isn't going to want to give up that budding love of his or her life.

Twin #1 may decide not to step back into the mess #2 has made, or at least not until Twin #2 cleans up the mess. A variation on this is that Twin #2 may block Twin #1 from returning to his or her life until Twin #2 has straightened out the mess Twin #2 is now embroiled in.

In all of these scenarios, it's entirely possible Twin #2 toys with permanently taking over Twin #1's life. If this happens, conflict between the twins may grow quickly toward a crisis if Twin #1 wants his or her life back.

BLACK MOMENT:

The middle of this story has so many possible complications that I can't suggest a specific black moment for each and every one. But several major elements will be consistent in the black moments of this trope:

--the external plot conflict that one or both of the twins are dealing with implodes

and goes to pieces

--the reason the twins switched places or the misidentification of a lookalike not

only becomes a crisis but goes terribly wrong

--any conflict between the twins explodes into a huge confrontation

--the love interest has to choose one twin over the other and chooses wrong...in

whose eyes that choice is wrong will depend on who your main character is and

who you've painted as the most heroic and sympathetic character in your story

with whom your audience most relates

--the relationship between Twin #2 and the love interest falls apart spectacularly

It would seem obvious that the switch or substitution of Twin #2 for Twin #1 happens in the black moment. The big reveal to the love interest and other major characters may provoke the black moment as opposed to being the black moment. The black moment may also force the big reveal to happen, which is to say the reveal of the switch or substitution may be fallout from the black moment that leads to the climactic confrontation at the end of the story.

THE END:

In the end of your story, the switch must be revealed if it hasn't been already, and all of the consequences of the deception ensue. These consequences of, and forgiveness for, the big deception may take up a lot of real estate in your story's final act.

The climactic confrontations all happen—the external plot problem that provoked the switch in the first place, any conflicts that arose between the twins as a result of the switch force a big show-down between the twins, there's a climactic confrontation between Twin #2 and the love interest, and perhaps also between Twin #1 and his or her twin and the love interest, particularly if you've established some sort of love triangle where the love interest is in love with both twins, now, and must choose one over the other. The act of choosing one twin over the other may provoke a whole new conflict between the twins that results in the story's climactic action.

One twin or the other must step aside for the lovers to get their happily ever after, forgiveness must be given to the twin who interfered in any existing romantic relationships, whichever twin put the other into the most difficult situation probably needs to be forgiven, as well. The love interest may need to forgive both twins for the deception. The twins need to forgive the love interest for not realizing (or for not realizing sooner) that the twins switched places. If it was an intentional switch of places in the story, whoever engineered the switch needs forgiving by everybody—assuming this person isn't the villain who was ultimately defeated.

KEY SCENES

--the first time the twin or look alike goes forth, intentionally masquerading as the other twin or their lookalike

--the first romantic encounter between Twin #2 and the love interest

--the moment when Twin #2 does the thing as Twin #1 that Twin #1 is not going to forgive him or her for doing, which is to say, the Moment Twin #2 crosses the line he or she should not have

--the moment Twin #1 finds out that Twin #2 crossed the line he or she should not have

--the moment the love interest realizes the depth of his or her betrayal by the twins (or by the lookalike) who kept the truth from him or her and played him or her for a fool

THINGS TO THINK ABOUT WHEN WRITING THIS TROPE

In the case of actual twins, why do they choose to switch places? Does it start out as a joke, or does it have a deadly serious reason for happening?

Have the twins switched places before? Do they have a history of stunts like this?

Who can actually tell the twins apart and figures out what's going on? When does this happen in your story, and what complications does it cause? Or do the twins have to actively avoid this person throughout the story?

In the case of lookalikes, why doesn't the look alike correct the mistake right away? What complication(s) ensues from not correcting the mistake that makes it impossible for the lookalike to tell the truth later?

Is the love interest romantically involved with Twin #1? If so, how quickly does he or she figure out that Twin #2 has replaced Twin #1? Does the love interest let on immediately that he or she is aware of the switch? Why or why not?

If an external person or organization has replaced someone with a doppelganger or clone, who is that entity, why do they do it, and for what purpose? How sinister is this group? Just how powerful is this group since it takes enormous resources to duplicate another human being closely enough to pass for that person?

How does Twin #1 or the person replaced by a lookalike, doppelganger, or clone find out what their replacement is up to? Does Twin #1 try to identity himself or herself immediately, or is there a compelling reason for Twin #1 to wait to reveal having been replaced? If so, what is that reason? Is it compelling enough for your audience to buy it as a reason not to reclaim one's life back immediately?

How does Twin #2 convince the love interest that he or she is the "real" Twin #1 in a way your audience will believe?

Who else besides the love interest is being deceived and why do they need to be deceived, too?

At what point does Twin #1 want to end the deception and Twin #2 NOT want to end it? Why does Twin #2 win that argument?

If the twins switch places, what elements of their twin's life do they each find incredibly alluring and what elements do they find surprisingly unpleasant?

Do the twins become much closer during this switch or does their relationship implode? What does this look like?

Does the love interest sense that secrets are being kept from him or her? Is he or she suspicious that something's off or wrong? Does this cause problems in his or her relationship with Twin #2?

What big external plot problem or crisis must be solved in your story? How does the act of the twins switching places or a lookalike stepping into someone else's life help solve this problem?

What event triggers the twins revealing their switch or the

replaced person revealing that he or she has been impersonated this whole time?

How does the love interest react to this big reveal?

How do the twins react to each other in the aftermath of the big reveal? How screwed up are each of their lives now and how much damage has to be unwound, repaired, or forgiven?

Who does the love interest ultimately choose to be with?

Who has to forgive whom in this story? What apologies, sacrifices, or grand gestures have to happen for the forgiveness to be granted and to be genuine?

TROPE TRAPS

Getting suckered by the notion that twins switching place is a lighthearted story or comic romp and not realizing that at its core, this is a story of a huge deception and betrayal of trust.

The twins don't have a compelling enough reason to switch places.

The twins don't have a compelling enough reason to STAY switched once they've switched lives.

If applicable, whoever placed the doppelganger or clone has no compelling reason to keep the original person alive and is a stupid villain for keeping the original person alive long enough to reclaim his or her life.

Just how dimwitted is the love interest (and family, friends, colleagues not to be able to tell the twins apart? Failing to give people who know Twin #1 well a compelling excuse for not recognizing that Twin #2 has taken Twin #1's place.

Failing to create a love interest the audience genuinely likes, roots for, and wants to be happy.

Failing to acknowledge that the love interest is a victim in this story. Failing to give him or her sufficient agency to protect self from emotional hurt or damage in your story.

Failing to give the love interest a real choice to exit the relationship with Twin #2 well before the big reveal at the end. In the absence of this choice, the love interest will appear manipulated, weak, gas lighted, and even traumatized by the events of your story. Even if you paint the love interest as not feeling this way, your audience, who is living the love interest's story vicariously, may feel all of these ways.

The problem that provokes the switch or results because of the switch isn't big enough or interesting enough to sustain the plot of your story.

Failing to give the audience a plausible reason for the big reveal and switch back to wait until the very end of your story.

Failing to give the twins a strong enough relationship/connection/friendship to forgive each other for the transgressions one or both of them has engaged in while living the other one's life.

Failing to think through seriously how the twins will forgive each other.

Failing to think through seriously how the love interest will forgive either twin for the gigantic betrayal of his or her trust, particularly if the love interest was engaged in a romantic relationship with both twins at some point.

Failing to show the twins learning major life lessons from this adventure.

TWINS SWITCH PLACES/LOOKALIKES TROPE IN ACTION
Movies:

- The Parent Trap
- Echoes
- The Princess Switch
- The Prisoner of Zenda
- Face Off
- Altered Carbon (TV series)

. . .

Books:

- The Prince and the Pauper by Mark Twain
- Faked by Karla Sorensen
- Someone To Watch Over Me by Lisa Kleypas
- Twin Crowns by Catherine Doyle and Katherine Webber
- I'll Be You by Janelle Brown
- The Holiday Swap by Maggie Knox
- Someone Else's Shoes by Jojo Moyes

39

APPENDIX A – UNIVERSAL ROMANCE TROPES LISTED BY VOLUME

Volume 1, THE TROPOHOLIC'S GUIDE TO INTERNAL ROMANCE TROPES

Accidental Pregnancy

Amnesia

Anti-Hero

Bad Boy/Girl Reformed

Beauty-and-the-Beast

Burdened by Beauty/Talent

Celibate Hero

Clumsy/Thoughtless/Bumbling Hero/Heroine

Cold/Serious/Uptight Hero/Heroine

Commitment Phobia

Damaged Hero/Heroine

Dangerous Secret

Disabled Hero/Heroine

Fear of Intimacy

Fresh Start/Do-Over

Goody Two Shoes

Hero/Heroine in Disguise

Makeover

Nerdy/Geek/Genius
Newcomer/Outsider/Stranger
Oblivious to Love/Last to Know
Only One Not Married
Plain Jane/John
Plus Size Love
Rebellious Hero/Heroine
Reclusive Hero/Heroine
Shy Hero/Heroine
Single Parent
Socially Awkward Hero/Heroine
Transformation/Fixer Upper
Ugly Duckling
Virgin Hero/Heroine
Widowed Hero/Heroine

Volume 2, THE TROPOHOLIC'S GUIDE TO EXTERNAL ROMANCE TROPES

Across the Tracks/Wrong Side of the Tracks
Best Friend's Sibling/Sibling's Best Friend
Best Friend's/Sibling's Ex
Best Friend's Widow/Widower
Childhood Sweethearts/Friends
Couples Therapy
Cross-Cultural/Interethnic/Interracial
Divided Loyalties
Everyone Else Can See It
Evil/Dysfunctional Family
Feuding Families
Fish Out of Water/Cowboy in the City
Following Your Heart
Forbidden Love
Friends to Lovers

Girl/Boy Next Door
Hero/Heroine in Hiding
Hidden/Secret Wealth
Home for the Holiday/Vacation Fling
Long Distance Romance
Love Triangle
Marriage Pact/Bargain Comes Due
Marriage of Convenience/Fake Marriage
No One Thinks It Will Work
Nursing Back to Health
On the Run/Chase
Quest/ Search for MacGuffin
Rags to Riches/Cinderella
Rescue Romance/Damsel or Dude in distress
Riches to Rags
Rivals/Work Enemies
Secret Baby
Secret Identity
Secret Organization/Secret World
Twins Switch Places/Lookalikes

Volume 3, THE TROPHOLIC'S GUIDE TO BACKSTORY ROMANCE TROPES

Back From the Dead
Billionaire
Burned By Love/Sworn Off Love
Bully Turned Nice Guy
Chosen One
Enemies to Lovers
Engaged to/Marrying Someone Else
Estranged Spouses/On the Rocks
Family Skeletons
Finding a Home

First Love
Forgiveness
Guardian
Hero/Heroine is Ex-Con
Insta-Family
In Love With the Wrong Person
Is the Baby Mine
Left At the Altar/Jilted
Lone Wolf Tamed
Mafia Romance
Not Good Enough for Him/Her
Rebound Romance
Reconciliation/Second Chance
Recovery/Rehabilitation
Redemption
Reunion
Revenge
Rivals
Ruined/Ruined Reputation
Runaway Brides
Scandalous Hero/Heroine
Separated/Marriage in Trouble
Spinster/Bluestocking/On the Shelf
Step Siblings/Stepparent
Survivor Guilt
Teenage Crush
Tomboy Reformed

Volume 4, THE TROPOHOLIC'S GUIDE TO HOOK ROMANCE TROPES

Arranged Marriage
Baby On the Doorstep
Boss-Employee
Bodyguard
Coming Home
Deathbed Confession
Disguised as a Male
Drunk/Vegas Wedding
Fake Fiancé(e)/Boyfriend/Girlfriend
False Identity
Fated Mates/Soul Mates
Fling/One Night Stand
Grumpy/Sunshine
Innocent Cohabitation
Love At First Sight
Love-Hate Relationship
Matchmaker/Matchmaker Gone Wrong
May-December Romance
Mistaken Identity
Nanny/Teacher & Single Parent
Online Love/Pen Pals
Opposites Attract
Pretend/Celibate Marriages
Raising a Child Together
Right Under Your Nose
Road Trip/Adventure
Running Away From Home
Secret Crush/Secret Admirer
Stop the Wedding
Straight Arrow Seduced
Stranded/Marooned/ Forced Proximity

Terms of the Will
Treasure Hunt
Tricked into Marriage
Unconsummated Marriage
Unrequited Love

ALSO BY CINDY DEES

THE TROPOHOLIC'S GUIDES:

UNIVERSAL ROMANCE TROPES

Volume 1, The Tropoholic's Guide to Internal Romance Tropes

Volume 2, The Tropoholic's Guide to External Romance Tropes

Volume 3, The Tropoholic's Guide to Backstory Romance Tropes

Volume 4, The Tropoholic's Guide to Hook Romance Tropes

NOTE: I've chosen not to make future volumes in this series available as pre-orders because I'm committed to getting each book right instead of hurrying to meet a deadline.

If you'd like to be notified when the next volume goes on sale, please visit www.cindydees.com/tropes and sign up for my (rather infrequent) tropes newsletter.

FICTION

Second Shot, A Helen Warwick Thriller

Double Tap, A Helen Warwick Thriller

The Medusa Project

The Medusa Game

The Medusa Prophecy

The Medusa Affair

The Medusa Seduction

Medusa's Master

The Medusa Proposition

I've received and heard your requests (with great delight, I might add) for more books covering the tropes of specific genres of fiction.

I'm currently developing lists of tropes for what I expect will amount to something like a dozen more genre fiction books covering genres including but not limited to:

- The Tropes of Sexual Tension
- Historical and Paranormal Romance
- Sweet, Clean & Wholesome, and Inspirational Romance
- Cozy Mystery
- Noir Mystery
- Crime Fiction
- Thrillers
- Horror
- Science Fiction
- Fantasy
- Paranormal
- Action/Adventure

If I've missed any genres you'd like to see books on, please feel free to contact me at www.cindydees.com and let me know!

ABOUT THE AUTHOR

New York Times and USA Today bestselling author of over a hundred books, Cindy Dees has sold over two million books worldwide. She writes in a variety of genres, including thrillers, military adventure, romantic suspense, fantasy, and alternate history.

Cindy is the creator and executive producer of an upcoming Netflix television series based on her Helen Warwick thriller novel series about a woman assassin, and Cindy has multiple additional television and film projects in development.

A two-time RITA winner and five-time RITA finalist, she is also a two-time Holt Medallion winner, two-time winner of Romantic Times' Romantic Suspense of the Year Award and a Career Lifetime Achievement Award nominee from Romantic Times.

Cindy taught novel writing courses for seven years at a major university and has taught dozens of workshops on every aspect of writing, screenwriting, and the publishing and TV/film industries.

A former U.S. Air Force pilot and part-time spy, she draws upon real-life experience to fuel her stories of life (and sometimes love) on the edge of danger. Her social media links are at www.cindydees.com and www.cynthiadees.com.

For more information on:

- Cindy's upcoming books on genre tropes (including cozy mystery, noir mystery, thrillers, sci fi, fantasy, horror, action-adventure, and various sub-genres of romance, and more)
- deep dives into individual tropes
- analysis of popular movie, book, and TV show tropes
- and much, much more

visit www.cindydees.com/tropes to sign up for her Tropoholic's newsletter.